Thomas More
on Statesmanship

Thomas More (bottom center) at the Opening of Parliament, 1523.
The Royal Collection, © Her Majesty Queen Elizabeth II,
Windsor Castle, MS 1114.

Gerard B. Wegemer

Thomas More on Statesmanship

The Catholic University of America Press
Washington, D.C.

Copyright © 1996
The Catholic University of America Press
All rights reserved
Printed in the United States of America

This paperback edition, incorporating minor corrections,
published 1998

The paper used in this publication meets the minimum requirements of
American National Standards for Information Science—Permanence of
Paper for Printed Library materials, ANSI Z39.48-1984.
∞

LIBRARY OF CONGRESS CATALOGING-IN-PUBLICATION DATA
Wegemer, Gerard B., 1950–
 Thomas More on statesmanship / Gerard B. Wegemer.
   p. cm
 Includes bibliographical references and index.
 1. More, Thomas, Sir, Saint, 1478–1535. Utopia. 2. More, Thomas, Sir,
Saint, 1478–1535—Contributions in political science. 3. More, Thomas,
Sir, Saint, 1478–1535. 4. Statesman—England—Biography.
 I. Title
HX810.5.Z6W45 1996
321'.07—dc20
    95-12682
ISBN 0-8132-0836-X (cloth: alk. paper)
ISBN 0-8132-0913-7 (pbk.: alk. paper)

Contents

Acknowledgments — vii
Abbreviations — viii

Introduction — 1

I. More's Understanding of the Statesman's Work

1. Can Reason Rule the Free? — 23
2. First, Self-Rule — 37
3. Ruling Citizens: What Is Needed? — 54

II. *Utopia*: A Statesman's Puzzle

4. Literature and the Acquisition of Political Prudence — 77
5. *Utopia 1* and *2*: Dramatizing Competing Philosophies of Life — 91
6. *Utopia 1*: Ciceronian Statesmanship — 109
7. *Utopia 2*: Augustinian Realist — 128

III. Issues in More's Career as Statesman

8. The Limits of Reason and the Need for Law — 153

9.	Reform over Revolution: In Defense of Free Will and a United Christendom	161
10.	The Limits of Government and the Domain of Conscience	183
	Conclusion	205
	Notes	215
	Works Cited	237
	Index	249

Acknowledgments

Expressing gratitude at the end of a long and difficult project is a great pleasure indeed. Special thanks go to the University of Dallas and the Bradley Foundation for making possible full-time work on this project during the academic year of 1992–1993. Then thanks are especially due to Fr. Ernest Fortin, who first sparked the inquiry of many years that this book represents. Other major contributors to that quest have been Drs. Christopher Wolfe, Damian Grace, Ward Allen, and Fr. Germain Marc'hadour, as well as many of my colleagues and students at the University of Dallas. I am also grateful to the National Endowment for the Humanities and to Dr. Richard Strier and the participants of his 1991 NEH Summer Seminar for College Teachers, "Renaissance and Reformation in Tudor-Stuart England," for the fruitful conversations that seminar made possible.

Grateful acknowledgment is made to Yale University Press for permission to reprint extensive excerpts from these volumes of *The Complete Works of St. Thomas More*: vol. 3.2, *Latin Poems,* ed. Clarence H. Miller, Leicester Bradner, Charles A. Lynch, Revilo P. Oliver, © 1984; vol. 4, *Utopia,* ed. Edward Surtz and J. H. Hexter, © 1965; vol. 8, *Confutation of Tyndale's Answer,* ed. Louis A. Schuster, Richard C. Marius, James P. Lusardi, Richard J. Schoeck, © 1973.

Abbreviations

Corr	*Correspondence of Sir Thomas More*
CSPS	Great Britain. *Calendar of State Papers, Spanish*
CSPV	Great Britain. *Calendar of State Papers, Venetian*
CW	*The Complete Works of St. Thomas More*
CWE	*Collected Works of Erasmus*
EA	Sylvester and Marc'hadour, eds., *Essential Articles for the Study of Thomas More*
EE	*Epistles of Erasmus*
EW	*English Works of Sir Thomas More*
LP	Great Britain. *Letters and Papers of Henry VIII*
SL	*St. Thomas More: Selected Letters*

Thomas More
on Statesmanship

Introduction

> The very root of writing well . . .
> Is to be wise; thy matter first to know;
> Which the Socratic writings best can show:
> And, where the matter is provided still,
> There words will follow, not against their will.
> He, that hath studied well the debt, and knows
> What to his country, what his friends he owes,
> What height of love, a parent will fit best,
> What brethren, what a stranger, and his guest,
> Can tell a *statesman*'s duty, what the arts
> And office of a judge are, what the parts
> Of a brave chief sent to the war: He can,
> Indeed, give fitting dues to every man.
> —Horace's *Art of Poetry*, Ben Jonson's translation[1]

"Statesman" is a word that enters the English language during the Renaissance as a result of a widespread return to the Greek and Roman classics. No Englishman contributed more to the recovery of that concept than Thomas More,[2] and no classical thinker contributed more to his understanding than Plato.

The Statesman (*Politicus*) and *The Republic* (*Politeia*) are the two most famous Platonic dialogues investigating the qualities needed by a political leader who dedicates himself to the advantage of those he rules, not to his own. Plato contrasts this true guardian of the state with the tyrant, who strives to satisfy his own passions and will. He makes this contrast vividly by comparing the statesman to a doctor, a ship's captain, and a shepherd; the tyrant, to a quack, an unskilled hireling, and a wolf.[3]

The Statesman is part of a trilogy that invites careful reflection upon the immense theoretical difficulties involved in determining the elements of genuine good rule,[4] and *The Republic* remains one of the most influential and debated texts in the Western tradition about the same topic. So influential were these two texts that subsequent thinkers, beginning immediately with Aristotle and Cicero, used them as their point of departure as they continued to reflect upon this fundamental issue of just rule.

Thomas More continued this tradition (often known as "civic humanism"), and he spent many years early in life studying the Greek and Roman philosophers. Among these, he "especially read Plato and his followers, delighting in their study because he considered their teaching most useful in the government of the state and the preservation of civic order" (Stapleton 13). More also spent many years of reflection upon the numerous controversies that had taken place among Christian thinkers during fifteen centuries of discussion over the fundamental issues of justice and good rule. In the end, More agreed with those who considered the statesman to be the virtuous leader who possesses both the science and the art of ruling. Not only did he agree, he spent his mature years deliberately cultivating those three important elements of statesmanship: the science, the art, and the personal virtue presupposed to that science and art.

To master the science of politics, More studied for over fifteen years after his formal education. These were years devoted especially to political philosophy and history. These studies culminated in his *History of King Richard III*, which gives his assessment of the political forces at work in England,[5] and in his *Utopia*, which refers to itself playfully but repeatedly as a "superior" version of

Plato's *Republic* (CW4 21/5,19; 19/23–27). During these fifteen years, More also continued studying and lecturing on the laws and customs of England, particularly through his active participation with the law school he attended and served, Lincoln's Inn.[6]

To master the art of ruling, More consulted with some of England's most accomplished rulers while he gained a wide range of experience throughout his fifteen years of political activity in London. Among his many activities, he was a member of the Parliaments of 1504 and 1510; he served as undersheriff[7] of London from 1510 to 1518; he was chosen to represent the merchants of London on two important foreign embassies in 1515 and 1517; and he had extensive involvement in the major legal controversies in London at that time. In addition, More spent over twenty years developing his rhetorical abilities, a skill that became of central importance in his legal and political careers. Already in 1515 he was chosen to be London's orator to welcome the Venetian ambassador; in 1518 he was the King's orator to welcome the papal legate; and in 1522 he gave the oration welcoming Emperor Charles V to England. During these years, More also developed a highly personal style of diplomacy characterized by a humor and irony that allowed him to speak the "full truth in jest"—or at least to hint at the full truth through a playful indirection (cf. CW9 170/36).

To acquire virtue was More's major preoccupation as a young man and throughout his life. As More insisted to his children's tutor, "put virtue in the first place among goods, learning in the second" (SL 105). By doing so, he was convinced that his children would "be inwardly calm and at peace and neither stirred by praise of flatterers nor stung by the follies of unlearned mockers of learning" (106). In adopting this position, More was agreeing with the common sense observation of classical writers such as Plato and Aristotle who understood that a person must have a stable character to see the world or oneself with any degree of objectivity. More also recognized the need for virtue in order to obey the dictates and duties that follow from what is seen. Unlike the tyrant, who does what he wills, the virtuous person is free enough from passion and impulse to do what is appropriate and just.

Like many of the other early Renaissance humanists in England, More was concerned throughout his life with the problems —both theoretical and practical—involved in achieving some measure of justice in the face of social unrest and the harsh exigencies of war, famine, and oppression that characterize much of political life. In coming to understand how to deal with these difficult issues, More drew heavily upon classical authors such as Plato, Aristotle, Thucydides, and his beloved Cicero, upon the early Church Fathers, and also upon the medieval and English traditions of common law and political practice. As we will see, he allied himself with these in arguing strongly for rule by law, not by arbitrary will.

If reason is to serve as the foundation for politics, then education and public deliberation are needed for its development. Nonetheless, More realized that to expect reason to exercise such power is almost utopian, given the fact that history seems to present more war than peace, more discord than harmony. The daunting task of good law and good education is, therefore, to strengthen and support reason against passion, prejudice, and thoughtless self-interest. The task is so difficult that most political philosophers after More have abandoned this educational project, which he and his classical ancestors saw as the irreplaceable support for just government. Yet conscious of all the difficulties involved, More remained eminently classical in his conviction that institutional arrangements could never substitute for personal virtue as the primary safeguard of political liberty.

In this light, the statesman's first task is to appeal steadfastly to reason in an effort to bring about a consensus on the common good through the slow development of law and tradition.[8] Rhetoric, political free speech, and the wide-ranging consultation and study encouraged by education are, therefore, necessary factors which the statesman must use and advance as much as possible. Hence, More's speech of 1523 urging free debate in Parliament (the first such plea on record in England) was but one manifestation of a consistent theory of statesmanship. So, too, was the education program he designed for his children. So, too, was his preference for the pen over the executioner's block as a deterrent to the revolutionary ideas entering England at that time—even though More did initiate and enforce executions prescribed by just law. More also recognized the necessity for prudent institutional arrangements, and he favored a representative form of government. Although he worked for a king, he wrote repeatedly about the dangers of investing too much power in one person.

For Thomas More, such issues were not mere matters for philosophic speculation. His whole upbringing and education immersed him in the pressing realities of the political world in which he lived. He was born in the heart of London during the Wars of the Roses, wars which were ended in large part by the most influential teacher of his youth, Chancellor and Cardinal John Morton. More remembered vividly the shock and terror caused by Richard III's tyranny.[9] He experienced personally the despotic rule of Henry VII. Throughout these and the many everyday conflicts of the busy capital and port city in which he was raised, young More was taught and advised by a father of unusual worldly wisdom.

John More was a lawyer from lowly origins, orphaned at sixteen and the eldest of six children. Nonetheless, he eventually rose to become a judge of the king's court. Thomas never wrote of his mother, Agnes Granger, who died when he was young, but he expressed the highest regard for his father.[10] John More and his family were thoroughly immersed in the life of the city. Although a commoner, John sent young Thomas to attend the best school in London, a sign of his ambitions for his unusually talented son. St. Anthony's School was located in the heart of the city, near the business district where the Mores lived, and Thomas attended there from roughly 1484 to 1489.

Thomas More's political education began in earnest, however, in 1489, when he began living in a place where few aspiring politicians could ever hope to be, even at the height of their careers—at the court of England's leading civil and ecclesiastical statesman: Chancellor, Archbishop, and soon to be Cardinal Morton. Young More was sent there by a father who recognized the rare gifts of his son, as did Morton himself. Morton was evidently a family friend, and as Roper tells us, Morton greatly delighted in young Thomas's "wit and towardness"; he "would often say of him unto the nobles that divers times dined with him, 'This child here waiting at the table, whosoever shall live to see it, will prove a marvelous man'" (3).

Morton did all that he could to help the young More, even to the point of persuading a reluctant father to send his son away from London to receive what John More probably considered a questionable education at Oxford. Therefore, from 1491 to 1493, More attended a school that was mostly for boys interested in the priesthood. After two years, however, John More insisted that his son attend an inn of chancery in London, the New Inn. This school provided the preparatory education needed for law school and for the social life demanded by the leaders of English society.

More's greatest educational debt to Morton, however, surely arose from within the halls of Lambeth Palace. To be able to see on a daily basis the leading men and women of the realm as they conducted business and enjoyed their leisure would alone have added a wealth of experience to a youth of More's intelligence and sensitivity. But his years with Morton were not simply years of observation: The fundamental purpose of serving as a page in such a household was to learn how to conduct oneself and, more specifically, to develop the virtues and abilities that would be needed for assuming leadership responsibilities. In addition, this arrangement began a friendship and an undisclosed number of conversations that were destined to continue for ten years, until Morton's death in 1500.[11]

Morton receives the most extensive tribute More bestowed upon any of his teachers. As More recounts in his two most celebrated works, Morton left a profound impression. In *Richard III* he describes how Morton "had gotten by great experience (the very mother and mistress of wisdom), a deep insight in politic, worldly drifts" (CW2 91). More credits this shrewd and learned doctor of laws[12] with bringing "infinite benefit to the realm" by craftily bringing about an end to the Wars of the Roses. This "bishop was a man of great natural wit, very well learned, and honorable in behavior, lacking no wise ways to win favor" (90). Significantly, these same qualities would later be attributed to More himself.

One lesson of particular value that More learned was Morton's habit of testing the character of those around him. Although More developed a different style, he admired the prudence and effectiveness of Morton's approach:

> In conversation [Morton] was agreeable, though serious and dignified. Of those who made suit to him he enjoyed making trial by rough address, but in a harmless way, to see what mettle and what presence of mind a person would manifest. (CW4 59)

More, too, tested character habitually. He carefully tested his own, for example, before deciding to be a monk or a layman. After four years of such testing, he decided to be a "chaste husband rather than a licentious priest" (EE, Nichols 394; CWE7 21). He also habitually tested the character of those around him, not by Morton's "rough address," but by his own irony and humor. So effective was this practice that people often doubted if he spoke seriously or in jest (CW6 68/35–69/2), thereby leading them to reveal their own mind or reaction. This practical use of comic irony he learned, in large part, from Socrates and Lucian.

Despite his admiration for Morton, More was not blind to his teacher's serious imperfections.[13] These he refers to respectfully and discreetly when he writes that Morton's last days were so godly that they "well changed his life" (CW2 91). Nevertheless, Morton received praise even from the highly censorious Hythlodaeus in *Utopia*.[14] Here, too, the qualities of More's early teacher would later be attributed to the student—or at least most of them:

> He was a man . . . who deserved respect as much for his prudence and virtue as for his authority. . . . His speech was polished and pointed. His knowledge of law was profound, his ability incomparable, and his memory astonishingly retentive, for he had improved his extraordinary natural qualities by learning and practice.
> The king placed the greatest confidence in his advice, and the com-

monwealth seemed much to depend upon him when I was there. As one might expect, almost in earliest youth he had been taken straight from school to court, had spent his whole life in important public affairs, and had sustained numerous and varied vicissitudes of fortune, so that by many and great dangers he had acquired a statesman's sagacity which, when thus learned, is not easily forgotten. (CW4 59–61)

One great difference between teacher and student was that More would wait many years before going to court. (Here, too, More may have seen the need to test—and train—his character before confronting the duties and temptations of high office.) Unlike his teacher, More waited over fifteen years after the end of his formal education before he entered the king's service. These were the years of reflection and study that formed the foundation of More's later career. During this time, in conjunction with his study and practice of English common law, More joined with some of the best minds in England and Europe to study Greek and Roman learning, together with biblical and patristic studies.

One of these early teachers of special influence was William Grocyn. This scholar not only taught More Greek; he also invited his young prodigy to deliver a series of lectures on Augustine's *City of God*. These lectures forced More to confront all the hopes and dreams of the Renaissance, at a time when he was trying to decide whether he should work in the city or leave that city to join a monastery. Why would More's teacher encourage him to study *The City of God* in such depth and at this time? Perhaps it was that Augustine challenged the city in ways that few others had done.[15] He also challenged the very possibility of all that the Greek and Roman classics promised: the prospect of building a noble and just city on earth, a city based on virtue. In *The City of God,* Augustine states flatly and repeatedly that earthly peace and justice will always and inevitably fail.[16] Therefore, it is no wonder that More would "treat this great work [not] from the theological point of view, but from the standpoint of history and philosophy" (Stapleton 7–8). In dealing with such issues, Thomas was grappling with the most basic issues of Renaissance political philosophy.

By 1503, More decided to work in the city, to marry, and pursue the law. He also decided to continue his study of Greek, especially Aristotle, with Thomas Linacre (CW15 101–3). Soon his Greek was so far advanced that he was competing in translations with William Lily and even Erasmus himself. More's genius became widely recognized (Pace 103–5, CWE7 24), and this seems to be the time he would have "devoted himself to the study of Greek literature and philosophy," especially Plato (CWE7 19, Stapleton 13). Not only would More write four Platonic dialogues that have come down to us, but Erasmus mentioned that More worked as a youth on a playful "dialogue in which he supported Plato's doctrine of communalism, extending it even to wives" (CWE7 23). During these years, More also continued his biblical and patristic studies with such eminent teachers as John Colet and the Charterhouse Carthusians.

After 1503, More became heavily involved in the life of the city. Already in 1504 he was elected a member of Parliament. This first term in Parliament was another major education in the realities of political life, and probably spurred More on to even deeper study of his beloved classical historians and political theorists. In this Parliament, More objected that the money Henry VII requested was unreasonably high. While debating the issue, More "made such arguments and reasons there against, that the King's demands thereby were clean overthrown" (Roper 5). Afterwards, the King remained so angry that More "was determined to have gone over the sea, thinking that being in the King's indignation, he could not live in England without great danger" (5).

Despite his setback with Henry VII, More achieved rapid professional success within the city of London. His influence and success as a civic and diplomatic leader became apparent in various ways.

Most obviously, he developed one of the largest private law practices in London. Roper wrote that More was making 400 pounds a year through his law practice—a large sum indeed when one considers that an average person lived on 10 pounds a year and the unusually well-paid headmaster of St. Paul's school received 35 pounds a year (Marius 5, Lupton 177n). After leaving his private practice, More worked for seven years in the king's service before matching those former earnings. Roper might have been exaggerating in stating that "there was at that time in none of the Prince's courts of the laws of this realm, any matter of importance in controversy wherein he was not with the one part of counsel" (5). Nonetheless, other evidence from that time indicates that More's judgment was valued and highly sought (Guy 1980, 3–7).

For example, in 1509, he was admitted "free and frank" to the Mercers' Guild, the most wealthy and influential of the London guilds at that time. This guild was probably most responsible for More's election in 1510 to serve as a burgess representing London's interests in Parliament. In 1511 he received the highest honor open to a young lawyer at that time when he was chosen to deliver the Autumn lectures at Lincoln's Inn. Shortly afterwards he also served as Governor of Lincoln's Inn. By 1514 More had become part of the Doctors' Commons, an association in London of preeminent lawyers and cultural leaders (McConica 51–53). These were all clear indications of the high esteem he had among his peers.

More's rapid success was not only caused by his mastery of law, although that mastery was of unquestioned and obvious importance. More taught law for three years at Furnivall's Inn, from 1503 to 1506. He was asked to give the guest lectures at Lincoln's Inn not only in 1511 but again in 1515, a distinction that, at age thirty-eight, positioned him for appointment as one of the highest-ranking judges of England.

In addition to his obvious legal expertise, however, More was also a master of rhetoric and diplomacy—skills that propelled him time and again into the major issues engaging first the city of London, then the English nation, and finally Christendom itself. More worked hard to acquire these skills.

To develop his rhetorical abilities,[17] More spent his earlier years "principally in poetry; after that came a long struggle to acquire a more supple style in prose by practicing his pen in every sort of writing" (CWE7 23). As a youth, he also took "delight especially in declamations," and Erasmus reports that "it would be difficult to find a more felicitous extempore speaker, so fertile are both his mind and the tongue that does its bidding" (23–24).

To develop his diplomatic skills, More had youthful training from his own accomplished father, Lord Chancellor Morton, and the inns of court. He also had years of professional experience, and he studied "with avidity all the historical works he could find," as well as those philosophers and poets most concerned with the city (Stapleton 13–14). More eventually became so accomplished in distinguishing principle from accidental factors that Erasmus marveled at More's ability to adapt himself to anyone in any situation in such a way that "nobody is less swayed by public opinion, and yet nobody is closer to the feelings of ordinary people" (CWE7 19).

Mastery of these political skills was part of the "renascence of good letters" which More sought to advance (CW15 18, SL 16).[18] This project of renewal which More and Erasmus advocated sought reform of society and church through the cultivation of reason and international cooperation. After More was established in government, for example, he said that "he owe[d] to his literary studies . . . the services he can now render to his country, . . . his increased adaptability to court society, to life among the nobility, and to [his] whole way of life" (CWE8 297). By proving that "good letters" could have such a powerfully practical effect, More became at least partially responsible for a type of education that would prevail for centuries among leading families throughout Europe and America. This unexpected result of More's success in "combin[ing] so much real wisdom with such charm of character" (lines 105–6) was pointed out by Erasmus:

> The result is that, while only a few days ago a love of literature was thought to be of no practical or ornamental value, there is now hardly one of our great nobles who would reckon his children worthy of their ancestry if they had no education in liberal studies. Monarchs themselves are thought to lack a good share of the qualities proper to a king if their knowledge of literature leaves much to be desired. (CWE8 297, lines 106–11)

Therefore, by the time that More entered the royal service in 1518, he brought a Europe-wide reputation based on an immense wealth of knowledge and experience. Apart from being recognized as one of the leading humanist scholars[19] of his day, he had been a city judge for eight years; a member of Parliament twice; an active and prominent lawyer; spokesman, negotiator, and member of the merchants' guild; a poet and public orator; founder and director of his children's school (the first co-ed school of its kind, giving the same education to girls and boys); and an ambassador on two foreign embassies.

Along with this wide-ranging practical experience, More entered King Henry's service with a well-developed political philosophy. Central to his political theory was the role of free will. When, therefore, Luther and his followers denied the existence of this human capacity, More considered that denial an attack on a fundamental pillar of political life. Later, when Thomas Cromwell, Henry VIII, and Thomas Cranmer decided to manipulate England's primitive parliamentary rule to advance Henry's imperial and despotic ambitions at the expense of the workings of private and collective conscience, More thoughtfully, respectfully, and effectively opposed their efforts.

The extent of More's political maneuvers at the end of his life has become better known in the last few years;[20] they were so effective, in fact, that his execution was deemed necessary, regardless of public reaction to killing a popular magistrate. Little attention, however, has been given recently to the theoretical underpinnings of his actions. This study, therefore, investigates the understanding of politics and statesmanship that led to More's well-known actions.

What this book shows is that Thomas More—as a civic humanist grounded in classical political thought, in biblical theology, and in English common law—offered an alternative to Machiavelli's absolutist prince, to Hobbes's institutional substitute for virtue, and to later social contract theorists. By synthesizing Cicero and Augustine with the pragmatic discoveries of English politics, More presented an alternative to the early modern theorists.

The greatest tests of More's theory and practice of statesmanship came at the end of his life.

First there arose reformers whom More considered to be revolutionaries: William Tyndale and Simon Fish, for example, who were Luther's English followers. In his last six years, More wrote seven major works against these reformers; during his tenure as chancellor, five people were tried and executed for heresy (Guy 1980, 164). What happened to political free speech and consultation? As I will show, these later actions of More must be considered in light of the danger that he and eventually Erasmus came to perceive. They saw these executions as the implementation of just law in the face of grave threats to peace and public safety. So grave did they consider these threats that they saw the very existence of Christendom to be at stake, as well as the entire humanist project, which they considered necessary to bring about a lasting international peace.

Peace and international unity based on education and cooperation were part of the ideal which More and Erasmus had long advocated. As they saw it, reformers like Luther and Tyndale were destroying the traditional supports for law and authority—and, therefore, of peace and unity—by denying free will, by emphasizing the corruption of human reason, and by limiting the Church to an elite group of "pure and spotless" individuals who claimed a nonrational access to the truth of reality. These emerging new theories rooted conscience in private inspiration, not in reason informed by tradition. At stake here, they argued, was an issue fundamental to all law and peace; at stake, in the words of James McConica and Stephen Greenblatt, was the very principle of intelligibility (Greenblatt 63, 58–59) and, hence, the entire humanist project. Both More and Erasmus predicted that, if the power of reason was denied and if will and private inspiration were to become reason's substitute, the result would be widespread chaos and increased violence.

The second great test More would face arose when Henry VIII decided to assume imperial powers, making himself the head of both church and state. In this final contest, More wrote extensively against Christopher St. German, a legal scholar who became Cromwell's leading propagandist against the prevailing "two swords theory," whereby distinct and separate authorities existed to rule separate jurisdictions. More strongly defended the co-existence of these two distinct authorities, each having its own laws and courts, which could serve as effective checks to the limitations inherent in each and could thus strengthen the pursuit of justice within individual countries and in Christendom at large.

By writing against St. German, More was writing against King Henry's caesaropapist plan to eliminate the Church's independent status. More's writing campaign, plus other forms of indirect opposition, became so effective that he was imprisoned and later executed. Even in prison, however, More continued to write, always it seems with the conscience of the King in mind. Of course, More was not writing for Henry or his own times alone; he knew well that many of the underlying issues and forces he faced were the same that faced every generation. Hence, the counsels to Henry within these last works were also addressed to all the "other caesars and their governors" who would betray the flocks entrusted to their care (CW14 545).

Several recent studies have suggested that Thomas More was far ahead of his time in advocating a "distinctively modern" government, thus being the first—even before Machiavelli—to recommend the separation of morality and politics. Instead of government based on personal virtue, as advocated by the classics, these studies suggest that More proposed a "systemic approach" to the problems of social injustice, substituting "social institutions and political practices" for the approach of "moral instruction" advocated by the classical and medieval theorists (Logan 254–70, 38, 104–11; Starnes 106; Fleisher 8). In such interpretations, all of which are based exclusively on More's highly controversial *Utopia,* the implication is that the moral leadership of statesmen need not and even should not play a determining role in government.

Other recent studies virtually ignore More's theory of statesmanship, since they assume that More had a repressed sexuality which led him to adopt a nonrational position that burst forth in rage when he could no longer understand or control his world. Therefore, unconscious drives, not principled choice, dictated what More wrote and thought.

The time now seems ripe for renewed reflection on the entire span of More's writings to appreciate more fully his understanding of government and statesmanship. Since Yale University Press has completed its monumental thirty-five-year project of publishing *The Complete Works of Saint Thomas More*,[21] a comprehensive reassessment of More's thought is in order. Such a reassessment will take decades of further discussion and judicious scholarship. Just the editing and notes of the *Complete Works* have taken an extremely talented team of scholars approximately three times longer than anyone expected. Now that they have done the difficult work of preparing the land and planting the seed, it may well take another thirty-five years for More scholars to reap a full harvest.

Most people's knowledge of More is limited to his highly ambiguous *Utopia*; yet this book is but one small part of a very productive life. In the last fifteen years, only Richard Marius (1984) and Alistair Fox (1983) have attempted assessments of More's entire corpus. Both are based on a psycho-historical approach, and both try to explain apparent inconsistencies in More by postulating sexual repression. I examine many of the same apparent inconsistencies, but in the context in which More, Erasmus, and the other civic humanists of Europe understood them: in the context of the numerous and diverse difficulties involved in achieving some measure of peace and justice in an imperfect world—a context that gave rise to the humanists' project of gradual reform through law and education.

Drawing upon G. R. Elton's portrait of More as one given to rage and distorted perceptions because of his uncontrolled passions,[22] Marius and Fox present More as a melancholy man. This type of character is exactly what More cautioned against; it is also a character portrait that opposes every previous historical account given of Thomas More—even the most critical. As we will see throughout this book, More firmly maintained that one could not see clearly without the stability that comes only from virtue; hence, the state of one's character does influence perception and action. Therefore, if More were dominated by the passion of melancholy throughout his life and by rage as soon as power came into his hands, then his life was divided indeed and his political actions went contrary to all that he wrote and admired.

But *was* More melancholy throughout his life? In contemporaneous accounts, no such evidence exists. Richard Pace called More "the son or successor of Democritus," the laughing philosopher (105). Erasmus marveled that More was "always friendly and cheerful, . . . disposed to be merry rather than serious or solemn" (CWE7 17). Vives notes his sweetness of temper (41). Roper, after living with More for sixteen years, "could never perceive [him] as much as once in a fume" (19). Among the recollections of More's natural and adopted children, no evidence whatsoever exists of melancholy, but only its opposite.

Alistair Fox, the strongest proponent of the melancholy theory, recognizes in a footnote that only one source "publicly acknowledged the melancholic aspect of More's personality" (1983, 27n). Astonishingly enough, this source dramatizes the exact opposite characteristic. *The Book of Sir Thomas More* is a highly unlikely place to find a melancholy More. In this play, composed in part by Shakespeare, More is portrayed as a person distinguished by his marriage of wit and wisdom, a person capable of both playing "merry jests" and quelling a city riot. After becoming chancellor, More gives a soliloquy on the importance of humility, followed immediately by several jests of "merry Sir Thomas." Not long afterwards, having proclaimed "I love to be merry" (Greg 37, Munday 154), More jumps in and improvises the part of Good Counsel in a play-within-a-play entitled *The Marriage of Wit and Wisdom*. After several other scenes showing Sir Thomas as both wise and merry, we come to the evidence Fox gives in support of his melancholy theory. The speech takes place at what would roughly be the end of act 4. More has resigned from his office as chancellor, and he is speaking with his distraught wife. Here he begins by speaking "like More in melancholy," but the speech is not even over before he encourages his wife with these words:

> For, so God pardon me, in my saddest hour
> Thou hast no more occasion to lament
> . . . .
> Than to behold me after many a toil
> Honor'd with endless rest. Perchance, the King,
> Seeing the Court is full of vanity,
> Has pity lest our souls should be misled
> And sends us to a life contemplative.
> Oh, happy banishment from worldly pride,
> When souls by private life are sanctified.
> (Greg 66–67, Munday 222–23)

These lines hardly portray a person overcome by melancholy. Nor is there any evidence in the rest of the play to indicate that More was overcome by that passion or malady. Instead, the equivalent of act 5 repeatedly acclaims More's merry virtue. He is praised by his jailer: "A wiser or more virtuous gentleman / Was never bred in England" (Greg 53, Munday 186). And after an old client calls him "gentle heart, . . . the best friend that the poor e'er had" and another Londoner calls him the wisest, merriest, and most honest gentleman in the universal world, More is seen jesting all the way to his execution (Greg 54, 56; Munday 188, 190).

The second type of evidence Fox presents is the "contrary impulses" he finds in More's writings, impulses that reveal the "tragic sense of apparent futility, injustice and absurdity of the world" (1983, 9). As we will see throughout this book, More never rejected a Christian view of life in favor of Fox's sixteenth-century version of a twentieth-century absurdist philosophy.

Yet if unresolved conflicts and melancholy did not stand at the core of More's character, what did? The revisionists point us to the best place to find the answer: More's own writings. Here is the strongest evidence of More's mind and character. Yet More's writings are subtle. To understand them, one must pay close attention to the literary genres, the intended audience, and the many other literary factors at play in More's writing. As More himself reminds us, "By neglecting the figures of speech," people "very often miss the real sense" (CW14 295–97).

After years of reflection on his treatment of these topics, I have been most surprised at the little space More devoted to law and government, the very activities that filled most of his waking hours. Instead, he concentrated on topics which provide the foundation for law and government, especially the nature and requirements of sharp-sighted reason and deep-rooted virtue.[23]

The second great surprise of this research was the discovery that More considered literature,[24] not law, to be the primary civilizing force—even though he recognized law to be indispensable for the success of this undertaking. From the early 1500s, More was an active participant of the "renascence of good literature" (SL 16, CW15 18/13), which the humanists saw as the foundation for a larger project of reform aimed first and foremost at strengthening the use of reason over superstition, prejudice, passion, and provincialism. As More explained it, literature is the most effective means to achieve "a good mother wit," that "one special thing without which all learning is half lame" (CW6 132). Such a wit is necessary in governing because it alone can give rise to impartial laws as well as just and prudent institutional arrangements.

That literature could play this important role in civilization was a central idea that More and his fellow humanists inherited from the ancient Greeks and Romans. More refers, for example, to Horace's famous dictum that literature should instruct and delight (CW3.1 3/5–6, CW3.2 644/6–7, CW4 1/4, Horace 343–44), but he makes clear that both the delight and the instruction should be ordered to the development of conscience (SL 106) and hence of political justice. As we will see, the assumption behind More's work and writings was that personal and civic harmony could be achieved only if reason ruled, not passion or pride. And to allow reason to rule, More saw the absolute need for literature and law to reign as well.

Part 1 of this book sets forth Thomas More's theory of statesmanship, drawing heavily from the entire corpus of his work.[25] Part 2 opens with a chapter presenting his understanding of literature. Following this general explanation are three chapters that apply More's understanding to *Utopia*. Finally, part 3 looks at the historical More and analyzes several major political issues he confronted. In all three dimensions of More's life—his political theory, his literature, and his political practice—one finds a consistent and principled approach to statesmanship.

The relevance of statesmanship to our own day should be evident by a simple reflection upon its common definition. A statesman is that "political leader regarded as a disinterested promoter of the public good" or the one "versed in the principles and art of government, especially one who shows unusual wisdom in treating or directing great public affairs."[26] More believed that such strong, well-trained, and vigilant leaders were absolutely necessary if political peace and justice were to prevail, even for a brief period. To bring about some measure of peace and justice, such leaders must first and foremost call upon the full force of reason, both past and present. This requires an appeal to the nation's conscience, calling it to remain faithful to its deepest convictions and commitments. These are generally best expressed in its laws and literature, those time-tested products of a collective reason that alone can provide a constitution[27] strong enough to resist tyrannical desire and arbitrary will.

Part One

More's Understanding of the Statesman's Work

1 Can Reason Rule the Free?

> [Herod's] table bears a severed head and a saint's countenance dripping with hideous gore. So too King Atreus, King Thyestes' brother, served as food to Thyestes the bodies of his two sons. Similarly, to the Thracian king his queen, a loyal sister but a treacherous mother, served their murdered son, Itys. Such delicacies as these mark the tables of kings; I assure you this is not a poor man's fare. (CW3.2, Epigram no. 227)

Like Plato and Augustine, More never articulates his political theory in any one place. Only by long and careful consideration of his entire corpus can that theory be appreciated.

Most fundamentally, however, More considered government to be a natural product of human beings who are genuinely free. Human beings are so free, in fact, that they can choose a tyrannical life supported by cruel dominion over the weak and innocent. Such savage behavior has always marked history, and it forces any thoughtful person to ask when and if reason will ever rule for long in political life.

For Thomas More, the limits of reason in politics are most clearly evidenced by the horror, the power, and the prevalence of tyranny. The nature of tyranny and the ever-present danger of its development are the most distinctive themes of his youthful writings.[1] The problem explored repeatedly in his early literature is well represented in the epigram above. As it shows, kings and queens often do not act like guardians of the state, but rather act in the most unreasonable and violent ways. Why is this so? And what can the true statesman do about it?

More shared the humanists' assumption that true reform depends on the power of reason, yet he constantly dramatized the many forces overshadowing reason. Enigmatically, the man who immortalized the Utopian life of pleasure also wrote the sinister life of Richard III. And the man who composed delightfully witty epigrams also dwelt upon the darkest forms of human folly. What are we to make of this contrast? Alistair Fox concludes "that there was, to speak metaphorically, a pendulum swinging throughout More's life," going from "manichean pessimism to undiluted optimism" (1983, 49). Yet, as we will see in these chapters, beneath this apparent dualism lies an assessment of political life that has unusual subtlety and depth.

In his early writings, More drew attention to the wide range of irrational, ridiculous, and destructive behavior. The panorama of human folly which he vividly sets forth leads one to laugh, but also to wonder why people act in such unreasonable ways. For example, several epigrams present the folly of the miser, who could increase prosperity for himself and others but actually impoverishes all by his unprofitable lust for the money itself rather than the greater goods it could bring. Others show the doctor who could care for his own and his patient's health, but who actually harms both by his obsession with drink. And closest to home for understanding statesmanship, other epigrams present the ruler who could use his power to shepherd his flock, but who perversely becomes a wolf, ravishing his own sheep.

What lies behind such widespread irrational behavior? Is it possible for reason to rule in this present human condition? Or should the wise take Raphael Hythlodaeus's advice and retreat from a public life dominated by ungovernable and even tyrannical fools? The question here is a serious one that lies at the heart of the Renaissance disputes about politics. Should the wise abandon the city and seek the refuge needed for contemplative life? Or should one serve the city and risk the corruption that Raphael predicts will infect all who try?

One indication that reason can rule, at least under certain conditions, is that most people laugh at—and thus recognize—human folly. Therefore, such satire as More writes in his epigrams and translates from Lucian can influence behavior, or at least this was the judgment informing the classical theory of poetics which More and his fellow humanists accepted: that literature can help shape civic behavior by assisting people to be more reflective and thus more deliberate in their actions. "Powerful" literature shames ridiculous actions by artfully bringing them to light; it honors the noble and good in the same way; it profoundly influences behavior by leading attentive readers to see the consequences of different ways of acting. This was the conviction behind Greek civilization from its earliest days. Hence Homer, the one poet to whom More gives unqualified praise in his *Epigrammata,* could be called the teacher of the Greek people. And hence drama, epic poetry, history, and philosophy have been seen as preparing the way for the Athenians' unprecedented form of democratic government based on law. But are these *bonae litterae* powerful enough to repress the tyrant and to curtail foolish behavior? This is a critical question that will be addressed in coming chapters.

As we will see, More's political theory is inextricably tied to his poetic theory, and in this way he is eminently classical. According to those classical authors More most loved, literature is not only something beautiful; it is also something useful and indeed necessary in shaping human action and in allowing political life to develop inasmuch as it artfully leads one to exercise reason freely. The poet helps many to see created reality and one's own tradition for what they are. Not only can he lead others to see beyond appearances to what is ultimately represented, but even more importantly, he can winningly engage the reason of those who normally ignore its demands. How? By the delight, fear, wonder, and intellectual intrigue he creates. What distinguishes More's understanding of statesmanship is his reliance upon the full power of literature to bring citizens to love and choose the good while fear-ing the consequences of evil.[2] At the same time, he also relies upon the full power of law to foster and protect the cultural values enshrined in that literature. More, like Cicero and the great poet-statesmen of the past, understood society's fundamental need for persuasion and personal free assent on one hand along with vigilance on the other to guide human beings who are genuinely free. So strong is the hunger and thirst for freedom that the pleasure of the freedom itself can lead to rebellion against the very conditions of freedom.

In the present chapter, however, we will concentrate on two questions underlying both politics and poetics: why does so much folly and unreason exist? And from the statesman's point of view: can reason rule in the face of so much perverse folly, especially tyranny?

The first and most fully developed reason More gives for folly in his early writings is the same one that Shakespeare points to most frequently: we are easily deceived by appearances because of ignorance or pretense. As a result, we confuse true goods with false goods, true pleasures with the "counterfeit image of pleasure" (EW 461). Instead of seeking true goods and their corresponding pleasures from the soul, we often settle for counterfeit images of pleasure arising from fragile and fleeting goods that appeal to the senses (335).

Such deception is the common theme of More's earliest English poems. In the first of his "Nine Pageants," for example, Childhood admits that "in play is all my mind" and that "I lead my life always in play" (EW 332–33).[3] The second pageant shows Manhood leading the same kind of life, except that his play is no longer "to cast a . . . ball" or to set a top, but "to hunt and hawk" and "to bestride a good and lusty steed" (333). By the time old age arrives, the dominant pleasures become the pride and power of office, and in later pageants this vain old man is still preoccupied with yet another form of pleasure: dreams of his own fame. So vain is this old man that he foolishly scorns the very one who will soon defeat him: "O cruel death, thy power I confound" (334).

Only after we have seen the whole pageant of this epicure's life does the Poet enter to warn his readers to distinguish between counterfeit pleasures and true pleasures—between the "elusive goods of this perishable world" (such as "pleasures, praise, homage," which all "quickly disappear") and "the love of God, which endures forever" (EW 335; CW3.2, no. 272).

"A Rueful Lamentation" also warns against "put[ting] your trust and confidence / In worldly joy and frail prosperity" instead of "heavenly things" (EW 335, 337). The longest of these early poems, "The Book of Fortune," develops the nature and cause of this confusion. It warns against Lady Fortune's "fair countenance and deceitful mind," which cause her followers "to crouch and kneel" and to gape after her trinkets of temporary bliss "as a dog does for the bone" (339). These mistaken people give up their liberty for bondage "in a fool's paradise"; true liberty, however, is achieved only by loving moral excellence and virtue, a way of life that actively seeks detachment from Fortune's transitory treasures. Throughout this poem, More reminds his readers that they are free to choose. "Each man has of himself the governance," we are told in the first part. And at the end of the poem, those who chose Fortune—even after More's warnings—are reminded, "Blame ye not me. . . . For it is your own fishing and not mine. . . . Do as you like, [for no man shall bind you]" (344).

Throughout his epigrams, More makes the same point about the consequences of choosing deceptive and fleeting pleasures. For example, "Exhortation to True Virtue" begins by lamenting that "alas, whatever in this miserable world attracts miserable man withers at once and dies like the spring rose." It then concludes: "Drink in the virtues; abstain from vain joys. True joys are the companions of the noble spirit" (CW3.2, no. 68). Not only do these vain joys wither, but they can also gravely harm those determined to enjoy them. For instance, the epigrams on overzealous lovers of drink show how this immoderation can turn people into savage beasts (no. 232) who are blind to the very world in which they live (nos. 210, 214). The same transformation occurs in souls who pursue their immoderate thirst for power and fame, a beastly thirst that can lead to the most disastrous type of blindness, the mad blindness of tyranny.

This image of blindness, usually representing the darkness of reason, occurs frequently in More. At one point, More explains what causes the "blindness of us worldly folk": neglecting to plant and cultivate the counsels needed in the gardens of our souls (EW 460–61).[4] Only nourishing and medicinal principles can adequately strengthen the eyes of the soul so that they are able to see clearly. Unfortunately, the seedlings of good counsel are often foolishly neglected because of the delight that arises from earthly pleasure; as a result, the "taste of spiritual pleasure" is never developed (461). Since earthly pleasures cannot nourish the soul, an over-preoccupation with them will eventually produce a sickness whereby the soul loses "the natural light of reason" (462). The only cure is to pull out by the root those "weeds of fleshly voluptuousness" so that one can "plant in their places, not only wholesome virtues, but also marvelous ghostly pleasure and spiritual gladness, which in every good soul arises from the love of God" (462–63). This skillful planting and eradication require the skill of the statesman, one able to tend the soul with the knowledge and care of a good physician.

A good physician of the soul recognizes how strongly human nature is attached to earthly goods and pleasures. Only the skilled physician knows how to accomplish the essential work of education—that is, how to cultivate a love for the goods of the soul over the earthly goods of the senses. The "whole study and labor" of the skilled philosopher, for example, is "to sever the soul from the love and affections of the body while they be together" (467). But this severance cannot be done abruptly or without tact. Only by using delight and measured instruction can the soul "flee vain pleasures of the flesh that keep out the very pleasures of the soul" (476).

More understood well, therefore, what was behind Aristotle's statement that "the whole concern of both virtue and of political science is with pleasures and pains" (*Nicomachean Ethics* 1105a, CW12 74/7–9 and note). Why, then, to return to our initial question, does so much folly exist? Because we human beings tend to confuse passing pleasures with true goods.[5] In light of this answer, it is not surprising that pleasure and clear perception are principal themes throughout More's writings.

However, as attractive as this first answer to the question of folly may appear, it is not complete. In fact, this initial formulation might give the somewhat Socratic impression that all vice can be attributed to ignorance, and all virtue to knowledge. However, More's comprehensive assessment of this issue points to other important factors at play. Ignorance and deception alone will not explain, for example, the phenomenon of knowing the good and yet deciding to go against it anyway, regardless of the consequences. An example of this type of irrational behavior appears early in More's *History of King Richard III*. There we see Edward IV rejecting his own weighed judgment and the wise advice of his friends and family on the politically sensitive question of his marriage. Instead of following what he recognizes as the reasonable course of action, he "tak[es] counsel of his desire" and ends up with a marriage that predictably causes grave civil unrest (CW2 61; Fox 1983, 79–80). Why do rational beings act so irrationally, even when they know what they should do instead?

More's most fully developed assessment of this question appears at the end of his life in *A Treatise upon the Passion*, his commentary on the biblical account of the Fall. Here the question becomes particular and concrete, rather than abstract and general: Why were Lucifer and Adam and Eve so foolish as to go against what they knew to be good? Ultimately the answer More gives is the same given by Augustine in his *City of God*: free will, the very property that Luther and his followers denied. We will have to see why this denial roused More and eventually Erasmus to denounce these reformers as potentially destructive of an entire civilization. What will become clear is that one cannot understand More without understanding the centrality of free will in his thought.

According to More's explication, God created rational beings in his own image and likeness (CW13 12/8, CW12 12/7–10, EW 387–88) so that they could be partners in his goodness (CW13 4/11). Only with the responsible liberty arising from a free will and intellect could they do good in a way analogous to God's free and benevolent way of acting. With this freedom, however, they could also choose to use their powers for their own pleasure, not for benevolence towards others (CW13 4–25). Lucifer, for example, performed the first act of perverse folly in choosing to behold his own beauty and to enjoy his will to power rather than continue his friendship with the God who created and loved him (5, compare with *City of God* 12.1). Lucifer's pride "made him so frantic that he boasted that he would be God's [equal] in deed" (5/10–11). Later he seduced Adam and Eve to delight in the same vain fantasy: that "you shall be as gods" (16/9; 19/16,25).

But what could possibly lead a rational creature to act in this way? More's answer is intimately connected with human freedom and is summarized in the word *pride*, that perversion of the rational creature's highest and most distinctive power of free will (cf. *City of God* 12.6).

Pride is the central and most pervasive theme in More's entire corpus. It is pivotal to all his earliest English poems. It underlies the "proud enterprise of [Richard III's] high heart" (CW2 86). Pride in its many forms is satirized in More's epigrams; *Utopia* calls pride "the chief of all plagues";[6] *The Four Last Things* calls it "the root of all sin"; *A Treatise upon the Passion,* "the head and root of all other sins and of them all, most pestilent" (CW4 243, EW 477, CW13 9/22–23). In *A Dialogue Concerning Heresies,* More agrees with Augustine that pride is "the very mother of all heresies" (CW6 423), a foundational idea that underlies all of More's other polemical writings (e.g., CW8 662, 1336). In setting forth his educational objectives for his children, More is most concerned that "this plague of vainglory may be banished far from my children" (SL 106). Even his very last writings on Christ show that "all the work . . . our Savior instructs and exhorts His apostles to, is the work of humility. . . . And since the devil that fell himself by pride is ever most busy to tempt everyman to the same sin . . . , our Savior therefore . . . in sundry places again and again gives His apostles . . . special counsel against the prick of pride" (CW13 116–17).

Pride is the great perversion because rational beings were created as "partners of the creator's goodness" (CW13 4/9), not gods in the idolatrous fantasies of their own minds. In every case, the proud person "boldly frame[s] himself a conscience, with a gloss of his own making after his own fantasy" (CW13 112/12–13). Just as Lucifer and Adam and Eve willfully interpreted God's commands according to their own desires rather than diligently attending to their reason, so every person has the freedom of will to do the same.

Pride, therefore, arises from the soul's intrinsic power to imagine what it wants and then to will freely to delight in that image regardless of its truth or goodness. With this spiritual freedom, rational creatures can will to devise "worldly fantasies"[7] of their own creation that are actually opposed to what exists (CW13 226/14, 81/12; CW12 61/18,27, 154/23,27, 210/5–6, 211/17, 225/1,17), thus leading them to neglect the good and true in order to attend to their own passion or pleasure. Hence, the power of free will is such that what one perceives can be willfully distorted according to one's own wishes, desires, and expectations. Given this fundamental freedom, all people are capable of rebelling against the indications of the intellect.

Augustine explains this same phenomenon at some length in *The City of God*. The proud person chooses "to live according to himself," rather than "abide in the truth" (14.3). By "falling away from the work of God to [his] own works," such a person comes to prefer "to rule with a kind of pomp of empire rather than to be another's subject" (14.11). This "self-pleaser" therefore "abandons Him to whom [he] ought to cleave as [his] end, and becomes a kind of end to [him]self" (14.13); he thus chooses "not to live as he was made to live," but "according to a lie" of his own making (14.4). By so "refusing subjection and revolting from Him who is supreme," the proud person actually "falls to a low condition" by debasing his true nature (14.13). It is the humble person who fulfills and actually exalts his nature by recognizing and accepting his status as a creature. As Augustine puts it, "humility enables us to submit to what is above us; and nothing is more exalted above us than God; and therefore humility, by making us subject to God, exalts us" (14.13). Augustine then goes on to give the essential difference between the city of God and the city of man:

> Humility is specially recommended to the city of God as it sojourns in this world, and is specially exhibited in the city of God and in the person of Christ its King; while the contrary vice of pride, according to the testimony of the sacred writings, specially rules his adversary the devil. And certainly this is the great difference which distinguishes the two cities of which we speak, the one being the society of the godly men, the other of the ungodly, . . . the one guided and fashioned by the love of self, the other by love of God.

This opposition of humility and pride, of love of self and love of God, of the city of man and the city of God is critical to a proper understanding of More's political philosophy.

A favorite metaphor More uses to explain pride is sickness arising from poison (e.g., CW13 16/13ff). Pride is like the venom slyly injected by the subtle serpent; once in the body, this poison gradually turns a reasonable and sane person into one who becomes frantic and mad, and who eventually dies. The only medicine that can bring about a cure is self-knowledge, together with diligent remembrance of who we are: limited creatures who have received all that they are and possess from their benevolent Creator.

Treating the gifts of the Creator as if they were one's own gives rise to yet another of More's favorite metaphors: pride as theft. In his picturesque way, More gives the example of the woman who abuses her gift of beauty by proudly stealing the glory from God. This kind of woman foolishly "stands in her own light and takes herself for fair, weening herself well liked for her broad forehead, while the young man that beholds her marks more her crooked nose" (CW13 8/2–4). In another example, More marvels at those who glory in themselves because they possess a certain amount of gold, which is "but of the earth, and of nature no better than is the poor copper or tin, nor to man's use so profitable as is the poor metal that maketh us the ploughshare, and horseshoe, and horse nails" (8/13–15). Just as vainglorious is the servant who holds himself in godlike honor because he can strut around in the borrowed gown of his master (8/32). Through these and other examples, More makes his point clear: everything that any creature has belongs to God, and to take the glory oneself for mere possession is theft. "'What have you,' says Saint Paul, 'that you have not received? And if you have received it, why do you glory as if you had not received it?'" (9/5–8, 1 Cor 4:7).

Pride occurs, then, "when any creature falls into the delight and liking of itself" rather than the One who brought that creature into being (CW13 7/12–13, 9/28). Yet like the poison in the body, pride does not spread at once. The first step is simply neglect—neglect that may, for example, take the apparently harmless form of vain delight in praise or flattery (7/14, 10/25). Then, by continuing to glory in themselves, people "become secondly thieves unto God, and finally from thieves they fall to be plain rebellious traitors, and refuse to take God for their God, and fall into the detestable pride that Lucifer fell to himself" (10/26–29). In other words, pride develops; and in developing, it can definitively change one's character. For this reason, More strongly warns his readers to "beware of this horrible vice, and resist well the very first motions thereof" (10/30–31). For this reason, More also considered the greatest challenge in life to be the governance of one's pleasures, imaginings, and passions. Such governance requires a deliberate and lengthy education so that good habits can act as what Aristotle calls "a second nature" in support of what is good and true, and not what is merely pleasurable. With such an education, one can eventually come to enjoy spiritual goods more than temporal ones—but only if one has freely chosen such a process as worthwhile and if one has deliberately taken steps to develop the virtues involved.

One of the worst developments of unchecked pride is evidenced in the tyrant, whom More analyzes in *Tyrannicida*. The tyrant, "puffed up by pride, driven by the lust of power, impelled by greed, [and] provoked by thirst for fame" has become as "cruel and violent" as "beasts living by prey . . . , on whom hunger alone has stamped certain marks of a tyrannical nature" (CW3.1 100). Once such a person is hardened in his will to do as he pleases, he will "trample on the laws of men, scorn those of gods, [and have] no respect for life" (100). Significantly, this description is given nearly a decade before More writes his *Richard III*, a work often faulted for presenting Richard's character unrealistically as one-dimensional. Yet to understand More, one must reflect on his conviction that human beings are free enough (or depraved enough —see CW12 151/22) to choose a tyrannical way of life, a life ruled by unrestrained desire rather than the demands of reason. More— like Plato, Thucydides, the Bible, Dante, and Shakespeare—asks his readers to consider whether the Herods, Judases, and Richards as depicted in literature reflect a type of human being that actually does exist. If one acknowledges that such individuals as Hitler and Stalin do pose a perennial threat to peaceful and rational society, then one can appreciate what More considered to be the greatest danger faced by the statesman of any era: the perverse folly of irrational behavior. To counter this tendency, society has an interest in using all the legitimate means at its disposal to encourage its citizens to seek the common good and to acquire a love for goods that are common and health-giving rather than idiosyncratic and destructive.

In the long debate that continues about *Richard III*, one must keep foremost in mind what More makes clear within its pages: he writes so that future generations can learn the lessons of tyranny as fully as story form ("historia") will allow. One central lesson is that unchecked pride can culminate in the triumph of tyranny. To illustrate this as dramatically as literature permits, More, as poet, incorporates tales that are useful to his purpose. The legend of Richard's hunchback, for example, uses an alleged physical deformity to reveal a spiritual deformity which many people do not see—until too late. Since evil triumphs primarily through deception, the role of the poet is to help his readers not only to learn to be discriminating and sharp-sighted but also to remember those lessons vividly.

What allows tyranny to triumph in *Richard III*? Certainly Richard's own deceptiveness and lust for power are important factors. But why does no one detect Richard's deception during his long and difficult ascent to the throne? A close reading of the story shows, with surprising force, that the civil and ecclesiastical leaders are the ones responsible. Why? For one simple reason: these nobles and clergy are no statesmen. Instead, they seek personal favor, fortune, and power to such a degree that they are willing to prostitute their reputations and even their souls to befriend Richard. Lord Hastings, for example, uses his good name to defend Richard's unjust arrest of Lord Anthony Rivers and Richard Grey. With powerful dramatic irony, Hastings "advised [his fellow nobles to] beware that they judged not the matter too far forth ere they knew the truth" (CW2 23/16–17); yet a few lines later the narrator tells us that Lord Hastings partly believed his own argument and knew part to be false. The Duke of Buckingham is also willing to "take it upon [his] soul" to dissuade the Queen from the need to seek sanctuary to save her young son (28/20–21). Even the Archbishop of Canterbury, in a servile effort to please Richard, "durst lay his own body and soul both in pledge" to persuade the Queen to leave the sanctuary. Yet the Queen herself is not without fault (Fox 1983, 92). Her self-interest alienated those who could have protected her sons; her imprudence left these children without the necessary protection; her lack of fortitude led her to give up the protection of sanctuary despite her better knowledge; and her lack of political sophistication left her powerless before lawless forces.[8] Yet the first and most obvious cause of Richard's rise is King Edward's premature death—caused by Edward's own lack of virtue in leading a life of "fleshly wantonness."[9] In addition, Edward bears even greater responsibility because of the dissension he caused by his imprudent marriage, a dissension which served as "a sure ground for the foundation of all [of Richard's plans]" (CW2 10). In each of these cases, leaders failed to lead.

As the story unfolds, there are numerous signs of Richard's ambitious plans, but these are repeatedly ignored, leading the narrator to lament "the blindness of our mortal nature" (52/13–14). Yet as the narrator makes clear, this blindness is of the leaders' own making. The Mayor of London, for example, "upon trust of his own advancement," knowingly enters into Richard's plot and even solicits his own brother to spread the slander that Edward V's mother was an adulteress (59). With such widespread complicity in hardened vice, traitorous tyranny easily triumphs—especially because no just leader invokes the law for protection. Instead, only Sir William Catesby and Richard use the laws, manipulating them for their own advantage. Hence "Richard Duke of York, a noble man and a mighty" was able "not by war, but by law, to challenge the crown" and eventually to exercise his tyranny (6/14–15).

As *Richard III* shows, therefore, laws alone are not enough to stop the tyrant. Vigilant statesmen, too, are needed, those with a strong-rooted love for liberty, a love sufficiently tested and educated to withstand the power and deception and ingenuity of evil.

Why so much evil? In summary, More agreed with the classics that ignorance is a major factor; but he also agreed with Augustine's dissent from the classics in his recognition that pride is a cause more fundamental and more difficult to cure—and at times impossible,[10] since the will is truly free (*City of God* 12.3,6,7; 13.14; 14.11,13).

Under such conditions, therefore, can reason rule the free? It can, but only if individual persons and nations exercise the utmost vigilance and possess true virtue.

2   First, Self-Rule

> Each man has of himself the governance. (EW 339)
>
> Is it not a beastly thing to see a man that has reason so rule himself that his feet may not bear him, but . . . rolls and reels until he falls into the gutter? (EW 495)
>
> I beseech our Lord make us all so wise as that we may every man here . . . wisely rule ourself. (Corr 519)
>
> For in man reason ought to reign like a king, and it does reign when it makes itself loyally subject to faith and serves God. For to serve Him is to reign. (CW14 509)
>
> Better to reign in Hell, than serve in Heav'n. (Satan in Milton's *Paradise Lost* 1.263)
>
> You can't be a king unless reason is king over you. (Erasmus CWE27 243)

To rule others justly, leaders must first rule themselves. No political task is more urgent; none is more difficult—as proved by the recurrence of this theme throughout world literature. Homer, for example, shows the tragedy that results when Achilles does not rule his anger. In deliberate contrast, Virgil shows the many political benefits that follow when duty-bound Aeneas eventually comes to rule his emotions for the sake of the common good. Among all of Aeneas's many difficult adventures, however, none proves more difficult and none requires more heroic effort than the struggle to achieve mastery over himself; yet, by the end of the *Aeneid,* Virgil's epic hero still falls short. The greatest king of the Old Testament faces the same challenge of self-rule, and he fails repeatedly. David has far less difficulty conquering giants like Goliath than he does in conquering his own unruly passions. To achieve mastery of himself, David wages battles until the very end of his life, and not without significant defeats.

More's earliest writings are concerned with this same fundamental issue, one that More understood firsthand. When he was sixteen, for example, More experienced the overpowering force of ungoverned emotion. Writing about this experience from the perspective of twenty-five years' distance, More describes his first experience of youthful love:

> I was helpless, as though stunned by a lightning-stroke, when I gazed and continued to gaze upon your face. Then, too, our comrades and yours laughed at our love, so awkward, so frank and so obvious. Thus did your beauty take me captive. (CW3.2, no. 263)

Reflecting on this encounter with Venus and Cupid, More goes on to comment on possible causes:

> Either yours was perfect beauty, or I lent it more perfection than it had; perhaps the stirring of adolescence and the ardor which accompanies the approach of manhood were the reason, or perhaps certain stars we shared at birth had influenced both our hearts.

But whatever the cause, the results were irrepressibly strong. As More writes in the same poem, "On this account a chaperon was imposed upon us, and a door strong enough to thwart our very destiny kept apart a pair whom the stars wished to bring together."

The difficulty of self-rule, or virtuous living, was one of More's lifelong preoccupations and is evident in his first works. More's three earliest poems all center upon the choice of virtue or vice, which in turn is based on the choice of what one will love: heavenly or earthly goods. Throughout "The Book of Fortune," for example, More reminds his readers that they are free to choose. "Each man has of himself the governance," we are told (EW 339). "Blame ye not me. . . . For it is your own fishing and not mine. . . . Do as you like, [for no man shall bind you]" (343–44). More makes clear, however, that this choice has lasting effects upon one's life: the choice is for misery or happiness, slavery or liberty.

To begin to appreciate More's preoccupation with the difficulties in living virtue, one must consider why More would choose to publish *The Life of John Picus* as one of his earliest works. The standard account is that More took Pico as a model for his life as a layman. This explanation, however, goes against the central point of the *Life* itself. According to the surprise ending, the good and pious earl lands in purgatory instead of heaven largely because he ignored his vocation to be a monk and remained a layman instead—a layman who did not know how to rule.

Furthermore, according to the biography, Pico led the life of a scholarly recluse, not that of an active civic humanist and family man. How then could such a person be a model for a man soon to be embroiled in all the cares and duties of a husband, father, lawyer, and politician? By the time he actually published this *Life*, More had four children, a large law practice, and served in Parliament. Pico had experience in none of these areas.

To increase the perplexing character of this work, More found it necessary to add passages and to edit from his translation certain features of Pico's life such as Pico's long preoccupation with the cabala and Pico's supposedly divine nature.[1] In addition, More eliminates seven pages discussing Pico's theological studies and writings and two significant references to the pope.

What, therefore, was of such interest to Thomas More in this famous philosopher who was an earl but should have been a monk and ended up burning in purgatory for neglecting his call? To answer these questions, one must reflect deeply on the dominant theme of the *Life* itself as amended by More.

Overall, the *Life* and all its appendices are primarily concerned with the difficult requirements of living a virtuous life, a life of self-rule. More immediately draws our attention to this facet in the two introductory sections which he adds. Here he refers to "virtue" at least ten times and explains in his dedication that his *Life of John Picus* is meant to help bring about the "gracious increase of virtue" (EW 347). Two pages later, More focuses on Pico's importance in apprehending the true substance of virtue:

> But Picus, of whom we speak, was himself so honorable, for the great plenteous abundance of all such virtues the possession whereof very honor followeth (as a shadow followeth a body) that he was to all them that aspire to honor a very spectacle, in whose conditions, as in a clear polished mirror, they might behold in what points very honor standeth: whose marvelous cunning and excellent virtue though my rude learning be far unable sufficiently to express . . . (EW 349)

At first, this passage seems to praise Pico for his virtue, but looking closely at More's characteristic use of irony, one notices that the work as a whole confirms that Pico is not necessarily such a praiseworthy model of virtue after all. Instead, he may tend to be that "very spectacle" "to all them that aspire to honor," honor being but a shadow of virtue. In other words, in reading Pico's *Life* carefully, one can learn—by understanding where Pico fell short—the true nature of virtue as well as the arduous warfare needed to achieve it.

The first part of More's translation emphasizes Pico's wondrous birth, his noble heritage and appearance, and the extraordinary learning he achieved while still a youth. At this point, More adds his own assessment within the text he is translating: "Full of pride and desirous of glory and man's praise (for yet was he not kindled in the love of God) he went to Rome, . . . coveting to make a show of his cunning" (EW 351). Here More points to what he considers to be Pico's fundamental character defect. This pride is most manifest when Pico goes to defend his nine hundred propositions at Rome, where, instead of winning acclaim as he expected, he is charged with heresy and is thus shamed and endangered. This experience leads to Pico's conversion, which More describes in a brief paragraph that replaces seven pages originally devoted to his theological and philosophical writings. Instead of focusing on these intellectual achievements, More tells us that "from thenceforth [Pico] gave himself day and night most fervently to the study of Scripture" (353).

What follows seems to be a truly exemplary life, one spent in fasting, generous almsgiving, and dedicated study whereby, "in the inward affections of the mind, he cleaved to God with very fervent love and devotion" (359). Especially in light of this glowing section that appears to be pure virtue, the aftermath of Pico's life comes as a considerable shock to the reader: Pico ends up not praising God in heaven, but crying forth from the fires of purgatory.

This surprise ending is again typical of the More one finds in those witty epigrams whose effectiveness usually depends on an unexpected turn (Grace 1985, 117). The unexpected twist in Pico's *Life* plays the same dialectical function as the surprising turn in the epigram: it forces the readers to rethink their initial perceptions and to read again in trying to understand what led to this abrupt end. In this *Life,* we must reconsider our entire notion of virtue and try to discover where Pico went wrong, where he did not adequately rule himself.

More gives three possible reasons for Pico's failure: he was either not

> kind [i.e., grateful] enough for so great benefices of God, or called back by the tenderness of his flesh (as he was a man of delicate complexion) he shrank from the labor, or thinking haply that the religion had no need of him, deferred it for a time. (EW 361)

These three deterrents to true virtue—ingratitude due to lack of love, negligence due to comfort, and sloth due to rationalization—deserve special note, partly because they will appear as major themes in More's writings until the very end of his life. They are also among the greatest obstacles to the development of the statesman.

At this point one must ask, what is More's understanding of true virtue if the great and pious Pico should fall so short? And what can less talented mortals do to acquire it? In getting us to ask such questions, More has succeeded in using the surprise ending to engage his readers in the dialectical process which will lead them to appreciate the material he appends to this biography.

Of Pico's fifty published letters, More selects and translates only three. All deal with the problems of statesmanship. Two show Pico's philosophy of self-rule; the other subtly shows the fundamental flaw in Pico's actual rule of himself, the flaw that accounts for his ending up in the flames of purgatory.

The first and third letters are addressed to Pico's nephew John Francis, who is struggling to live as a statesman in a corrupt and worldly court. More writes a lengthy introduction to the first, commenting not upon the many Christian elements that fill the letter, but upon the classical image of Circe which Pico merely mentions in passing.

Circe is the classical figure often used to explain how individuals can allow themselves to be turned into beasts, and this figure illustrates the interior "warfare" needed if one is to achieve virtuous living. More explains that Circe's power comes from an enchantment whereby the lure of sensual pleasure "changeth us from the figure of reasonable men into the likeness of unreasonable beasts" (363). He then cautions his readers not to look for such enchanted beasts outside of ourselves; rather, the greatest beasts are the "brutish appetites" within. If we leave these appetites ungoverned, More warns, "we deform the image of God in our souls, after Whose image we be made, and make ourselves worse than idolaters" (363–64).

In focusing upon Circe, More brings to the fore the same question posed by his *Life* as a whole: how is one to be truly virtuous in a world of powerful charms and deceptive allurements? The answer Pico gives in this first letter is a clear and unambiguously Christian answer: one lives virtuously by loving God ardently above all else. Curiously he says nothing about duties to one's country and fellow citizens. Ardent love of God is achieved, according to Pico, in this way: "If thou covet to be happy at the last—let no day pass thee but thou once at the leastwise present thyself to God by prayer, and falling down before Him flat to the ground with an humble affection of devout mind" (368). He then sums up by advising two things which More, too, would advise throughout the rest of his life[2]:

> Now to make an end with this one thing, I warn you . . . never forget these two things: that both the Son of God died for you and that you shall also yourself die shortly, live you ever so long. With these two, as with two spurs—that one of fear, that other of love—spur forth your horse through the short way of this momentary life, to the reward of eternal felicity. (368)

Pico's dual counsel—to consider Christ's love for us and to remember the inevitability of death—makes the task of living virtuously appear quite simple. In contrast, More's final version of Pico's *Life* shows that task to be so difficult that no one[3] can be assured of success, not even those who appear to be most pious.

Pico's third letter is quite similar to the first, since it is written to the same person, who now faces even greater adversity. Pico urges John Francis to continue living virtuously amid his many travails, and he tells him from the first word to the last line of the letter to do so joyfully—because in this way he will imitate Christ. True virtue "should have God alone to please" (372). This idea he repeats again and again: "Stop therefore thine ears, my most dear son, and whatsoever men say of thee, whatsoever men think on thee, account it for nothing, but regard only the judgment of God" (373).

In contrast to the clear Christian teaching of these letters, Pico's last letter poses a significant problem, one that suggests more evidence why Pico ends up doing time in purgatory. In this letter Pico responds to his close friend Andrew Corneus, who has told Pico just what Giles and Morus tell Hythlodaeus in *Utopia*: that he should apply his philosophic learning to civic life. Pico gives a passionate defense of his liberty, arguing that his most princely activity is the pursuit of philosophy itself. Philosophy makes its practitioners

> kings of kings; they love liberty; they cannot bear the proud manners of estates; they cannot serve. They dwell with themselves and be content with the tranquillity of their own mind; they suffice themselves and more; they seek nothing out of themselves. (370)

The phrasing of this unstatesmanlike reply could be mistaken for Hythlodaeus's, especially since both refuse civic service. But what Christian could say these words in an unqualified way? More, in his introduction to this letter, points to this incongruity by stating unambiguously what the letter explicitly denies: that one *can* legitimately "use" philosophy for the common good (369). While Pico denounces all "useful" applications of philosophy as mercenary, More argues that it can rightfully be studied "for the instruction of [the] mind in moral virtue"—the same position which Cicero and other civic humanists strongly advocated.

More seems to draw our attention to the unchristian side of Pico in another subtle way: by the dating of the letter. The actual letter was written in 1486, the year before Pico's conversion (according to the dating in More's biography). If More had given the actual date, the reader would have another indication of the change that took place in Pico. More "errs," however, and dates the letter October 1492, a few months *after* his second letter to John Francis. What is the literary effect of this error?[4] It seems to show a continued ambiguity in Pico's motives after his conversion—an ambiguity which seems corroborated by the fact that Pico is punished in purgatory. Overall, this letter helps one appreciate the subtlety of pride and the difficulty that even Pico encountered in achieving genuine virtue and clear-sighted self-knowledge.

By so posing the difficulty which the great Pico himself experienced in living virtue, More prepares the way for the final section of poems, the section that is largely More's own addition to a work which is otherwise mostly translation. Here More develops Pico's short aphorisms, which present the need for a vigilant and carefully studied warfare within each individual.

But before including these poems, More translates one of Pico's many devotional commentaries. The only one chosen is designed to stir the reader to the ardor and meditation advised in letters 1 and 3. More also includes Pico's "Interpretation of Psalm 15," which focuses again upon the difficulty of acquiring virtue. It warns that the "one peril" of the good man is to "wax proud of his virtue" (375). The way to avoid this peril is "if a man had God always before his eyes as a ruler of all his works, and in all his works should neither seek his own lucre, his glory, nor his own pleasure, but only the pleasure of God" (379). To achieve this objective, Pico advises prayer and meditation, since "of every meditation we should always purchase one virtue or other" (377). Once again Pico makes the acquisition of virtue sound relatively simple, in contrast to the impression More leaves.

More's first series of poems, "Twelve Rules of . . . Spiritual Battle," expands Pico's twelve short prose apothegms into five pages of verse.[5] It begins by dispelling the utopian desire for the virtuous life to be easy. Showing More's usual common sense reasoning, the narrator of rule 1 explains that one must suffer now or suffer even worse in the afterlife. He goes on to explain in rule 2 that even this world requires great labor and effort if the fruits of the earth are to be acquired. One must therefore expect "war continual" and battles sharp and long. Rule 3 continues developing the same thought, but turns to the example of a militant Christ to illustrate the effort needed to acquire genuine virtue:

> Consider well that folly it is and vain
> To look for heaven with pleasure and delight.
> Since Christ our Lord and sovereign *captain*
> Ascended never but by manly *fight*
> And bitter passion; then were it no right
> That any servant, ye will yourself record,
> Should stand in better condition than his lord.
> (381, emphasis added)

More, following biblical tradition, uses battle imagery in depicting the struggle for virtue. This fight must not be a grudging one, according to rule 4: "[W]e not only should not grudge / But even be glad and joyful of this fight" (381). Why? So we can delight in imitating Christ. Curiously characteristic of More, this rule is the longest of the entire poem and exhorts the soldier to be joyful like Christ. All five stanzas of this rule focus the reader's attention on Christ's humble and valiant way of life; they end with a call for the reader to see in every difficulty and in every battle an opportunity to develop some virtue.

The next two rules counsel constant vigilance in this battle for virtue. They encourage the reader to take the offensive by striving always to perform "some good virtuous act," while being on guard for the blinding power of pride.

Rule 8 continues to counsel and excite the soldier to virtue: before battle he must keep himself in shape; in battle he should fight "as though thou shouldest after that victory / Enjoy for ever a perpetual peace"; yet after battle, he must be ready to fight immediately again.

This readiness for war should not lead to presumption, however, as rule 9 cautions: we are but "frail glass" and "he that loveth peril shall perish therein." The next rule also gives important advice to creatures who are weak and fallen: resist evil from the very beginning, for "Too late cometh the medicine if thou let the sore / By long continuance increase more and more."

Rule 11 introduces considerations that are indispensable once the battle becomes "bitter, sharp and sour." Here the narrator explains that the greatest pleasure comes from the virtue which conscience beholds, not from the outward pleasures of the body. As he did in rule 3, the narrator again calls for "manly defence" that will bring "honor, peace and rest / In glorious victory, triumph and conquest."

Finally, the last rule addresses the soul under severe siege, perhaps verging on despair. The counsel given is biblical and pinpoints again the one great danger of any spiritual combat: pride.

> Remember the glorious apostle Saint Paul
> When he had seen God in His perfect being,
> Lest such revelation should his heart extol,
> His flesh was suffered rebel against his soul:
> This did almighty God of His goodness provide
> To preserve His servant from the danger of pride.
>
> (385)

This pride is "the very crop and root of all mischief." And what is the solution? How does one best fight against this root of all evil? The "Rules of Spiritual Battle" concludes with the answer that recurs in at least a dozen other works which More writes:

> Against this pomp and wretched world's gloss
> Consider how Christ the Lord, sovereign power,
> Humbled Himself for us unto the cross:
> And peradventure death within one hour
> Shall us bereave wealth, riches and honor:
> And bring us down full low both small and great
> To vile carrion and wretched wormes meat.
>
> (385)

Meditation on Christ and the reality of death—these themes continued to be central in More's writings throughout the rest of his life.

Following these rules of spiritual combat is a poem on "The Twelve Weapons of Spiritual Battle." Again More greatly expands Pico's work; for each of Pico's twelve phrases, More composes a seven-line poem. These weapons are actually counsels we should "consider well" "when the pleasure of a sinful temptation comes to mind" (386). The first seven are reminders of the fleeting character of earthly pleasures and of earthly life as compared to the eternal joy and enduring good of right action. The eighth recalls the nature and dignity of human beings: "Remember how God hath made thee reasonable / Like unto His image and figure" (387). The ninth is a reminder that the greatest source of joy this earth offers is a good conscience, i.e., "th' inward gladness of a virtuous mind" (388). The next two counsels recall the many benefits bestowed by a loving God who "daily calls you to His bliss" and who "dearly has bought" each one through "the piteous cross of woeful Christ." By considering God's many benevolent actions, the narrator appeals to the warrior's sense of justice, stirring him to remain diligent and loyal. This appeal is reinforced in the last poem by recalling examples of the great saints: "The witness of saints, and martyrs' constant sight / Shall thee of slothful cowardice accuse: / God will thee help if thou do not refuse" (388).

These twelve counsels, composed at the beginning of More's literary career, call to mind the "heap of good counsel" he composes at the end of his life in *A Dialogue of Comfort against Tribulation*. In that work, More reminds us that such advice is necessary for a life of self-rule, for a life of virtue (see, for example, CW12 7/22, 202/1–3, 282/1–15).

These two series of poems, therefore, point us directly to the underlying theme of Pico's *Life*: virtue or self-rule requires a constant and difficult battle, a battle which can easily be lost. Yet, as More's concluding poem indicates, warfare is not the most important activity; the love which motivates and directs that self-rule is. In his "Twelve Properties or Conditions of a Lover," More develops Pico's list of qualities into an elaborate and carefully structured poem about the nature of love. Each property is set forth in two stanzas: the first stanza describes the property as it is present at the peak of ardent human love; the second then applies that human quality to the love for God. This poem has special importance in dispelling the theory that More was somewhat manichaean in his outlook or that he undervalued the human side of life. More's affirmation of both the human and the divine is perhaps most clearly seen in his use of Petrarchan conceits in treating the tenth and eleventh properties of love, but this affirmation is present throughout the entire poem.

More also draws the reader's attention to the power of love in the last selection that he appends to his *Life*, "A Prayer of Picus Mirandula unto God." This passionate prayer ends with a view of God that More affirmed throughout his life, that of God as a "tender loving father."⁶

More's *Life of John Picus,* therefore, sets forth the requirements, and especially the great difficulties, of living virtuously—even for a man as learned and austere as Pico. The greatest obstacle is the lure of pride, which, as we have seen, is freely choosing one's own idea of the good over the Creator's.

While the *Life of John Picus* relies heavily upon biblical sources to present the nature and difficulties of living virtue, many of More's other early works do not. His three Lucian translations, for example, deal with this same phenomenon of self-rule, but from a nontheological point of view. In *Cynicus,* the Stoic philosopher describes the effect of following ungoverned appetite. Speaking to a critic who ridicules his self-discipline and austere way of life, the Stoic philosopher retorts:

> You yourselves bestow no thought on your own actions, basing none of them on rational judgment, but upon habit and appetite. Therefore you are exactly the same as men carried along by a torrent; for they are carried along wherever the current takes them, and you wherever your appetites take you. Your situation is just like what they say happened to the man who mounted a mad horse. For it rushed off, carrying him with it; and he couldn't dismount again because the horse kept running. Then someone who met them asked him where he was off to, and he replied, "Wherever this fellow decides," indicating the horse. Now if anyone asks you where you're heading for, if you wish to tell the truth, you will simply say that it's where your appetites choose. (CW3.1 167)

As the Stoic makes clear, self-rule requires freely chosen restraints and deprivations. However, the masterful irony of this dialogue is such that it leaves the thoughtful reader wondering if the Stoic himself has acquired adequate self-rule. For not only must the appetites of the body be governed, but so also must the appetites of the mind, as shown in More's translation of two other Lucian dialogues. Both satirize the excesses of the supposed philosopher.

In *Menippus,* a youth goes "to the men whom they call philosophers . . . , begging them to deal with me as they would, and to show me a plain, solid path in life" (171). Bewildered by their "most contradictory of opinions," he resolves to visit Teiresias in the underworld to find out what is "the best life," the life that "a man of sense would choose" (172). During the visit, he decides that all the world is but a stage where Fortune "arrays the participants in various costumes of many colors" (176). And when he finally meets Teiresias, he learns that the simple life is best, one that allows "laughing a great deal" (179).

Lover of Lies also satirizes the ways of supposed philosophers, showing that "a powerful antidote to such poisons" as their own fantasies is found "in truth and in sound reason brought to bear everywhere" (196; chapter 4 below gives a detailed analysis of this dialogue).

Sound reasoning is surely an indispensable element in self-rule, but as seen in chapter 1, sound reason cannot exist apart from virtue, at least not for long. Since we are rational creatures, our reason is meant to discern the laws of that creation of which we are a part. Unless practiced in virtue, however, the mind will easily be lured to vainglory instead of truth. Without virtue, one will not submit to laws and authorities outside of oneself, a submission that is, paradoxically, needed for the freedom that comes from self-rule. In this light, one can understand why More summed up the whole of his educational intent as putting "virtue in the first place among goods, learning in the second" (SL 105). More knew that virtue was needed to develop in his children a good conscience, i.e., "the inner knowledge of what is right [*conscientia recti*]" (SL 104, also 106). Without such a foundation in both virtue and truth, he judged that a person "ever wavers between joy and sadness because of other men's opinions" (104). The acquisition of virtue must have first place, since only a well-ordered soul can prevent the blindness or folly that comes from following disordered passion, especially pride.

According to More, the "whole fruit" of education "should consist in the testimony of God and a good conscience" (SL 106), which should also give rise to an inward calm and peace (106). Instead of this calm clear-sightedness, pride brings "a blindness almost incurable" (EW 478), since pride presents to the soul a mad or vain fantasy (478), a counterfeit (461ff) or "false imagination" (476), instead of reality itself.

As we have seen, the main problem of cultivating the disposition needed for rational behavior is that the will and the intellect are drawn more immediately and forcefully to temporal goods of the body than to the eternal goods of the soul (CW12 108/26–109/2). Hence the first affections are directed to comfort and pleasure, not to virtue and contemplation. To acquire these more satisfying "spiritual affections," one must actively temper the demands of the senses while engendering, planting, and watering the spiritual affections "many a time and oft" (205/9; 282/7–8,12). This requires a development in self-knowledge, frequent contemplation, "substantial advice and good counsel," and a "right imagination and remembrance" (238/7–8, 198/25–33, 202/2–3, 312/11–12). The result, achieved after much effort over many years, is "a fervent longing" for the soul's greatest joys (306/29–307/1).

More warns, however, that it takes "labor, travail, penance and bodily pain" to achieve the "sweetness, comfort, pleasure and gladness" of that highest good and greatest pleasure possible, i.e., that "ardent and lasting love" of eternal goods (EW 463–64). Just as cultivation of the transitory earth requires considerable labor, effort, and time, so does cultivation of the immortal soul.

Good precepts and affections must be planted and nourished, while the "nettles, briars and other . . . barren weeds" of pride and deceptive pleasures must be carefully and consistently rooted out (SL 105; EW 460–64; CW4 99/31–32; CW12 13/13ff, 282/14–17). Only after "considering deeply" and "pondering well" the "good seed" of wise counsel, can the soul achieve a depth of love for things eternal (EW 492, 486, 476). This depth can be achieved only "by a long continuance, a strong deep-rooted habit—not like a reed ready to wave with every wind, nor like a rootless tree scantly up on end in a loose heap of light sand, that will with a blast or two be blown down" (CW12 204/13–17). Only such a steadfast conscience can provide the greatest joy possible in this life (EW 365, 388, 386, 381–85).

Without virtue, reason will never be able to enjoy that calm and stability needed to see clearly. In *A Dialogue of Comfort,* for example, Anthony discusses the dangers of a mind controlled by the passion of fear. As Anthony explains, a soul in such disorder fails to see things as they are (CW12 111–12); instead, it sees fantasies and vain imaginings. Anthony gives the example of an army that stays awake all night. They are terrified of their enemies, who seem to be entrenched just a short distance away. At daybreak, however, they discover that the "enemy" was nothing but a farmer's hedge (110).

Another example Anthony gives is the fear involved in the "most horrible" temptation to suicide (122ff). To cure a soul shaken and disordered by this extreme fear, Anthony distinguishes several steps which a physician of the soul must take. First, the physician must find out about the person and his situation—a knowledge he can attain only if, like Socrates, he can get the person to speak his true mind. Then, having entered into conversation, the "cunning physician" must give warnings of the danger in "a sweet and pleasant manner"—using fictitious stories if necessary. Why are stories important? Because they allow an objectivity not usually possible in self-examination; in short, they allow reason to operate, unimpeded by passions and self-interest. By considering and discussing the characters of a story, one can come to see principles that apply to one's own situation. Through such stories, the suicidal person can gradually come to see the difference between imaginary and real apprehensions.

Yet more basic than stories to the curative process is the clear-sighted reasoning that good stories can stimulate—the type of reasoning the Greeks called dialectics, i.e., rigorous conversations that can bring sure knowledge and that can distinguish "fond fantasies" from "substantial truths." Throughout the *Dialogue,* we see old Anthony skillfully directing such a conversation. By the end of the book, he has helped Vincent to conquer his own fears and false imaginings.⁷ He has brought Vincent to a clearer perception of the true nature of his situation by cunningly eliciting his doubts and apprehensions, while calling him to remember true principles as opposed to the illusory ones.

Wise Anthony has a twofold task in bringing about this cure. He must discover the ideas and fantasms which occupy Vincent's thoughts, and he must lead young Vincent to see or to recollect ideas that correspond more closely to the nature of things. In this dialogue, therefore, More dramatizes the traditional Platonic metaphor in presenting old Anthony as a skillful physician whose wisdom and wit permit him to devise the proper educational strategy to help young and passionate Vincent to achieve self-rule by acquiring greater wisdom and control.

Throughout all three books, Anthony shows that the best defense against unruly passions is a conscience which rests firmly in truth. Anthony, therefore, resembles Plato's true statesman, who not only possesses both true knowledge and virtue himself, but can also educate others by "implanting" these goods of knowledge and virtue in the souls of his fellow citizens (*Statesman* 309). He stands in stark contrast to the dissembling sophist who uses the art of dialectic to make himself a hero of debate and a merchant of learned wares (*Sophist* 23).

As this *Dialogue* makes clear, virtuous and clear-sighted persons need a "heap of good counsel" to help in their deliberations about the many unknowns in life. This supply of counsel is especially needed in the realm of ever-changing political events that arise from the often unpredictable actions of people who are genuinely free by nature. The "heap of good counsel" Anthony gives is from the same source as the counsel More himself gave: from the long tradition of classical, Christian, and native English authors.

To achieve self-rule, therefore, one needs a virtue that is adequately supported by good counsel and that has been sufficiently tested to withstand the storms and unknown dangers that will always arise.

3 Ruling Citizens: What Is Needed?

> Any man who has command of many men owes his authority to those whom he commands: he ought to have command not one instant longer than [the people] wish. Why are impotent kings so proud? Because they rule merely on sufferance? (CW3.2, no. 121)
>
> There can be nothing more helpful than a loyal friend, who by his own effort assuages your hurts. Two beggars formed an alliance of firm friendship—a blind man and a lame one. The blind man said to the lame one, "You must ride upon my shoulders." The latter answered, "you, blind friend, must find your way by means of my eyes." The love which unites shuns the castles of proud kings and prevails in the humble hut. (CW3.2, no. 32)

In his early epigrams, More indicates that the good ruler must be humble if he is to be effective. Epigram 32, quoted above, is one of the most striking and original in a series of poems dealing with government. This poem shows humility's capacity for uniting and fostering friendship through the recognition and acceptance of limitations, an attitude in sharp contrast to the cruelty and violence of proud tyrants. As the other poems in this series imply, great skill is involved in the ability to match up deficiencies in such a way as to make a society work. This skill is precisely the one needed for good rule.

In his later works, More repeatedly makes the same point about humility. One of the most striking examples occurs with the only direct reference to Henry VIII in More's final books. In his *Treatise upon the Passion,* More is commenting on Christ's washing his disciples' feet, a custom continued throughout Christendom by many princes during Passion Week. Of the princes who practice this custom, More comments that none performs it "I suppose nowhere more godly than our sovereign lord the King's Grace here of this realm" (CW13 114). Having contrasted this attitude of humble service with King Saul's proud insistence upon his own ends (112), More observes that all Christ "instructed and exhorted His apostles to is the work of humility." He then concludes by giving special warning to the "governors of His flock" against "the prick of pride" in the proper use of their authority (116).

In these last works, proud King Saul emerges as the recurring example of the great danger facing any ruler—and quite pointedly, the danger facing Henry VIII. Saul was chosen by God and entrusted with enforcing the laws of Israel, and he began as a just and energetic advocate of Israel's common good. Yet faced with tribulations, Saul became impatient and "murmured, grudged and distrusted God" (CW13 213). Because of the "framed reverence of his own stand," Saul "followed his own wit" after "boldly fram[ing] himself a conscience with a gloss of his own making after his own fantasy" (112). By following this fantasy, he ended up consulting witches, a practice explicitly forbidden by a law that Saul himself proclaimed (CW13 213, CW12 62, CW14 153). Soon, civil war ensued because of his grave injustices, and in the end the kingship had to be taken away from him.

Since pride allows one to choose a "fond fantasy" over the dictates of conscience, it presents the statesman with his greatest difficulties of good rule. In cases such as King Saul's, it occasionally becomes necessary to remove from authority those who abuse it; in other cases, it becomes necessary to prevent fellow citizens from exercising a free choice that goes against the common good, or even a good of their own.

As we have seen, suicide is an example of the latter case that More dwells upon in his *Dialogue of Comfort* (CW12 122ff). Because of a mad fantasy and the desperate passions it arouses, persons can attempt to take their own lives. What should one do? If the person is truly free, should not that person be able to choose to end his own life?

In dealing with this example, old and wise Anthony shows that such a person may not be free at all, but rather enslaved by a delusion or passion—"maddened" by some grave disease of the soul. The statesman must, therefore, have a profound understanding of the human soul[1] and must know how to identify the many illnesses that can afflict it, always respecting the individual's fundamental freedom, but always attentive to the demands of the common welfare at the same time.

Considering the statesman as a physician of the soul is a concept that goes back to classical times. In Plato's trilogy on statesmanship, for example, the Eleatic Stranger explains clearly how a proud soul is cured:

> [Educators] cross-examine a man's words, when he thinks he is saying something and is really saying nothing, and easily convict him of inconsistencies in his opinions; these they then collect by the dialectical process, and placing them side by side, show that they contradict one another.... He, seeing this, is angry with himself, and grows gentle towards others, and thus is entirely delivered from great prejudices and harsh notions ... [thus] produc[ing] the most lasting good effect on the person who is the subject of the operation. For as the physician considers that the body will receive no benefit from taking food until the internal obstacles have been removed, so the purifier of the soul is conscious that his patient will receive no benefit from the application of knowledge until he is refuted, and from refutation learns modesty; he must be purged of his prejudices first

and made to think that he knows only what he knows, and no more. (*Sophist* 230)

The physician of the soul must purify the soul by first helping it to learn modesty; only then can the soul benefit from the knowledge it acquires.

In one of his earliest letters, More comments that only the most skilled physician can treat those vices of the city which arise from the "feigned loves and honeyed poisons" of accomplished flatterers (SL 4–5). Such poisons can affect the health of the whole person and all those around him (CW15 285, 291). Only a skillful physician knows "when and how long some certain medicine is necessary, which at another time ministered or at that time overlong continued, might put the patient at peril" (CW12 147). Unless properly treated, moral cankers can eat through the flesh and "catch the bone," making normal remedies impossible (EW 384).

Good reform depends upon a true statesman who is immensely learned in the laws and customs of his people, since there are "many things [in those laws and customs] to be pondered and weighed by his wisdom" in effecting a suitable cure. Just as with a "physician for whom there are many good books written to give good light and instruction," a statesman cannot find all the cures in casebooks. He must use "the discretion of his brain" and not be restricted to books to bring about the most prudent and effective cure (CW6 261–62). Given the many peculiarities and circumstances of each case, the statesman must have the knowledge and judgment—the prudence—of the best of physicians. He must also have the skill to implement those laws effectively, primarily by eliciting the people's good will and cooperation. This reliance upon good will is imperative because "when their hearts are once fixed upon their blind affections, a man may with as much fruit preach to a post as reason with them to the contrary. For they nothing ponder what is reasonably spoken to them, but whereto their fond affection inclineth" (433).

More considered the "best and kindest of physicians" to be

Christ (CW14 95), and he presented a rather detailed analysis of the rhetorical skill involved in Christ's attempt to cure his three most trusted apostles and Judas, the known traitor. The example More chooses to analyze occurs after Peter, James, and John have fallen asleep while supposedly watching with Christ in the Garden of Gethsemane. With these individuals, Christ uses skillful rhetoric to appeal to the conscience of each. As More's context makes clear, the apostles represent rulers who should be vigilantly governing. Here Peter, along with James and John, acts as a ruler who "neglects to do what the duty of his office requires," and "like a cowardly ship's captain who is so disheartened by the furious din of a storm" that he "deserts the helm . . . and abandons the ship to the waves" (265).

The first medicine Christ applies to Peter consists of two rhetorical questions, an exhortation, and an admonition:

> Simon, are you sleeping? Could you not stay awake one hour with me? Stay awake and pray that you may not enter into temptation. For the spirit indeed is willing, but the flesh is weak. [Mt 26:40–41, Mk 14:37–38]

More observes that "this short speech of Christ is remarkably forceful: the words are mild, but their point is sharp and piercing" (CW14 161).[2] Pointing out the "barbed implications" of "our Savior's gentle words to Peter" (163), More observes that this first application of medicine did not succeed in rousing Peter and the others "to complete vigilance but only to such a startled, half-awake drowsiness that they hardly raised their eyes to look at Him . . . [and] still they slipped back into sleep the moment He went away" (195).[3]

When Christ returns later to find his disciples asleep once more, he again "undercuts them with . . . a serious and weighty kind of irony" (289) that may "shock" the "pious" who are "not sufficiently versed in the figures of speech" (293).[4] Like Horace and the Eleatic Stranger, Christ is well aware of the power of language; even so, his forceful appeal to conscience does not effect an immediate cure to their negligence. Nonetheless, Christ patiently continues his appeal to their consciences, inviting them "to cooperate with the promptings of His inward assistance" (199). In addition to his "kindness and patience" (199), however, he does not hesitate to use severe rebuke (483). Like a good surgeon, he will "wield with vigor that sword of the word, whose stroke, like that of a scalpel, lets the pus out and heals by wounding" (479). Eventually this "diligent care" (195) does bring about such a cure that Peter, James, and John all will die rather than neglect their duties. This cure depended upon the patient and artful development of conscience in each.

Such is not the case with Judas, however, whose pride prevents him from learning from the gentlest of rebukes (CW13 76–78). Nevertheless, even during Judas's actual betrayal, "Christ as a most conscientious physician tries both ways of effecting a cure" —i.e., by diligently using "words both gentle and harsh . . . so that if anyone should be suffering from a disease that does not respond to treatment, he may not blame the failure on . . . negligence but rather attribute it to the virulence of his own disease" (CW14 403).

More explains these two ways at some length:

> Employing first of all gentle words, He says "Friend, why have you come?" When he heard himself called "friend," the traitor was left hanging in doubt. For since he was aware of his own crime, he was afraid that Christ used the title "friend" as a severe rebuke for his hostile unfriendliness. On the other hand, since criminals always flatter themselves with the hope that their crimes are unknown, he was blind and mad enough to hope . . . that his villainous deed had escaped Christ's notice.
>
> But because nothing could be more unwholesome for him than to be duped by such a futile hope . . . , Christ in His goodness no longer allows him to be led on by a deceptive hope of deceiving but immediately adds in a grave tone, "Judas, do you betray the Son of Man with a kiss?" He addresses him by the name He had ordinarily used— and for this reason, so that the memory of their old friendship might soften the heart of the traitor and move him to repent. He openly rebukes his treachery lest he should believe it is hidden and be ashamed

to confess it. Moreover, He reviles the impious hypocrisy of the traitor: "With a kiss," He says, "do you betray the Son of Man?" (405–7)

In dealing with Judas, Christ first uses irony—a mild but penetrating appeal to conscience. However, when such medicine does not work, Christ resorts to strong and open rebuke, even using his power to cause Judas to draw back and fall to the ground (413). Despite the care of this good physician, Judas exercises his free will and deliberately rejects the medicine that would cure his conscience, a conscience "full of guilty sores" (457). Yet since all of creation works together against such madness (461/10–11), Judas—like Richard III—is unable to ignore the demands of conscience for long.

Conscience and free will are two factors of fundamental importance that inform More's understanding of statesmanship. Throughout his writings, More presents the governed as free and thinking citizens to be loved and respected, not as slavish subjects to be abused. As Damian Grace has pointed out, More speaks of "citizens" and the "people" of a nation, not "subjects" of a monarch (1988, 133–36). As such, "these terms imply a political community and not merely a multitude which gains its corporate being from monarchical rule" (135). These terms also imply that human beings are free and self-governing. In Epigram 121, for example, More articulates a view of political authority that was grounded upon free consent:

The Consent of the People both Bestows and Withdraws Sovereignty
Any man who has command of many men owes his authority to those whom he commands: he ought to have command not one instant longer than his [people] wish. Why are impotent kings so proud? Because they rule merely on sufferance? (CW3.2)

The view of politics behind this epigram is based on a conception More derived from both the classical political philosophers and his native English tradition as well as from the Bible.

Aristotle, for example, points out in the first chapter of his *Politics* that "when, according to the rules of the political science, the citizens rule and are ruled in turn, then [the ruler] is called a statesman" (1252a 15–17). Later he states that "constitutional rule is a government of freemen and equals" (1255b 19–20) where "citizens at large administer the state for the common interest" (1279a 39–40). Cicero agrees with Aristotle but emphasizes the importance of freedom and self-rule in a new way (see chapter 5 below). In addition, English legal theorists like John of Salisbury and Sir John Fortescue articulate clear notions of equality under law and self-rule (e.g., *Policraticus* 28, 67 and *De Laudibus Legum Anglie* 31, 79). Of particular significance, Fortescue draws attention to Augustine's definition of a people in *City of God* 19.23: "A people is a body of men united by *consent* of law and by community of interest" (31, emphasis added). This observation may have been of considerable importance to More in his early lectures on *The City of God*.

More also learned the importance of self-government from his reflections on the biblical understanding of human freedom and responsibility. More held that reason by itself "has no full and perfect instruction without help of revelation" (CW8 996). Thus, revelation can show how God intended political life to be governed, as seen in the way God governed Adam and Eve, both before and after the Fall.

In his exegesis of Genesis, More points out that human beings are created in the image and likeness of God and are thus free and rational. These characteristics are, then, fundamental elements that must always be respected in determining the best way of ruling others.

Before the Fall, for example, political authority did not include the use of force, nor did one person have dominion over another. More illustrates this when Eve falls to the temptation of Satan. In assessing this incident, More blames Adam for not ruling properly. Although Adam "had as then no dominion given him over her, yet his reason might show him that to give her good counsel he should have kept her company, which if he had done, the serpent had not deceived her" (CW13 21). So powerful was reason before the Fall, that government's task was one of good counsel alone. Reason, however, requires free choice, and Adam's love of self led him to neglect its proper use. As More presents it, Adam's negligence was twofold.

First, Adam was "so negligent in looking to sensuality that he let her over-long alone therein, and chose not to do his diligence in driving that sinful suggestion from her" (CW13 22). Hence, "by wandering another way from her, he suffered her to miscarry and be infected" (21). Drawing out the implications of this event for us, More comments that such negligence should serve as a

> warning to every man in this world to do the diligence that he possibly can to keep every other man from hurt. For as holy scripture says: "God has given every man care and charge of his neighbor" [Sir 17:12]. And harm creeps from one to another by more means than men are aware of. And he that cares not if his neighbor's house fall on fire may happen to lose his own. (21)

If such harm proceeds from the neglect of one person's neighbor, even greater harm follows upon a statesman's neglect of his country. More explains:

> This lesson . . . pertains most specially to those that have over other men the special charge given unto them, that our Lord therefore by the mouth of Ezekiel terribly threatened them in this way: "If when I say to the wicked man you shall die, you do not show it him, nor do not speak to him that he may turn from his wicked way and live, both shall that wicked man die in his wickedness and yet the blood of him shall I require of your hands" [Ez 3:18]. (21)

As he continues his commentary, More emphasizes the importance of the good ruler's diligent use of reason:

> This is a fearful work, lo, to those that have the care over other folk and a necessity to take good heed to their flock, to guide them well, call upon them and give them warning of such ways as they may perish in. For otherwise shall the sheep not only perish and be punished, but the scab of the flock shall catch and consume shepherd and all for his negligence. (21–22)

As he does here and throughout his writings, More singles out this vice of negligence as one of the ruler's greatest sources of failure.

Adam is guilty of another instance of negligence, one quite similar to his first. After Adam became aware of Eve's fault, he then neglected to direct his reason to determine the right and just course of action. "For as tenderly as Adam loved Eve," he gave his reason "over to sensuality" (22) and sought to please Eve rather than God (16, 22).

Because Adam and Eve freely chose to neglect the voice of reason, God devised a method of governing human beings that would help them be more vigilant in attending to their highest powers. As More puts it, God orchestrated the negative consequences of free will to serve as a "double help" to insure "double diligence." The double helps are at first surprising since they are "two enemies . . . , the devil and [one's] own sensuality" (CW13 47). Nonetheless, they require constant diligence by each person "to keep sure watch to resist them"; they also serve as a "double help" by requiring each person "to call double so much unto almighty God for grace" (47). Given the presence of these two constant reminders of one's dependence upon God, a person "is more able and more sure now to subdue them both, than with less looking for God's help he was before" (47).

As part of his governance of Adam and Eve, God provided three other major "safeguards" in the very nature of the human beings he created (CW13 12–13). The first was to make "the body of man of the slime of the earth," while creating the soul in the image and likeness of God. This fleshly mortal body would be another constant reminder of the human being's status as a limited creature ordered within a larger universe (12).

The second "safeguard of their persons from pride" was "precepts and commandments, whereby they should remember and consider themsel[ves] to be but servants" (12). Among these were the positive command to work and the negative prohibition from eating the fruit of the tree of knowledge. Once again, these commands served to remind Adam and Eve of their responsible positions within an ordered universe.

As for the third way "of repressing all occasion of pride" in human beings, God "graciously fenced and hedged in their hearts" with fear of punishment if they disobeyed (13). This fear in its many forms was therefore meant as a necessary motivational help in achieving the most difficult goods of life.

Despite these safeguards and despite their satisfying love for a personal God, Adam and Eve indulged their "foolish proud affection" to be like gods, thus delighting in their godlike powers rather than in God himself (CW13 16–19, 7). If Adam and Eve had diligently attended to reason, they would have seen the need to turn to their Creator for counsel and assistance. As it turned out, untried Eve was seduced by the vain and impossible fantasy suggested by the wily serpent, and uxorious Adam was "seduced and brought into a foolish hope" by his pleasure of Eve's fellowship (14–20). Instead of seeking advice and help from God, Adam and Eve were "weakened by thoughtless drowsiness" (CW14 563). Thus, they became complacent and forgetful of the forces working against their happy state.

Faced with a talking serpent who promised them the world, they would have acted reasonably if they had consulted their Creator's design instead of rashly acting as they did. To use one's godlike powers properly, powers that necessarily surpass the experience and expectations of any creature, each person must humbly ask God's help in order to avoid using them unreasonably and foolishly. Such a request, however, presupposes a freely chosen way of life that entails a recognition of one's creaturely limitations. This recognition leads to a continuous struggle for virtue, motivated in part by the awareness that failure is always possible. The fear that results is "a singular grace of God" since it leads to diligence and vigilance in using one's godlike powers. A person who does not fear God—for example, a person who proudly enjoys great worldly success—will not be able to "know himself" as the limited creature he is (CW13 24, 47; CW12 48).

To avoid the destructive effects of pride, one must strive for "diligent remembrance" of human nature's true situation. Because this remembrance and even the exercise of reason depend on free initiative, the pursuit of true liberty requires a virtuous character, one habituated in vigilant attention to reason. Just as a vigilant and well-prepared country is less apt to suffer invasion than a negligent and weak one, so a vigilant person is less apt to fall prey to external or internal enemies.

The good ruler or statesman should, therefore, act as a vigilant guardian or watchdog, not as a tyrant or wolf ravaging the flock (CW3.2, nos. 133, 109, 115; CW2 24/30). He is the head of a people whom he should see as part of his own body (CW3.2, no. 112). He is the ruler of a free people, not a master of slaves (nos. 121, 198, 120, 201, 206). He should act as a devoted father towards his children, not as a master dominating his subjects (nos. 111, 109). Nowhere, however, does More compare the statesman to the physician—a noticeable absence which reflects a significant break with the classical tradition over the role of church and state.[5]

The ruler has political authority in order to give—first and foremost—good counsel, i.e., reliable guidance to a reasoning people created to be self-governing. As such, the ruler will govern according to laws which the people and their ancestors worked out by collective deliberation (CW5 277, 281). By governing in this way, the good ruler appeals consistently to the nation's conscience as it has long been formed by law and tradition.

This view of politics explains in part why More made his famous request for free speech in Parliament (Roper 8–9) and why he preferred representative government to monarchy. In his speech before King Henry and Parliament in 1523, More argued that giving "right substantial counsel" depended upon the free exchange of ideas. Since "in matters of great importance, the mind is often so occupied in the matter that a man rather studieth what to say than how," it would be impossible to have a true examination of issues unless everyone "of your Commons were utterly discharged of all doubt and fear how anything" they might say would be taken by the king. Unless such assurances were given, the wisest and most discreet would be "put to silence from the giving of their advice and counsel" (8–9).

The same concern for good and prudent counsel also lies at the heart of the following epigram that compares monarchy and representative government:

> Perhaps it is difficult to find a group of good men; even more frequently it is easy for a monarch to be bad.... An evil senator is influenced by advice from better men than he; but a king exercises the only influence on his advisers. A senator is elected by the people to rule; a king attains this end by being born. In one case blind chance is supreme; in the other, a reasonable agreement. The one feels that he was made senator by the people; the other feels that the people were created for him so that, of course, he may have subjects to rule. A king in his first year is always very mild indeed. So it is that a consul—one who shares his power—will be at any time as good as a king is in the beginning of his reign. Over a long time a selfish king will wear his people out. If a consul is evil, there is hope of improvement. (CW3.2, no. 198)

The comparison clearly points to the superiority of representative government since elected officials are more receptive to reasonable advice than are most kings, and they can be held more accountable to "reasonable agreement."

Elsewhere More discreetly undercuts the supposedly exalted status of kings (CW3.2, nos. 39, 201, 206, 243, 244), and he calls attention to the one vice most harmful to proper rule and most responsible for the tyrannical soul: pride. And why is pride so dangerous to a ruler? Because it distorts his judgment (Grace 1985, 125; CW3.2, nos. 114, 121; CW4 243/22–245/2) and thus leads him to misuse his authority (CW3.2, nos. 19, 80, 109, 115, 243).

In his later writings, More continues to present the monarch not as an absolute and infallible instrument of God's dread judgment and majesty, but as a fallen human being with a special function in society[6]—yet a function so important that it calls for consecration and the greatest of respect (CW9 50, CW8 595). More's attitude stands in contrast to the custom of the day, certainly in contrast to King Henry's conception of himself. For example, More makes sparing use of Romans 13:1, the biblical quote most often quoted to support the absolute character of kingship. More uses this passage only twice in his writings: once to support the authority of the Church (CW5 197) and once in quoting Henry VIII's own defense of his power (270). More did not emphasize the extent of the king's power; in fact, he warned against so doing on the grounds that "if a lion knew his own strength, hard were it for any man to rule him" (Roper 28). Even midway in his career at court, when many were optimistic about Henry VIII's character and when he himself was receiving special favor, More expressed his deep understanding of the monarch he served: "Son Roper," he said, "I may tell thee I have no cause to be proud thereof, for if my head could win him a castle in France . . . it should not fail to go" (12).

This distrust in the power of kings arose from his understanding of human nature and of history. According to More, anyone who knows only power and prosperity is incapable of true self-knowledge and is therefore particularly vulnerable to pride (CW12 58/25–26, 59/11; CW13 47/5–9). In fact, More's whole perspective on human nature supports the prudential need to limit power: "Unlimited power has a tendency to weaken good minds, and that even in the case of very gifted men" (CW3.2, no. 19/90–91). Since no one is perfect, no one can be invested with unqualified and absolute authority—whether by inheritance, election, or divine right. Furthermore, all civic leaders need the help of public deliberation and prudent counsel.

Regardless of the form of government, however, More considered the rule of law the fundamental criterion of a government's justice. Human laws, which are "the traditions of men," arise as the work of prudent civic leaders concerned for the common good (CW5 281/14–15). They provide a "sure and substantial shield" (CW6 262/8) that is absolutely necessary for true freedom and a relatively just society (368–72, 403–5). Although no law is perfect (CW10 164), "people without law would rush forth into every kind of crime" (CW5 279). As a result, even unjust laws deserve respect. In the face of such laws, More advises that one wait for a "place and time convenient" to advocate change. He, therefore, strongly disapproves of "open reproof and refutation" (CW9 96–97; repeated and further defended at CW10 193, 228–30). This he showed in his own life by his manner of respectful resistance and by his serene acceptance of death when confronted with a law he could not obey.

Law has such an important place in More's political philosophy that it becomes the determining factor in considering the justice of any ruler's action:

> If you take away the laws and leave everything free to the magistrates, either they will command nothing, and then magistrates will be useless, or they will rule by the leading of their own nature and imperiously prosecute anything they please, and then the people will in no way be freer, but, by reason of a condition of servitude, worse, when they will have to obey, not fixed and definite laws, but indefinite whims changing from day to day. And this is bound to happen even under the best magistrates, whom, although they may enjoin the best laws, nevertheless the people will oppose and murmur against as suspect, as though they govern everything, not according to what is just and fair but according to caprice. (CW5 277–79)

Since law provides a stable and disinterested standard of justice, one can understand More's statement that he would give even the devil justice, for the sake of the common good (Roper 21–22). Law is society's clearest expression of reason and, potentially, one of its strongest safeguards against injustice. Since law often arises from a body such as Parliament, it is no surprise that More held throughout his life that Parliament, not the king, was "the supreme and highest authority in England" (CW15 320/22–23, Roper 42, Derrett 468ff).

Given this dependence upon laws that have arisen from the collective wisdom of tradition, statesmen would not be concerned with achieving the theoretically "best" form of government. Instead, they care "as best they can" for whatever form their people have developed (see CW4 99/28). More indicates just this point in his epigram "What Is the Best Form of Government?" (CW3.2, no. 198). There, as we have seen, More begins by weighing the pros and cons of a king and of a senate. Throughout this poem, he shows a preference for a representative form of government in which virtuous individuals have the possibility of being elected for limited terms. At the end, however, he takes a characteristically surprising and abrupt turn to acknowledge that rarely can one choose one's form of government:

> But say, what started you on this inquiry anyway? Is there anywhere a people upon whom you yourself, by your own decision, can impose either a king or a senate? If this does lie within your power, you are a king. Stop considering to whom you may give power. The more basic question is whether it would do any good if you could.

Here More demonstrates his clear-sighted realism or, one might say, his sober English pragmatism: the best must always be considered in light of the existing traditions and customs of a country. This same idea is expressed by *Utopia*'s Morus in these words: "What you cannot turn to the good, you must at least make as little bad as you can" (CW4 101/1–2).

Does this mean, then, that laws are superior to statesmanship in bringing about justice? Or to put this in its most extreme form, can laws and their attending institutions be a substitute for the personal virtue of the one executing the laws?

For More, law is absolutely indispensable for the relative peace or justice of any society, but the law "leaves many things to be pondered and weighed by [the judge's] wisdom" (CW6 261/33–34). Even the best of laws can easily be abused (CW12 225).[7] As we have seen, Richard III came to power "not by war, but by law" (CW2 6), and it was a respected man of laws who bore special responsibility for Richard's triumph (45).

More says explicitly that no law or set of laws can totally protect the innocent (CW10 163ff). Therefore, those administering the laws must treat them with the greatest respect—but prudently, as a physician who uses all the means at his disposal to bring about a cure (CW6 261). Laws, like medicines, can be applied only by individuals; the justice that results will be proportionate to the prudence and courage and temperance of those who apply them.[8]

In this light, one logically looks to More's writings to find examples of such prudent statesmen; but, as usual with More, one finds the unexpected. Every possible model of statesmanship found in his writings is substantially defective. From his first published work, for example, one might have high expectations of learning about statesmanship; after all, *The Life of John Picus* is about an earl, "a great lord of Italy," a descendant of the Emperor Constantine, and a person famous for his learning. Yet these expectations are soon dashed by the fact that Pico, despite his great learning, was a person who did not know how to rule. In fact, he showed such disregard for the management of his servants and his estate that "his negligence and setting naught by money gave his servants occasion of deceit and robbery" (EW 358). By some accounts, this negligence even led to his early death, Pico having been poisoned by these same servants (Copenhaver 176).

From the Bible, the three great kings of the Old Testament generally appear as examples of kingly failure and human frailty rather than success. King Saul is overcome by passion, abandons God, and in the end is removed as king (CW8 50, 161; CW12 62; CW13, 112, 213; CW14 153). Even humble King David abuses his power in order to serve his own passion, misusing his kingly position to commit adultery and even manslaughter (CW6 394, 401; CW8 529ff).[9] The gifted Solomon also fell into wanton folly, causing his people to become impoverished by his own lavish living and eventually prompting ten tribes to fall from him (CW6 42–43, CW12 53). From the New Testament, More shows Herod as inebriated by passion and capable of the cruelest tyranny (CW3.2, nos. 224, 226–27). From the classical world, More gives many examples of the tyrant, but none of the model king.

From his contemporary world, More seems to praise two rulers as just and prudent; however, when considered closely, even these instances are qualified praise. Upon first view, Cardinal Morton appears to be the prudent ruler praised in *Utopia* and credited in *Richard III* for ending the Wars of the Roses. However, as we have seen, he is also described as ending his life in a manner "so godly that his death, with God's mercy, well changed his life" (CW2 91). What, one must ask, so badly needed to be changed in his life? A ready answer is suggested by reflection on this spiritual leader's political maneuvers in *Richard III*.[10]

The second instance of what, at first glance, seems to be unqualified praise is the ode addressed to King Henry VIII at the beginning of his reign. Nonetheless, this coronation ode should be considered in the context of the 257 other poems that accompanied its publication, some of which point to the changes that kings usually undergo as their reigns wear on (see esp. no. 198). Indeed, towards the end of that collection More seems to undercut his original hopes for Henry's good rule in a surprisingly direct juxtaposition of epigrams:

> 243 *On Lust for Power*
> Among many kings there will be scarcely one, if there is really one, who is satisfied to have one kingdom. And yet among many kings there will be scarcely one, if there is really one, who rules a single kingdom well. (CW3.2, no. 243)
>
> 244 *On the Surrender of Tournai to Henry VIII,*
> *King of England*
> Warlike Caesar vanquished you, Tournai, till then unconquered, but not without disaster to both sides. Henry, a king both mightier and better than Caesar, has taken you without bloodshed. The king felt that he had gained honor by taking you, and you yourself felt it no less advantageous to be taken. (CW3.2, no. 244)

When these two epigrams are considered together (Grace 1985, 120; Adams 76), especially in the context of Henry's lack of attention to English domestic affairs and More's disagreement with his costly and senseless wars for foreign territory, Henry does not come off well.

Yet even if one were to consider the coronation ode by itself, the very structure and diction of that poem would lead the attentive reader to be cautious. On the surface, the poem paints a picture of good rule by praising Henry's promising beginnings. And indeed this poem presents all those qualities of good rule that appear elsewhere in More's writings.[11] Nonetheless, the poem never lets us forget that Henry is just beginning his reign and that all of these qualities depend on his continued exercise of virtue. Halfway through the poem, for example, is where the narrator reminds his readers that "unlimited power has a tendency to weaken good minds, . . . even in the case of very gifted men" (CW3.2, no. 19/90–91). This reminder is enough to make any attentive reader wonder what can prevent Henry from suffering just that decline, especially since a significant portion of the poem criticizes the unjust elements of his father's reign.

One reason for More's sober assessment of all past statesmen is his conviction that all human beings suffer the effects of the Fall; thus, all err and fail in virtue. As Scripture has it, even the just person falls seven times a day (Proverbs 24:16, CW6 395, CW9 108). For this reason, More says emphatically that he did not trust any human being completely. Even the learned and holy Fathers of the Church err (CW15 213–17), and as More put it at the end of his life, "I never intend, God being my good lord, to pin my soul at another man's back, not even the best man that I know this day living; for I know not whither he may hap to carry it" (Corr 521).

A second reason is related to the first: like Aristotle, who praises poetry and philosophy over history, More distinguishes what ought to be from what is. As we have seen in chapter 1, a person can see clearly the truth and justice of some law or course of action and yet fail to exercise the fortitude needed to act in accord with that knowledge. This is the drama of history, the drama of free will, in which the struggle for justice is a constant, unending, and imperfect one. Convinced of the fallen human condition, More could see the ideal[12] and yet know that all will fall short in striving to achieve it.

In this view, history unfolds as a result of individual free actions, but always guided by a provident God who does not hesitate to intervene, often through the great individuals he brings into existence. Every period of history is essentially the same in that each presents a sufficient level of difficulty to test and reveal the character of the individuals given dominion over that order. More looked at his own age in just this light. As we will see in chapter 9, More saw Luther and Tyndale as men acting upon a fond fantasy, just as his friends Martin Dorp and John Battenhouse had done.[13] Against them he used the same medicine, relying first and foremost upon the prudent force of reason.

Since human beings were created to rule themselves freely, More saw no substitute for conscience, while also recognizing the need to use prudently the force mandated by law and authorized by lawful authority. Well aware of the dangers and difficulties of life, More never took a passivist stance, and he had no hesitation, for example, in advocating armed resistance to the Turks who were sweeping over Europe in their cruel exploits (CW6 415). Nor did More hesitate to use language with the surgical force needed to reinstate the health of reason. Nor did he refrain from advocating the force of just war.[14]

More could have certainty that virtue and conscience were the surest foundation for politics because of revelation. He believed in a created order which human beings could come to know and which included an objective law of nature written in the human heart, one that anyone can know by reason (CW6 141). Since all have free will, however, all can ignore this law as made known by conscience and follow the "foolish fantasy" of their own proud imagination—but only for a limited period of time, since the violation of conscience always causes grief (EW 461–62, CW13 258, SL 238), even in the most hardened and cruel tyrant (CW2 87/8–21, CW14 457). Conscience, then, provides the metaphysical foundation and the ultimate binding force of law, arising from the very structure of one's being and not merely as the result of threatened punishment as Raphael implies in *Utopia*.[15]

The genuine statesman, therefore, is the one who humbly recognizes this order and binds himself to administer its laws, accepting this as his chief duty and the only safeguard of justice. To achieve the common good, statesmen courageously and vigilantly tend their sheep, watching diligently for the attacks of the wolf, attacks which will always come in this fallen world. Lax leaders will permit the flock to be scattered and seriously harmed (CW13 22/2–4). Nonetheless, More was confident that after such poor leadership, a strong and energetic Moses would arise to introduce some semblance of peace and justice again (CW8 794/6–8, CW6 142/5–9). This Moses would not be perfect, however, and neither would the justice he achieves. Each Moses is a fallen human being, leading other fallen human beings—all capable of using their freedom to build justice or to destroy it.

Part Two

Utopia: A Statesman's Puzzle

4 Literature and the Acquisition of Political Prudence

> [Oxford students] must also learn prudence in human affairs.... And I doubt that any study contributes as richly to this practical skill as the study of the poets, orators, and histories. (CW15 139)

> Albeit poets be with many men taken but for painted words, yet do they much help the judgment, and make a man among other things well furnished of one special thing, without which all learning is half lame. What is that, quod he?
>   Mary, quod I, a good mother wit. (CW6 132)

How can poets help develop good judgment in human affairs? And what lies beneath More's claim that no other "study contributes as richly to [prudence in human affairs] as the study of the poets, orators, and histories"? These are the questions this chapter will address.

More considered the study of good literature to be an important part of the statesman's education in prudence—i.e., in that ability to see and to make judgments in light of what actually exists without the distortions that often arise from one's own desires or expectations. To appreciate the difficulties in achieving such prudence and such objectivity in perception is to appreciate why Plato makes epistemology the central issue in his exploration of statesmanship.[1]

Because More appreciated these difficulties, we must be careful not to simplify More's subtle understanding of the epistemological and psychological underpinnings of literature. One leading critic, for example, has concluded that More's writings are the product of "a rigidly dualistic cast of mind" which radically segregates the physical and the spiritual in manichaean fashion (Fox 1983, 33–34). At first sight this view might seem to be supported by the apparent contradictions in More's writings: the *Utopia* seems to offer the refreshing promise of freedom and pleasure, while its companion piece *Richard III* shows the darkest aspects of life; the *Epigrammata* presents a similar contradiction, joyfully affirming the earthy and sensuous and at the same time calling for the renunciation of everything worldly for the sake of virtue. Yet these conflicting dimensions are in fact present in human life; and that being the case, More could be interpreted as an exceptionally true-to-life artist. Leicester Bradner and Charles Lynch seem to advocate this assessment, noting that it is precisely this "vivid interest in life in all its aspects that makes More's *Epigrammata* incomparably the best book of Latin epigrams in the sixteenth century" (CW3.2 63).

Moreover, an important epistemological factor explains this apparent dualism: rational thought demands it. To appreciate the apparent dualism in More's works is to enter into the deepest and most significant aspect of his thought: for no one can "see" what the philosopher and poet "see" without going beyond the surface appearance of reality and word. For such sharp-sightedness, figures of speech are needed—especially dialectics and irony. After all, what is dialectics but the careful weighing of two opposing points of view? And what is irony but a figure of speech which involves "something which is the opposite of what is actually said" (Quintilian 9.2.44)? It is surely no accident that Socratic dialectics is tied inextricably to Socratic irony and that these figures of speech are More's favorites.[2]

For More as well as for Socrates, irony and dialectics are integral parts of the highest work proper to the soul, the work of perceiving the true and the good. This work of seeing requires thorough training in dialectics, and it requires that one bring to bear all of one's powers.

In his "Seventh Letter," Plato shows the difficulty and the necessity of dialectics in seeing what actually is. He maintains that dialectics involves great labor because each of the four instruments used by the mind (names, definitions, images, and intellectual perceptions) has inherent limitations. Although "each of these four instruments is defective by nature," Plato explains, "by the repeated use of all of these instruments—passing in turn from one to another, up and down—knowledge is implanted with difficulty" (343d–e). This process of weighing and reconsidering is dialectics, but dialectics ordered to the discovery of what is beyond the sensible:

> Only when all of these things—names and definitions, and visual and other perceptions—have been compared with one another and tested, proving them by kindly proofs and employing questionings and answerings that are void of envy—only then, when reason and knowledge are at the very extremity of human effort, does there burst out the light of intelligence and reason regarding the nature of any object. (344b)

Here as elsewhere, Plato stresses the great difficulty in seeing the essential characteristics, the truth, of something. His *Republic, Theatetus,* and *Phaedrus* all attest to the long and arduous climb involved in ascending from a hazy vision of shadows in the dark of opinion to the clear sight of truth in the light of the Ideas. Such sight comes, he tells us, only when the mind has repeatedly exercised all of its powers to their utmost limits, and it constitutes what many Greek philosophers considered to be the work most proper to human beings.

More also drew attention to the immense difficulties involved in first seeing and then representing human nature accurately. In *The History of King Richard III,* for example, the narrator marvels at Richard's ability to deceive even those who knew him best, and he points out the blindness of the human condition. The most explicit statement of this theme occurs after Hastings has been executed, having ignored clear signs and warnings. The narrator exclaims: "O good God, the blindness of our mortal nature! When he most feared, he was in good surety; when he reckoned himself surest, he lost his life" (CW2 52).

The difficulties of seeing and then representing human nature accurately are also indicated in the *Epigrammata*'s twelve poems which deal with the art of painting. The problem is most succinctly posed in Epigrams 93 and 94. Epigram 93, "On an Accurate Portrait," claims that "your likeness is so truly portrayed in this picture that it is not your picture, but your mirror." Epigram 94, however, "On the Same Portrait," contradicts Epigram 93 by calling attention to the great "discrepancy between you and your portrait." By first presenting the commonplace that art should mirror nature and then by repeatedly denying that this is so (see also CW3.2, nos. 87, 88, 92, 97, 98, 185, 186), More alerts his readers to art's proclivity for distorting what it presents and to reason's limited grasp of the reality that art proposes to represent. This distortion arises in part from the art form, but mainly from the mind. As Epigram 88 indicates, it is often "himself the painter has revealed" in his portrait, not the person or object ostensibly portrayed. As More suggests, artists more often than not actually go counter to the real workings of nature, even in dealing with "the innermost secrets of nature" (no. 185).

This human tendency to perceive nature falsely underlies both the satires of the *Epigrammata* and its *ridiculum* poems, which comprise at least half of the collection. What lies beneath More's portrayal of human life as having a largely defective and ridiculous character? Is More's depiction of this state of affairs a mirror image of human nature or a distortion? The very fact that we are led to ask these questions shows that we have been drawn into the dialectical inquiry that lies at the heart of More's epistemology.

More points clearly to the role dialectics plays in literature when he is called to defend his work as a poet. In response to one critic who calls his work "but an imagination that never could come to pass" (CW8 938/32), More indicates that the reader must be dialectically involved with the literary text:

> I answer him that if he so say, he shall speak very unlearnedly. For be the thing never so false and impossible too, yet may it be put and admitted, to consider thereby what would follow or not follow thereupon, if it were both possible and true. (938/33–36)

In great literature the reader must exercise his judgment and consider what would or would not follow if that fictional world were "both possible and true." This dialectical involvement and response are integral parts of the reading process of learned people.

In answer to another critic who rejected all learning except Scripture, More explains in greater detail the role of the reader's judgment in literature. First he leads his young interlocutor to reflect upon what actually goes into an interpretation of Scripture:

> Now in the study of Scripture, in devising upon the sentence, in considering what you read, in pondering the purpose of divers comments, in comparing together divers texts that seem contrary and be not, albeit I deny not but that grace and God's especial help is the great thing therein, yet uses he for an instrument man's reason thereto. (CW6 132)

Every reading of literature, be it secular or sacred, involves considering, pondering, and comparing sentences and "divers texts." As More goes on to explain, these dialectical powers of reason must be exercised like any other human faculty:

> God helps us to eat also but yet not without our mouth. Now as the hand is the more nimble by the use of some feats; and the legs and feet more swift and sure by custom of going and running; and the whole body the more wieldly and lusty by some kind of exercise; so is it no doubt, but that reason is by study, labor, and exercise of logic, philosophy and other liberal arts corroborate[d] and quickened, and that judgment both in them, and also in orators, laws and stories, much ripened. (132)

Here More compares the exercise of the body to that of the mind: just as physical exercise makes the body more "nimble," "swift," and "lusty," so the study of the liberal arts "quickens" and "much ripens" the judgment. This striking image seems designed to help his young interlocutor see what has been blinding him to the value of secular learning. The youth's untested opinion that Scripture can be simply interpreted led him to ignore the many sophisticated intellectual skills which provide the normal access to any written text.

Finally, More explains the special role of literature in this process of ripening judgment:

> Albeit poets be with many men taken but for painted words, yet do they much help the judgment, and make a man among other things well furnished of one special thing, without which all learning is half lame.
> What is that, quod he?
> Mary, quod I, a good mother wit. (CW6 132)

In a perceptive commentary on this passage, Alistair Fox argues that this "good mother wit" afforded by literature is "a sense of the realities of the human situation." Like Chaucer, More believes "in the power of everyday experience, especially as illuminated by poetry, to inculcate wisdom" (Fox 1978b, 22). It is precisely such common sense wisdom—the ability to judge accurately—that is implied in the phrase "good mother wit." As Fox explains:

> Human experience, for More, was characterized by paradoxical and ironic complexities, so that "good mother wit" is not simply a matter of naked intelligence or reason—these can provide the basis for sound judgment only when fertilized by an *accurate perception of the nature of things*. (1978b, 22; emphasis added)

More states explicitly that true dialectics leads to "the very nature of things" (CW15 34/1, 72/18). He also points out that this activity of dialectics is presupposed in his own literature. Appended to the second edition of *Utopia* is a letter in which More explains how one should read his *Utopia*—or any similar literary work.³ He is responding to a report from Peter Giles regarding the confusion of "an unusually sharp person" upon reading *Utopia* (248/2). More censures this unnamed critic for failing to be, "as the Greeks say, 'sharp-sighted'" (248/23), but he praises this same critic for succeeding in three areas: (1) for censuring More's apparent lack of judgment regarding certain customs in *Utopia*, (2) for reading the *Utopia* "slowly and carefully as to weigh all the details intelligently," and (3) for singling out certain points for criticism "not thoughtlessly but discreetly" (248/10–21). Through this praise, More reminds the sharp-sighted reader what the reading of any serious literary work demands: active participation through dialectic study and careful weighing of the ideas involved.

Yet because of the fallen state of human nature, even those who possess the best dialectical skills will sometimes err. Therefore, More states categorically that he will "take no one man's word unconditionally" (CW15 69) and that he will never be "so committed to anyone's opinions that [he] will not freely disagree with him where [he has] good cause" (201). This sober assessment of reason's fallibility would explain why one of More's principal aims in education was to have his children "love good advice" (SL 106). Why? Because informed judgment is impossible without it, since judgment necessarily involves a dialectical weighing of facts and perspectives. It is no wonder, therefore, that More also had such a high regard for Aristotle as a teacher of "true dialectic and true philosophy" (CW15 23), since Aristotle recognized clearly that dialectics requires weighing carefully and often these differences.

Literature helps develop prudence by creating true-to-life situations that pleasantly induce the reader to exercise all those faculties of mind that go into making complex judgments, a process that requires the reconsideration of one's own highly prized ideas of the good. Because of the ever-present danger of pride, this confrontation with one's own prejudices constitutes the most difficult aspect of acquiring prudence.

As More put it, received opinion is able "to pervert even sound minds and judgments" (CW15 27). Such perversion is easily understood if we consider that the "real task [of dialectics] is to press us along with true reasoning" (37) until we come to "the nature of things [*rerum natura*]" (35, 73). Unless dialectics is ordered to the perception of things as they actually are, the goal of truth can never be achieved. For More, the goal of those who "treat human concern seriously" is "the truth, and not winning a quarrel" (75).

Yet such persons seem rare. Indeed, many people prefer lies to truth—as seen in the three dialogues of Lucian which More translates before publishing any of his own major works. To understand the importance of dialectics and irony for Thomas More, we must reflect upon Lucian, one of his greatest teachers of literature, a teacher More might seem to hold on a par with Plato, at least in literary effectiveness.

More's understanding of literature appears to have changed once he read and translated Lucian. His four earliest English poems are more didactic, less ironic and dialectic in structure, than those that come later. More explains his high regard for Lucian's style:

> If . . . there was ever anyone who fulfilled the Horatian maxim and combined delight with instruction, I think Lucian certainly ranked among the foremost in this respect. Refraining from the arrogant pronouncements of the philosophers as well as from the wanton wiles of the poets, he everywhere reprimands and censures, with very honest and at the same time very entertaining wit, our human frailties. (CW3.1 3)

The maxim referred to here comes from the *Art of Poetry*, where Horace says that poets, in imitation of Socrates, should "look to life and manners for a model [*respicere exemplar vitae morumque*] and draw from thence living words" (lines 317–18). But to do so, as Horace shows in his own poetry, one must use irony.

To appreciate more deeply how irony produces the living words that lead to a dialectical penetration of appearances, we can profitably turn to the longest of these three Lucian dialogues, *Lover of Lies*, which is marked by "a measure of Socratic irony"

(CW3.1 5). "Whether this dialogue is more amusing or more instructive," More considers it "hard to say" (5). The amusement comes mostly from the irony; the instruction, from the dialectical activity that the perceptive reader must exercise. Yet the irony constantly invites and even presupposes some level of dialectical inquiry.

Nowhere in this dialogue does anyone directly answer Tychiades's opening question, "What in the world makes many men so fond of lying?" (CW3.1 180). At first, we get caught up in the story's captivating humor without noticing that this central question is never explicitly answered. The thoughtful reader, however, wants to answer such a fundamental question and begins a second but more attentive reading.

Lover of Lies begins with Philocles's giving a reasonable answer to Tychiades's opening question: people lie because it is useful. Tychiades agrees that a useful lie can be understandable, even praiseworthy, but he is "speaking of those men who put sheer useless lying far ahead of truth, liking the thing and whiling away their time at it without any valid excuse" (180). This kind of behavior seems to mystify Tychiades. Philocles then suggests another reason: folly. Why else would anyone "choose the worst course instead of the best?" (180). Tychiades rejects this answer, too, on the basis that he "could show you many men otherwise sensible and remarkable for their intelligence who have somehow become infected with this plague and are lovers of lying" (181). Such "sensible and remarkable" people include Herodotus and Homer, as well as "even cities and whole peoples." Philocles then suggests yet another reasonable but inadequate answer: by using such tall tales, poets add "delectability" to their tales, and cities can increase the profitability of their tourist trade! (181). Philocles goes on, however, to join Tychiades in his mystification at those who "have no such motive and yet delight in lying" (182). He concludes that such behavior is "utterly ridiculous." As we have seen from More's *Epigrammata,* much of life is ridiculous. Nonetheless, the question remains: *why* do so many people behave in this way?

The rest of the dialogue is Tychiades's account of the visit he has just had with Eucrates, known as a "trustworthy person . . . a man of sixty, and a great devotee of philosophy" (182)—and yet a man who lies wildly, telling the most incredible tales. By the end of the account, Philocles is fearful that he, too, might be susceptible to the strange madness that has overcome Eucrates. Tychiades offers him this reassurance: "We have a powerful antidote to such poisons in truth and in sound reason brought to bear everywhere. As long as we make use of this, none of these empty, foolish lies will disturb our peace" (196).

The message of these last lines is quite similar to the lesson More himself draws from this dialogue. In the introduction to his translation, he says the lesson is "that we should live a life less distracted by anxiety; less fearful, that is, of any gloomy and superstitious [lies]" (CW3.15). As More restates this same idea elsewhere, sound reasoning should lead to "the inner knowledge of what is right," which in turn should result in an inward calm and peace—for a "mind must be uneasy which ever wavers between joy and sadness because of other men's opinions" (SL 104, 106).

Up to now, Lucian has helped us see the ridiculous, as does More in many of his epigrams; this kind of seeing, however, is not necessarily the "inner knowledge of what is right." For example, seeing that lying is ridiculous does not answer the question as to *why* people lie. Can we see further, beneath the ridiculous, to find the reason for lying? As I hope will become apparent, the brilliance of Lucian's dialogue rests precisely in his ability to lead his careful readers to discover the "why" of gratuitous lying.

This discovery requires a third reflective reading of Lucian's dialogue, one which is attentive to the "measure of Socratic irony" (CW3.15) that informs its structure. We might consider, for example, how the irony works in a simple sentence like the following: "[Eucrates] bade me sit by him on the couch, letting his voice drop a little to the tone of an invalid when he saw me, although as I was coming in I heard him shouting and vigorously pressing some point or other" (183). Why is this change of manner brought to our attention? What does Eucrates's deliberate change in tone imply? Why would a man capable of vigorous shouting suddenly subside to the whisper of an invalid when Tychiades enters?

To answer these questions and to help appreciate the dialectic activity involved, one might turn to H. W. Fowler's explanation of irony.[4]

> Irony is a form of utterance that postulates a double audience, consisting of one party that hearing shall hear and shall not understand, and another party that, when more is meant that meets the ear, is aware both of that more and of the outsiders' incomprehension. (295)

In the case at hand, the unobservant reader notices Eucrates's change, but sees no significance in it. The sharp-sighted reader, however, is aware that something important has been indicated. This reader either understands what Eucrates is doing or at least makes a mental note of it and then reads farther, trying to find more clues.

And what is the "measure of Socratic irony" at work? Here again Fowler is helpful:

> Socratic irony was a profession of ignorance. What Socrates represented as an ignorance and a weakness in himself was in fact a noncommittal attitude towards any dogma, however accepted or imposing, that had not been carried back to and shown to be based upon first principles. (295)

Tychiades is a Socratic figure feigning two types of ignorance: (1) ignorance about why people lie; (2) ignorance about the power of the superstitions revealed by Eucrates and his friends. As we will see, Tychiades seems to have an understanding based on first principles about the reason people lie; otherwise, he could not control the ironic tone of his tale with such mastery.

What occurs next in *Lover of Lies* is a series of "incredible," "truly miraculous," "amazing," and "wonderful" stories about fantastic cures, talking snakes, walking statues, and a 110-yard-tall woman who has snake feet and is accompanied by dogs bigger than elephants. Tychiades is sarcastic in questioning the truthfulness of these stories, but he also makes careful note of the effects that these stories have on Eucrates's other friends: "Ion, Deinomachus, Cleodemus, and the rest of them, open-mouthed, were giving him unwavering attention, old men led by the nose, all but doing obeisance to so unconvincing a colossus" (CW3.1 189).

This "open-mouthed" reverence towards Eucrates points us to what seems to be Eucrates's deepest motive. Towards the end of the dialogue, that motive is revealed with the greatest clarity that dramatic irony allows when Eucrates says, "You might think that I was bragging about myself beyond belief" (195). That is exactly what the attentive reader comes to know is the truth about Eucrates. After weighing all the evidence, the reader sees Eucrates as a vainglorious, proud braggart out to get the "unwavering attention" and applause of his friends (189).

As we have seen, More himself indicates that pride or vainglory is the "mischievous mother of all manner of vice" (EW 477, CW13 9) and the greatest obstacle to clear-sightedness. As he writes to his children's tutor:

> You will scarcely find a man, however old and advanced in study, whose mind is so fixed and firm as not to be tickled sometimes with desire of glory. But, dear Gonell, the more do I see the difficulty of getting rid of this pest of pride, the more do I see the necessity of getting to work at it from childhood. (SL 106)

Throughout his writings, More points to pride as "the most dangerous habit there is" (CW15 303). In its hardened form, it brings a "blindness almost incurable" because it "covereth the eyes of their soul" (EW 477–78). In this assessment, More finds a fundamental agreement between the Greeks and the biblical authors.

As we have seen in chapter 1, More believed that pride begins with a fantasy or a vain imagining that is one's own creation. Then, given the tendency to become enamored with whatever is one's own, this "counterfeit image" is taken for truth itself, thus substituting "a false imagination" for a "very true contemplation" (EW 486, 461–62, 476; CW15 279–81; CW13 226/14, 81/12; CW12

61/18,27, 154/23,27, 210/5–6, 211/11, 225/1,17). This explains why "my" opinion can often "pervert even sound minds and judgments" (CW15 37): love for one's own idea prevents that idea from being tested and appraised by the light of dialectics.

In contrast, the true work of reason begins by considering and contemplating varying opinions and images from different points of view, usually with the help of good conversation (the ordinary form of dialectics). Pride enters when one prematurely ends this process, arbitrarily taking one's own image or opinion of the good as the definitive one. Given the tendency in every person to fall into this trap, one can appreciate the difficult role of the great poet in making a literary work that will delight readers in ideas other than their own while simultaneously challenging their most deeply rooted prejudices, the ideas that stand in the way of seeing the truth.

Homer, the only poet to receive unqualified praise in More's epigrams (CW3.2, no. 51), provides one of the greatest examples of this deft art. Homer is faced with instructing warriors who have little concern either for justice or for the order of their souls. He delights these warriors by telling a wonderful story of excitement and depth like the *Iliad,* and in the process he instructs them indirectly. He does this by making the situation and the hero so filled with problems that thoughtful readers have always been led to question the entire cultural basis of both Greece and Troy.

Homer's poetry both delights and instructs—thus fulfilling what More considered the proper role of poetry to be. The poet's proper work, he says, is to "little by little instill [good opinions] in men's hearts with the sweetness of verses" (645/6–7, *"mellitis numeris opiniones bonae sensim inferendae pectoribus"*).

Homer's poetic genius lies precisely in this: that he genuinely delights and involves his readers to such an extent that he can implant images that are more accurate than those that previously restricted their sight.[5] For example, by incarnating Greek honor in the figures of Achilles and Agamemnon, Homer creates a series of images so complex and so true-to-life, that sharp-sighted persons can see the Greek ideal of honor in a different way after contemplating the story as a whole. No thoughtful reader could picture the proud Achilles in the same way after witnessing his traitorous plan to restore his own honor at the cost of his friends' lives, his bestial treatment of noble Hector's body, and his lament in the underworld over the tragic choices he made in life. Nor could a thoughtful reader picture the proud Agamemnon in the same way after seeing the repeated abuse of power that eventually leads to his shameful murder by his own wife. Homer consistently writes in a way that leads a thoughtful reader to reflect deeply on the very nature of the cultural ideal most prevalent among the Greeks.

This same type of dialectical engagement takes place in More's own masterpiece, *Utopia*. Even today it remains a source of much delight and discussion.

5 *Utopia 1* and *2*: Dramatizing Competing Philosophies of Life[1]

> If you cannot pluck up wrongheaded opinions by the root, if you cannot cure according to your heart's desire vices of long standing, yet you must not abandon the ship in a storm because you cannot control the wind. (CW4 98)

The dialectical puzzle of *Utopia* is embodied in the opposition set up between the characters of Hythlodaeus and Morus: whom are we to believe? Since *Utopia*'s publication, disagreement and uncertainty have marked discussions concerning these two. Some, for example, see Morus as "naive" or "a fictional caricature of author More's uncertainty," while others see Morus as the "spokesman for prudent judgment" or the "good Ciceronian humanist."[2] The character of Raphael Hythlodaeus has evoked similar dispute. Some condemn him as a lying, "irresponsibly selfish security seeker," "a burlesque of the humanist," or close-minded and humorless. In contrast, other critics see Raphael as "completely reliable" and "designed for the role of Plato's spokesman" or as author More's mouthpiece. If these two characters elicit such conflicting reactions then More has succeeded in creating true-to-life characters of considerable complexity. As we will see, these characters also dramatize two distinct philosophies of life.[3]

As general character types, both Raphael and Morus initially appear as fools,[4] Morus meaning "fool" in Greek[5] and Hythlodaeus meaning "learned in nonsense."[6] This playful ambiguity tells us nothing definite about the type of person each represents, since either could be a Christian fool or a worldly fool. A better clue to the question of character types comes when Morus identifies himself and Raphael as representing two types of philosophers—Raphael is the scholastic, while Morus is the civic humanist (CW4 98/6,10–11).[7]

To learn more about these characters, one must exercise prudence or good judgment, paying close attention to the individual attributes that serve to build up each persona. As Erasmus explains:

> A delineation of character is built up of all accompanying attributes; this could be nationality or country, and we could describe the physical appearance, dress, voice, language, gestures, gait, religious practices, cast of mind, and moral behavior. (CWE24 583)

Not surprisingly, More uses many of these attributes to delineate the characters of Raphael and Morus. For example, in *Utopia* we learn about Morus's and Raphael's homelands and the attitude of each towards his country. Morus, a devoted Englishman, willingly and actively serves the king, whom he admires and loves. Raphael, a onetime citizen of Portugal, left his country early in life, preferring the freedom of travel to the "servitude" to his king or to any other king (CW4 55/3–4). More also details important information about the physical appearance, dress, language, religious practices of each, inviting the attentive reader to discover how these reflect each character's cast of mind and moral behavior. Raphael, an older man, dresses in a slovenly manner, praises the religious practices of the Utopians more than his native religion, and speaks with an *insolentia* that reflects his intolerant and rigid behavior. Morus, in the prime of life, dresses according to his station, practices his religion, speaks and acts graciously, and displays throughout a tolerant, easygoing cast of mind.

Another element which Erasmus singles out as important for

character delineation is "the universal emotions [such as] the feelings of father for children, husband for wife, citizen for country, prince for people, people for noble, and all the others discussed in detail by Aristotle in his *Rhetoric*" (CWE24 584). While Morus clearly exhibits these strong emotions towards his children, wife, country, and prince, Raphael shows no positive emotion toward any of them. In fact, Raphael has gladly detached himself from these natural ties for the sake of the objects Raphael acknowledges as the locus of his own strongest emotions: study and travel.

Perhaps the most revealing element to consider and weigh in judging Morus's and Raphael's characters is their dialogue. As Erasmus points out in *De Copia*, dialogue plays a major role in character delineation:

> Particularly appropriate to character delineation is *dialogismos* or dialogue, in which we supply each person with utterances appropriate to his age, type, country, way of life, cast of mind, and character. (CWE24 586)

More employs dialogue throughout book 1 and at the end of book 2. In both places, the style and rhetorical structure reveal the distinct character of each persona.

A good example of this revealing rhetoric occurs after Morus tries to convince Raphael to use his learning and experience to counsel a king. Raphael adamantly refuses, insisting that the true philosopher cannot find a place in political life.[8] The concluding exchange of this disagreement between Morus and Raphael includes Morus's longest single response and his most direct criticism of Raphael's theories (CW4 98/9–100/3). In this speech, Morus adopts an argumentative style which reflects the *ethos* of his character: polite—*civilis*—conversation. In keeping with this conversational style, Morus uses plain sentence structure and diction, and significantly, he mitigates the possibility of the personal offense often engendered by such strong disagreement through the use of the parable, antanagoge, understatement, and litotes.[9] Intent more on polite and diplomatic instruction than on sophistical argumentation, Morus chooses rhetorical figures and schemes aimed at clarity of expression while establishing good will with his interlocutor. The structure of this reply as a whole reveals Morus's polite, civil, and Christian *ethos,* a light-hearted and playful *ethos* reinforced and revealed even in the rhetorical design of the individual sentences.

Ranging from a thirty-nine-word period to a direct four-word construction, each of Morus's sentences works to produce a clear but diplomatic and often playful design. Sentence 1, for example, opens with an emphatic negative connective (*imo*) contradicting Raphael's previous statement, followed by an emphatic affirmative (*est verum*), followed by another negative (*non huic scholasticae*). Once past this introduction of contradictory play, we must wait for six lines to ascertain *verum*'s meaning (compare this "indirect" approach with Raphael's rather harshly direct rejoinder). In the course of the intervening lines, More introduces the metaphor which he will develop into a parable in the next nine sentences: the metaphor comparing the philosopher to an actor on stage. Morus's playful, dramatic, and indirect method continues throughout this exchange. These three qualities, integral to Morus's rhetorical strategy, differ greatly from the qualities of Raphael's rigidly doctrinaire approach.

Morus does not begin his rebuttal with an abrupt and abstract confrontation, as Raphael does. Instead, he personifies *philosophia civilis* and creates a drama. Rhetorically, this approach serves to distance his criticism from the person criticized. Instead of attacking Raphael directly, Morus presents his strong disagreement as a parable, thus softening his criticism of Raphael's scholastic philosophy, "which thinks that everything is suitable to every place" (99/12–13). Morus dramatizes his disagreement. He places "another philosophy, one more political [*civilior*]" on stage so that Hythlodaeus and the readers may see the difference between the effects of each type of philosophy. Morus's philosophy "knows its stage [*scenam*], adapts itself to the play in hand, and [cares for] its role neatly and appropriately [*concinne & cum decoro tutatur*]" (99/13–16).[10] In this parable, Morus not only dramatizes the reason for his disagreement with Raphael, he also explains the rationale behind his own rhetorical and political approach: the philosopher cannot be a "scholastic," i.e., one who speaks in universals, removed from particular persons and surroundings. Instead, the effective philosopher must know, adapt to, and protect his *scenam*.[11] Throughout this passage, Morus speaks politely, but he also speaks clearly. Following Morus's parable comes a four-word periphrastic construction: "*Hac* [sic] *utendum est tibi.*" This gerundive construction expresses Morus's disagreement as directly and forcefully as language allows. Here, Morus tells Raphael that he ought to know his public and that he ought to accommodate himself to them. To do so, however, would require that Raphael "protect"—*tutatur*—his roles *concinne et cum decoro*. "*Tutatur*" in the context of sentence 1 and of the subsequent parable conveys a rich meaning since *tutor* means "to watch over" in its primary sense and "to care for, guard, or protect" in its secondary sense. This selection of words indicates that Morus does not imply that the philosopher—or Raphael—should protect his own personal part in the play. Rather, the effective philosopher cares for his fellow-actors by vigilantly watching for the interests of the play as a whole and by subsequently adapting his role gracefully and elegantly (*concinne et cum decoro*) to the needs that arise. The clarity and force of Morus's position are important to appreciate. Otherwise, one could too readily accept many critics' interpretation of Morus as an easily intimidated, naive persona.[12]

Overall, Morus's carefully constructed argument has three main parts: sentences 1 through 6 present Morus's disagreement by personifying the philosopher as an actor on a stage; sentences 7 through 10 expand this metaphor to the state and draw out its meaning; sentence 11 concludes Morus's case with irony and humor. As a whole, the figure of thought in sentences 1 through 10 constitutes a parable told with *anamnesis* (recalling past events) and *enargeia* (setting forth something in a vivid, lively manner), summarized and emphasized with two *sententiae*—all characteristic devices of polite, but truthful, conversation. Not only does Morus develop his argument through clear and vivid figures, he also adopts syntax and diction to serve the same end: to teach lucidly and forcefully while maintaining a charitable tone. Raphael, in contrast, aims at emotionally oriented persuasion, not dialectical illumination.

The two *sententiae* of this passage serve to dramatize and to make memorable Morus's one main point, that the philosopher should play his role in the city. In sentence 5, halfway through his response, Morus states:

> *Quaecumque fabula in manu est eam age quam potes optime.*
> [Whatever play is being performed, perform it as best you can.]

This *sententia* has a parallel in sentence 10, at the end of his argument:

> *Et quod in bonum nequis vertere efficias saltem ut sit quam minime malum.*
> [What you cannot turn to good, you must at least make as little bad as you can.]

Perhaps to balance the force of these maxims, Morus does not end on a heavy, moralizing note. Having made his point unequivocally in parable and passive periphrastic, and having reinforced the point with parallel *sententiae,* Morus ends this rejoinder in sentence 11 as one would expect from a charitable master of Renaissance wit—with irony, understatement, and wordplay.

> For in order that everything be good, this would not be possible unless everyone were good, which I do not as yet expect for several years to come. [*Nam ut omnia bene sit fieri non potest, nisi omnes boni sint, quod ad aliquot abhinc annos adhuc non expecto.*] (101/2–4, but my translation)

The first and second subordinate clauses, parallel in form and sound (*parison*), playfully bring together the political state of things—*omnia*—with the people—*omnes*—making up that state (*antimethathesis*). The irony of this sentence works upon understatement achieved through litotes. Morus could have said, "The state will never be completely good because men will never all be good." His actual formulation, however, softens the impact and makes his criticism more palatable. Here diplomacy rules without sacrificing either candor or clarity, and the structure of this reply as a whole reveals Morus's polite and Christian *ethos*.

In contrast, Raphael Hythlodaeus's style places clarity and candor before diplomacy, and he makes little if any effort to mitigate the harsh effect of his radical proposals. As with Morus, Raphael's word and act correspond in the *ethopopoeia* of his declamation. While the conventions of polite but truthful conversation guide Morus's rhetoric, *libertas* guides Raphael's. While Morus speaks in a pleasant, ironic, and politely succinct manner, Raphael speaks in an impolite, blunt, and unpleasantly long-winded manner (long-winded to the point that Raphael himself apologizes for this character defect; see 85/27–32). Raphael's response, three times as long as Morus's, consists of thirty sentences, nine being longer than Morus's longest, with one colossal 131-word period replete with the major devices of oratorical copia—a surprisingly long conversational reply.[13] Raphael also uses exaggeration and *ad hominem* arguments to sharpen the effect of his rather virulent attacks, while Morus uses numerous devices to soften the impact of his strong views.

Hythlodaeus begins his response by categorically and universally denying that any philosopher-advisor could do any good without eventually "sharing the madness of others" in his attempt "to cure their lunacy" (101/6–7). "Madness" and "lunacy," of course, embody the hostile and intolerant tone that pervades Raphael's argument. These opening words say, in effect, "By this approach of yours, Morus, you can accomplish nothing at all, other than sharing the lunacy of others." This critique extends not only to what Morus has said, but to all those persons and republics not in agreement with Raphael. As we see time and again, this failure to qualify and distinguish marks Hythlodaeus's impassioned address and his intolerant *ethos*.[14]

For example, the simplistic nature of Raphael's radical view becomes evident in his use of medicine as a metaphor. Morus used this same metaphor in 98/9–100/3, where he recognizes that the complete cure of the commonwealth is impossible; yet, he advises, "You must at least make [the commonwealth] as little bad as you can." In contrast, Raphael denies that medicine will do any good at all, and he offers no hope apart from his elixir for all social ills—complete communism:

> There is no hope, however, of a cure and a return to a healthy condition as long as each individual is master of his own property. Nay, while you are intent upon the cure of one part, you make worse malady of the other parts. (105/37–107/2)

This simplistic and dogmatic approach to the ills of the nations[15] confirms the validity of Morus's criticism of Raphael for thinking "that everything is suitable to every place" (99/12–13).[16] Not only does Raphael confirm the truth of Morus's criticism by his manner of speech, Raphael also confirms this criticism by his habitual behavior.

First, the tone Raphael adopts in his conversation with Morus is an important indication of Raphael's true character. Raphael's speech is *"sermo tam insolens"* (CW4 98/4) because "his own principles and philosophy require a blunt, abrasive style" (Kennedy 97). His tone is also highly emotional, arrogantly blunt, and thoroughly humorless. When juxtaposed with the absurdity of certain proposals, this tone helps create much of *Utopia*'s humor. For example, when Raphael recounts the incident with Cardinal Morton, he self-righteously describes the hilarious scene between the monk and the hanger-on, while completely missing the humor of the situation. Raphael also relates the marital inspection incident with grave seriousness, even when comparing the selection of a spouse to the selection of a horse.

The lack of humor and moderation which Raphael exhibits in his rhetorical style reflects the immoderation of his political beliefs.[17] Raphael's view of private property, for example, constitutes the premise underlying his position throughout books 1 and 2. In book 1, when Giles and Morus ask, encourage, and exhort Raphael to serve his country, Raphael adamantly refuses. First he argues that his service would be useless; then he defends his position by saying that the world is too corrupt to be reformed;

finally, after Morus's insistence, Raphael reveals the doctrinaire belief that ultimately justifies his own action: man's virtue depends upon the elimination of private property. Apart from a radical purge, society can never become just. As Raphael explains:

> Yet surely, my dear More, to tell you candidly my heart's sentiments, it appears to me that wherever you have private property and all men measure all things by cash values, there it is scarcely possible for a commonwealth to have justice or prosperity. (CW4 103/24–27)

After Morus immediately and unqualifiedly rejects this simplistic proposal, Raphael claims in defense that his doctrinaire solution not only could work, but actually has worked. Here Raphael claims access to a special knowledge and experience not open to Morus or to any living person of the known world. Based on this special knowledge, Raphael insists—again in absolute terms—that the Utopians have (1) "extirpated the roots of ambition and factionalism along with *all* the other vices" and (2) have eradicated *all* "danger of trouble from domestic discord" (245/9–11, emphasis added). Yet, by carefully studying Raphael's own account of Utopia, we can see that neither of these claims proves true.

Other important indications of Raphael's character occur when Raphael first appears in the work. Giles introduces Raphael to Morus as a great storyteller unmatched in his ability to tell tales of strange countries (48/25–27) and as a sailor who is more like Ulysses or Plato[18] than like Palinurus.[19] In the early Renaissance, such a comparison would immediately raise suspicions. As Erasmus states in *De Copia,* Ulysses must be "cunning, lying, deceitful, able to endure anything" (CWE24 584–85).[20]

After thus casually associating Raphael with one of the most notorious figures of the Renaissance,[21] Giles next reveals Raphael's full name. Not only the name but also Giles's manner of introduction seem rather unusual. Here, a close study of the text is helpful. Ralph Robinson translates the sentence in question as one would normally expect to find in such an introduction. However, Robinson's translation changes the actual meaning of the passage: "For thys same Raphaell Hythlodaye (for thys ys hys name) is . . ." (Robinson 26–27). Compare the Latin text with the following translations. Edward Surtz's translation comes closer to the actual text, and my translation renders the Latin as literally as possible.

> *Nempe Raphael iste, sic enim vocatur gentilicio nomine Hythlodaeus* . . . (CW4 48/31–32)
>
> Now this Raphael—for such is his personal name, with Hythlodaeus as his family name . . . (49/38–39)
>
> Now this Raphael, for such is he called, with the family name being Hythlodaeus . . .

Notice what a curious introduction Raphael receives. Why does the narrator make a distinction between what Raphael is called and what he is known to be? Such a formulation serves to raise yet another doubt in the mind of the perceptive reader about Raphael's true identity: Is this character a self-proclaimed healer of God ("Raphael"), or does he actually belong to the family of those well-learned in nonsense ("Hythlodaeus")?

After this mysterious introduction, we next learn what Raphael has done with his life. After abandoning his family and kin, he indulges his passion to see the world. What has he done with this great wealth of experience? This sixteenth-century Ulysses contrasts strikingly with the public servants whom he addresses. Both Morus and Giles appear in the opening paragraphs of book 1 as learned men who have sacrificed their personal interests for the good of their families, friends, and country. Morus, having signed the *Utopia* as "Thomas More, *Citizen* and *Sheriff* of the Famous City of London" (emphasis added), tells us the reason for his travel. He travels only to serve the king, and he praises Giles for similar loyalty and dedication to country, family, and friends.

When Raphael first appears, Morus thinks he is a ship's captain—an understandable and rather perceptive guess. Raphael does have a dignified air about him, and he reveals in his manner and dress the dominant passion of his life: travel. The question of Hythlodaeus's identity and credibility would naturally arise with any man of Morus's experience and position. Morus was, after all, chosen to be the King's negotiator and representative because of his worldly wisdom. As the undersheriff and a leading lawyer of London, Morus dealt with people from every walk of life and was constantly called upon to judge their opinions and conduct. Attention to character, therefore, was a professional necessity for a man like Morus.

Two other important clues about Raphael's identity appear in the introduction of book 1. First, Raphael Hythlodaeus claims that he circumnavigated the globe as Vespucci's "constant companion"—several years before even Magellan actually did so (Donner 1945, 17; Chambers 123). Raphael's boast goes too far here, since he violates known historical fact. The second clue arises when Giles mentions a book which "everyone is reading," a reference to the *Mundus Novus* or *The Four Voyages of Amerigo Vespucci*. This book, a forgery published in Vienna in 1507, became a best-seller throughout Europe. Like most preposterous tales, *Mundus Novus* was based on some fact: Vespucci wrote three letters about his *two* voyages, yet Raphael claims to have been with Vespucci on his *fourth*, a voyage which never took place. As one historian explains the motivation behind the fabricated voyages:

> Amerigo's genuine letters had been too dispassionate, and he had presented too calmly his startling, revolutionary idea of a New World. He had been too truthful. . . . The composers of the *Four Voyages* did their best to attract readers. Amerigo had written in a letter to Lorenzo that he had slept among the natives. The *Four Voyages* made him say that he slept with native women; it made him tell how the natives defecated; it made him suggest things he dared not tell. (Pohl 154)

Now if Raphael boasts of being Vespucci's constant companion during the last three voyages, and if two of these voyages never took place, what are we to think of him?

After these preliminary introductions, Morus and Peter Giles listen to Raphael about his journeys and his criticism of various regimes at home and abroad. Giles then asks Raphael why he does not use his knowledge to serve his king, his family, and his friends. Raphael replies that such service constitutes "servitude" (*seruitium*, CW4 54/26), which he will not endure. Giles and Morus both argue against this view throughout book 1, and Morus tells Raphael directly that "it is your positive duty, as a good man, to give [counsel to kings]" (86/9–10).[22]

In response, Raphael sets forth three examples showing the futility of such work, but each example becomes less real and more absurd (Sylvester 1968, 284–85). The first, taken from an actual visit to an actual statesman whom Morus respects as wise and good, argues against Hythlodaeus's position. In this first example, Raphael tells of a meeting with Archbishop Morton, the king's chancellor and chief advisor. Morton attentively listens to Raphael and agrees to try out Raphael's suggestions—a fact which argues against Raphael's claim that no ruler would implement his opinions.[23] Hythlodaeus's second example involves an imaginary council of "some" French king, and his third example involves an imaginary council of an imaginary king. Both of these latter examples, Morus dismisses as wholly impractical, and he objects:

> Frankly, I do not see the point of saying things like that, or of giving advice that you know they will never accept. What possible good could it do? That sort of thing is fun in a friendly conversation, but in the councils of kings, where matters are debated with great authority, there is no room for these notions. (CW4 96/32–98/8)

Raphael, as one would expect, takes this objection as one more support for his position that sound advice to kings will always be futile and that "there is *no* room for philosophy with rulers" (98/8–9, emphasis added). To this response, Morus gives his longest single reply and his most direct criticism of Raphael's theories:

> If you cannot pluck up wrongheaded opinions by the root, if you cannot cure according to your heart's desire vices of long standing, yet you must not on that account desert the commonwealth. You must not abandon the ship in a storm because you cannot control the wind.
>
> On the other hand, you must not force upon people new and

strange ideas which you realize will carry no weight with persons of opposite conviction.... You must handle everything as tactfully as you can, and what you cannot put right you must try to make as little wrong as possible. (98/25–100/3)

Raphael gives no consideration to such prudent accommodation. He criticizes it as lying and therefore wholly incompatible with Christian ethics (101/5–29). After angrily denouncing his opponents as madmen and liars (101/5–14), Raphael insists on the *a priori* superiority of Platonic and Utopian institutions, "where all things are common" (101/14–18). Then he repeats his dogmatic principle that any sane and open-minded person should agree that his proposals are "appropriate or obligatory to have propounded *everywhere*" (101/22–23, emphasis added).

The dramatic effect of Raphael's ranting in such passionate and absolute terms is comic, especially when, in a few pages, he will praise both the Utopians' tolerance and their prohibitions against the type of zealous proselytism he himself indulges throughout books 1 and 2.

Having used these strident ***ad hominem*** arguments, Raphael appeals for the second time to Christ and Plato to support his views. Raphael presents himself as the opposite of those nominal Christian preachers who,

> crafty men that they are, finding that men grievously disliked to have their morals adjusted to the rule of Christ and following I suppose your [Morus's] advice, accommodate His teaching to men's morals as if it were a rule of soft lead that at least in some way or other the two might be made to correspond. (30–35)

Here Raphael assumes the very worst about Morus. He compares Morus to an untruthful and hypocritical preacher, and he speaks —or rather, vehemently preaches—against Morus's immoral political compromises. This irony seems all the greater when we consider that Raphael himself boasts of the way he used compromise and accommodating rhetoric to escape from undesirable political situations he encountered. For example, when Raphael recounts the adventures of his journey from Utopia, he explains what they had to do to return successfully. He and his companions "began by degrees through continued meetings and civilities to ingratiate themselves" with a ruler who could help them (51/30–39). Yet when a counselor like Morus wishes to use a friendly rhetoric and carefully chosen examples, Raphael condemns such behavior as lying and unchristian conduct. The diplomacy that worked so effectively for Raphael on his return trip, Raphael denounces for Europe.

Next, Raphael tells Morus "there is no chance for you to do *any* good" because either your colleagues would corrupt you or else "you will be made a screen for the wickedness and folly of others. Thus you are far from being able to make anything better by that indirect [*obliquo*] approach of yours" (103/9–15, emphasis added). Once again, in absolute terms, Raphael condemns completely what Morus prudently tries to do. Morus's "indirect method" arises from the prudence recommended by a Cicero or a Xenophon, an Aristotle or a Plato.

Although Raphael opposes the indirect method advocated by Plato and Morus, Raphael nonetheless summons Plato against Morus as an authority for his own argument. I quote Raphael's account of Plato's argument in full, because of its importance in ascertaining Raphael's perspective:

> For this reason, Plato by a very fine comparison shows why philosophers are right in abstaining from administration of the commonwealth. They observe the people rushing out into the streets and being soaked by constant showers and cannot induce them to go indoors and escape the rain. They know that, if they go out, they can do no good but will only get wet with the rest. Therefore, being content if they themselves at least are safe, they keep at home, since they cannot remedy the folly of others. (103/16–23)

Raphael takes this example completely out of context. Furthermore, his reasoning here, like his interpretation of Christian ethics a few lines earlier, reflects ideas of his own making. Plato himself counseled political rulers of his day, and humanist philosophers of the Renaissance praised Plato for doing so.

In his reply, Raphael refers to book 6 of the *Republic* (486d–e), where Socrates argues that the philosophers should rule, since they understand people and politics best. Adeimantus objects, but Socrates counters with a long reply, and in the end Socrates convinces Adeimantus that philosophers should rule as kings. Raphael simply ignores this major and best-known idea of the *Republic*, that cities will achieve justice only when philosophers become rulers.

In this section of the *Republic*, Socrates discusses different regimes and their different attitudes towards the philosopher or potential philosopher. Some regimes would treat the philosopher "like a human being who has fallen in with wild beasts," or "as a man in a storm, when dust and rain are blown about by the wind." In such regimes, the philosopher prudently "keeps quiet and minds his own business" (496d). Under normal circumstances, however, the implication seems to be that the philosopher can participate in the city unless extreme circumstances such as a radically unjust populace or a dangerous political storm should make that involvement imprudent or impossible for a time. In Raphael's account, however, all philosophers should abstain from all types of regimes, except Raphael's own.

And what is Raphael's own? Complete communism:

> Yet surely, my dear More, to tell you candidly my heart's sentiments, it appears to me that wherever you have private property and all men measure all things by cash values, there it is scarcely possible for a commonwealth to have justice or prosperity. (103/24–27)

For fifty-five lines, Raphael goes on to proselytize about the miraculous social cures that will result from imposing communism upon every country. Raphael radically and incredibly ends by insisting that "there is *no* hope, however, of a cure and a return to a healthy condition as long as each individual is master of his own property" (105/37–39, emphasis added).

Morus immediately and unqualifiedly rejects Raphael's idea: "I am of the contrary opinion. Life cannot be satisfactory where all things are common" (107/5–6). Not only does Morus state that life would be less pleasant with such a regime, he enumerates the many positive evils it would bring about: want and sloth instead of the plenty and industry promised by Raphael; riot, continuous bloodshed, and the loss of all authority instead of the peace, harmony, and the complete obedience to authority depicted in Utopia (107/5–16).[24]

Raphael replies to this total rejection of his idea of the good in the only way he possibly could and still maintain his standing before such an authority as Thomas Morus. Essentially Raphael argues, "But I have actually seen it work." Rather than appealing to a common ground in this argument, Raphael now claims access to a special knowledge and experience not open to Morus or to any living person of the known world. This special knowledge comprises the core of Raphael's gnosticism.

That More has gnosticism clearly in mind can be seen by such details as the original name of Utopia and the name of Utopia's god. Utopia's former name was Abraxa, the highest of the 365 spheres governing Basilides's gnostic system, and Utopia's god bears the gnostic name Mythros. By presenting these and other details,[25] More invites us to consider the gnostic character of Raphael's thought. Gnosticism opposes traditional philosophy because it calls upon secret knowledge known only to the gnostic master. As gnostic scholar F. C. Burkitt explains, "Gnosis is based on two main factors: one is the personal authority of the teacher; the other is, indeed must be, the self-consistency of the new teaching" (5). This secret and absolute knowledge of the gnostic master stands in sharp contrast to that knowledge universally accessible to all men which Socrates dialectically sought (7).

Raphael Hythlodaeus epitomizes the gnostic tendency of criticizing the existing political order so radically that one can therefore lay claim to no personal responsibility at all, arguing that the order of all existing governments is so corrupt that one cannot serve without becoming part of that corruption. Raphael's philosophy of life bases itself upon a gnostic fabrication that ignores important human and political realities. Hence, when More identifies Hythlodaeus as a gnostic, he continues a traditional attack upon overly simplistic systems of thought. Just as St. Paul warns the early Christians against the *pseudonymous gnosis* ("false-named" or "pretended knowledge," 1 Timothy 6:20), More warns us against the nonsense of Raphael's Nowhere.

Morus stands in direct contrast to Raphael's refusal to involve himself in the political world as it exists. Morus is the dedicated father and public servant who travels and leaves his family only for duty. Erasmus draws attention to these qualities in his introductory letter (CW4 3/16–17). Erasmus marvels at More's many domestic, civil, and professional duties and wonders how Morus "finds time even to think of books" (3/21). Jerome Busleyden also writes of Morus as a man who "long devoted all [his] pains, labors and energy to the interest and advantage of individuals, but . . . also on the common good" (33/4–7). So pressing are More's many duties that he apologizes for the long delay in finishing his *Utopia*. These civic and domestic demands have allowed him to write the *Utopia* only by "filching time from sleep and food" (41/9–10).

William Budé also praises Morus for his involvement in civic affairs, but he laments the widespread abandonment of justice as understood by the classics (7/39–9/2). Budé then points out one telling reason why the classical notion of justice-as-virtue has given way to the prevailing notion of justice-as-power: "the humanistic scholars, living far from public business for the sake of relaxation or for the investigation of truth" are helpless before the "knotty bonds of pacts and contracts" made by the unjust (9/11–24). Raphael Hythlodaeus, one such scholar, epitomizes this civic helplessness while Morus epitomizes the Christian humanist's ideal of civic involvement.

Morus and Hythlodaeus, therefore, dramatize in speech and action the different philosophies they espouse. Each represents an alternate view of the best way of life. Raphael the gnostic abandons the known world and renounces all responsibility for it; in contrast, Morus the Christian humanist advocates and embodies a "more civil" (*civilior*) behavior. Raphael, as a gnostic master, uses a rhetoric that is direct, abrupt, and passionate; Morus, following his principles of Christian humanism, uses a rhetoric designed to establish friendly good will and civil rapport. Raphael's best way of life involves a condemnation of all existing political institutions of the known world; Morus's best way of life involves active political involvement with the very world Raphael rejects.[26]

6 *Utopia 1*: Ciceronian Statesmanship[1]

> But there is another philosophy, more practical for statesmen, which knows its stage, adapts itself to the play in hand, and performs its role neatly and appropriately. (CW4 99/13–16)

In this chapter, I will show how More carefully creates a pattern of Ciceronian allusions[2]—a subtext, if you wish—that provides another internal measure by which to weigh the arguments proposed by Raphael, who holds himself aloof from society, and Morus, who embodies the fully involved Ciceronian humanist. These Ciceronian allusions invite us to explore the deepest issues of classical political philosophy, and they reveal a level of Lucianic comedy previously unnoticed.

The conflict between those dedicated to the business of the city (*negotium*) and those who abandon the city for the sake of leisure (*otium*) constitutes, as Quentin Skinner has shown (1987, 126–31), one of the fundamental issues debated both in More's time and in the ancient world. Cicero's most distinctive position as a political theorist, in fact, arises precisely out of this debate. Cicero was the first to argue what became a common position among the civic humanists of the Renaissance: "that the noblest way of life is one of virtuous public service" rather than a life of withdrawal and contemplation (Skinner 1988, 450). Significantly, More not only chose Cicero's way of life for his own,[3] he also chose Cicero's literary method for exploring the underlying issues associated with that way of life. He chose the dialogue genre, filled with irony, deliberate ambiguity, and paradox. In so dramatizing this question concerning the best way of life, More and Cicero dialectically engage all those who had treated or would treat this perennial issue of personal and political well-being.

Cicero was perhaps the most highly regarded thinker among the civic humanists of the Renaissance (Seigel 3ff; Kristeller 1961, 297, 304–5; Trinkaus 343–44; A. Kinney 1986, 69; Skinner 1988, 414ff). Commentators today seem surprised at this claim, since most current critics consider Cicero inconsistent and eclectic at best.[4] If Renaissance figures considered Cicero so inconsistent a thinker, however, what would have attracted humanists like More to value him so highly? An adequate interpretation of *Utopia* may well depend upon our ability to answer this question, and our answer seems to require a fuller grasp of the classical tradition than we have at present. In the difficult task of recapturing this tradition, Thomas More's writings may serve not only as an example but also as a guide.

If we begin with the Renaissance assumption that Cicero is a preeminent thinker worthy of close study, we open ourselves to a depth in *Utopia* hitherto unclaimed. In light of this assumption, we will begin with a sketch of Cicero's understanding of the highest good, the best way of life, and the best state of the commonwealth. Then we can compare Morus's Ciceronian positions with Raphael's views.

Yet one must first ask: What alerts the perceptive reader to the Ciceronian subtext in *Utopia*? The title itself, *De optimo reipublicae statu. . . ,* would lead most humanists to think immediately of Cicero. Cicero had written his own *De re publica,* and one must not forget that Plato's *Republic* received its name from Cicero's Latin translation of the Greek *Politeia.* Not only the first words of *Utopia* but also the last would alert More's fellow humanists to the dominant role of Cicero in the work before them. The last two lines of *Utopia* restate almost word for word Cicero's famous judgment upon Plato's *Republic*: "There are very many features in the Utopian commonwealth which are *more to desire than to hope for*."[5] This parallel passage is significant because, in using it, Morus establishes the same distance between himself and Raphael's best regime as both Aristotle and Cicero established between themselves and Plato's best regime.[6]

The Yale editors of *Utopia* cite over fifty possible references and allusions to Cicero; at the time of the edition's publication in 1965, they called for a thorough study of the Ciceronian dimension of More's *Utopia*. This study was long in coming. In 1978, Thomas White suggested that "More may have deliberately echoed" Cicero's central concepts of decorum and utility (White 1978, 140n). He argued persuasively that these parallels exist, but he did not go further in explaining the place of such literary allusions in the work as a whole. George Logan in 1983 followed White's lead and pointed out other important allusions to Cicero, such as his treatment of *honestas*, civic humanism, and the debate over virtue and pleasure (Logan 51–52, 85–86, 102–3, 109n, 179–80).

Arthur Kinney was the first in recent times to explain the literary principle involved in More's use of Cicero.[7] According to his 1986 study, the numerous textual references and allusions to Cicero and other classical authors "are pointers for our reading of More's text" (72, 78). By alluding to previous great thinkers who contributed to the same discussion, More intentionally deepens and broadens his dialogue about the best way of life and the best state of the republic. In doing so, he invites his humanist audience to think through the same issues, considering what was said before in light of the new perspectives which he brings to bear.[8]

Cicero grapples throughout his writings with the question of the highest good and yet, imitating his "beloved" Plato and Socrates,[9] nowhere does he unequivocally state his final position. He frequently evaluates the positions attributed to or taken by others, but he maintains that he belongs to the school that follows the true method of Socrates most closely, i.e., the moderate skeptics of the Old Academy. For Cicero, the question of the highest good can be given a probable but not an absolute answer. In at least five of his major dialogues, he investigates this question by weighing the two positions most commonly taken in his own city of Rome.[10] The Stoics said the highest and only good was virtue; the Epicureans said pleasure. Cicero agreed that virtue was the highest good, but he sharply criticized the Stoics for being unrealistic in their claims "to explain with certitude and consistency all things" and for maintaining the extreme position that material benefits such as wealth and health were really not goods at all. Cicero and Aristotle and the Old Academy held that such benefits were not comparable to the highest good, but they were recognized as goods of a lower order. Cicero also criticized the Stoics for failing to provide a place for politics in their philosophy.

The Epicureans, however, were far more dangerous than the Stoics because they actively advocated withdrawal from political affairs. Also serving to undermine natural civic virtue and civic-mindedness was their theory of pleasure as the chief good.[11] For Cicero, pleasure is "that enemy which lurks deep within us, entwined in our every sense—that counterfeit of good, which is, however, the mother of all evils" (*De leg.* 1.17.47, also *Acad.* 2.46.140, *De off.* 3.33.116ff); virtue alone leads to happiness.

Although in places Cicero rhetorically argues against both positions (Nicgorski 1984, 569–71), he takes very seriously the fundamental option which they pose to all persons at all times. At the end of the *Academica,* for example, after reviewing the full range of positions on knowledge of the ends of life, Cicero says: "There remains therefore one match to be fought off—pleasure versus moral worth [*honestas*]" (2.46.140).

Just this match is dramatized in *Utopia*. There we find a society supposedly constructed upon the philosophically impossible amalgam of the Epicurean and Stoic views of the highest good. For the Utopians, the highest good is pleasure, but pleasure defined as the Stoics define virtue (CW4 163–67). How can this be? We also discover that the Utopians deny what both the Epicureans and the Stoics agree upon: the existence of free will (223/7–8).

How can this be? In raising these questions and many others like them, the observant reader must look more deeply into the Utopian view of human nature and the way of life that best completes human nature—thus launching us into the obvious intent of the book.[12]

To understand the importance of this issue, we would profit from a review of Cicero's rather comprehensive treatment of the subject. Such a view would go beyond the scope of this book, but we can reasonably assume that Thomas More would expect his humanist readers to be familiar with this most basic philosophic issue. The issue at stake is not an academic question of the relative worth of pleasure over correct moral action; the issue has to do with human nature and what will bring human nature to its completion or happiness. Succinctly put, the question becomes, "What is the best way of life?" For Cicero, this question has a definite answer, whereas the question of the *summum bonum* does not. Why? The second question is a speculative one, incapable of final resolution. Moving from the speculative to the practical realm, however, Cicero could from his own experience conclude that the life of virtue would lead people to happiness. If one decides against virtue and follows the life of pleasure, "many things fall in ruin, and especially fellowship with mankind, affection, friendship, justice and the rest of the virtues" (*Acad.* 2.46.140). Like Nietzsche, Cicero leaves open the speculative possibility that truth may not be beautiful or lovable. Practically speaking, however, no political order has ever recognized such a view of truth; nor could any city or civilization last if it did.

In exploring the questions about the nature of the person and the state, Cicero consciously adopts what he calls a Socratic approach.[13] He begins by asking questions about the human condition and—like Socrates—chooses to avoid speculation about broad, cosmic issues that lie beyond his own immediate experience. Cicero's philosophic reasoning begins by observing the person's many natural inclinations, including the strong inclinations toward truth, fellowship, independence, and security. For Cicero any position on the nature of the person and the best way of life must account for all of these inclinations. The decorous or proper way of life is one which forges these inclinations harmoniously under the guidance of reason.

Decorum refers to a quality of reasonable action that is both *honestum* and *utile,* morally right and useful. For Cicero, a person or commonwealth cannot act decorously without acting in a morally right and a prudentially appropriate or useful manner.[14] As we will see, decorous or fitting behavior provides a key to understanding Cicero's thought and that of Morus in *Utopia*. In Cicero's view, the best way of life unites the useful (*utile*) with the right (*honestum*) and accounts for the full complement of inclinations.

Cicero concludes that virtue, not pleasure, will bring happiness; thus the life of virtue is the best way of life. Such virtuous activity is appropriate (*decus*) and right (*honestas*) and arises out of each person's natural inclinations to do good. Virtuous behavior is "forged and fashioned" (*De off.* 1.4.14) by respecting the legitimate demands of nature while allowing reason to order them in a fitting or decorous manner (*De off.* 1.4.15). Yet how does one decide what is fitting or decorous given all of the many conflicting demands of nature? The difficulty of this task Cicero does not underrate, as anyone knows who has studied the second and third books of *De officiis*.

The best way of life is known by reason's reflection on the comprehensive requirements of human nature.[15] This reflection reveals the need for reason's ordering of these apparently contradictory inclinations; it also reveals the weakness and inability of an individual to achieve this order by his own power alone. As a result, law and rhetoric (products of reason) are both required to achieve the best way of life, a way of life that needs support from tradition or institutions for its implementation.

Cicero recognizes that all people, subject to passions and to other pressing demands of life, need external forms created by reason to enable their own reason to develop and to guide them to live virtuously. Law and rhetoric (rhetoric is an important component of literature) are the two external forms most effective in bringing about virtuous living. For example, law establishes the extent of citizen involvement and the order of government; it regulates the exercise of religion and the form of education; it determines policies of war and policies toward other nations; most importantly, it establishes and protects private property. In other words, law establishes institutions that arise from a people's collective use of reason in ordering life to respond more adequately to the needs of human nature.

Yet why is rhetoric necessary for reason to reign in the individual and in society? Cicero recognizes the innate craving of each person for independence. Because of this inclination, Cicero constructs his best form of government upon the free and rational consent of the citizens. Rhetoric plays an important role in what ideally is a deliberative process focused upon issues of civic import. As Cary Nederman explains in his recent study of Cicero, "While men always retain their natural inclination to congregate ... the recognition of this nature and its implications for their lives needed to be awakened in and drawn out of them by means of reason and persuasion. Men will only unite, in other words, when they become expressly aware that it is natural (not to mention beneficial) for them to do so" (5–6). Nederman's study helps us appreciate the depth and centrality of Cicero's conception of rhetoric. Reason and speech do not simply separate men from animals in some abstract sense; this faculty for rational discourse "renders possible the mutual understanding through which the sacrifices and burdens of human association may be explained and justified" (Nederman 7). Rhetoric leads people to accept law, and thus makes government possible. "Cicero held that social and political arrangements were the product of explicit common agreement among primitive men arrived at through non-coercive means, viz., through the application of reason and persuasion" (9). Without understanding the place of rhetoric and its role in free government, one could not understand how Cicero intended his best regime to be built upon bonds of love and reason, not upon the fear and compulsion which characterize the government of Utopia. Significantly, rhetoric marks the apex of a statesman's education for Cicero, but has no place in Utopian education or government. (Nor did it have a place in More's program of education for his own children, although it was one of the most important skills in his professional advancement.)

Cicero's best regime, then, rests upon free cooperation that proceeds from the good will of friendship and civic-mindedness, not upon fear, which Cicero considered the motive least effective and most foreign to healthy political life (*De off.* 2.6.22–2.8.29). This cooperation is fostered primarily through the free exercise of benevolence and liberality. Taking seriously the phenomena of duty and friendship, which arise from our nature as social beings, Cicero considers this social dimension of human existence to be so important that he concludes: "Nothing ought to be more sacred in men's eyes" than duties governing the welfare of their fellowmen (*De off.* 1.43.155). As a consequence, "the claims of human society and the bonds that unite men together take precedence over the pursuit of speculative knowledge" (1.44.157). Why? For the simple reason that a safe and well-ordered state is the precondition for achieving other goods.

In summary, Cicero considered virtue as the best way of life, and the best state of the commonwealth as one based on friendship and good will, protected by law and fostered by rhetoric.

In the opening of book 1, Morus lavishes praise upon his fellow civic humanists, singling out those qualities much admired by Cicero, such as skill in rhetoric, diplomacy, and law (CW4 47/27–30) as well as friendship and virtue, learning and wit (49/2–12). He also tells us exactly what interests him about Raphael's travels. He is not interested in Raphael's tales of Ulysses-style monsters and "stale travelers' wonders" (53/36), but rather in learning about the wise and prudent customs and institutions that other nations devised to enhance civic life (53/33–55/14). This statement reveals a great deal. First, it implies that Raphael told many tales which did not interest Morus. Secondly, what Morus here identifies as having potential interest—customs and institutions that promote civic life—he later judges absurd at the end of Raphael's account

(245/18). Why he does so makes sense in light of Morus's Ciceronian perspective.

After Giles and Morus both have encouraged him to devote his talent to the common good, Raphael strongly refuses, calling such service servitude and declaring his desire to live as he wills—"*sic uiuo ut uolo*" (56/1).[16] These words echo Cicero in *De officiis* 1.20.70, where he is speaking of the magnanimous man who would risk everything in defense of his liberty. It is appropriate for such magnanimous people, says Cicero, to live as they please ("*cuius proprium est sic vivere, ut velis*"). The liberty which Cicero praises is of a different kind than the liberty Raphael passionately defends for himself. Neither kind of liberty, however, is possible for the Utopians.

To defend his position, Raphael gives an historical example about John Cardinal Morton, a noted civic leader and counselor to the king. As various commentators have pointed out, this example does not support Raphael's position.[17] Raphael intended to argue that it is useless for a wise man to enter public life in an imperfect regime. Yet Morton demonstrates that one humanist can indeed influence the history of nations for the good and can even change the direction of civic policy for the better.

Morus, accomplished diplomat that he is, does not directly point out this discrepancy to Raphael,[18] but he does strongly argue that Raphael has a duty as a good man to give constructive advice and thus to contribute to the common good. Here Morus "echoes the sentiments and even the imagery of the *De officiis* almost word for word" (Skinner 1987, 133), but Raphael dismisses these common Renaissance sentiments completely in an insolent manner (A. Kinney 1986, 61). To justify this dismissal, Raphael cites two fictional examples. Morus considers both of these imprudent and inopportune, and he compares such advice to an actor who performs the way he wants without regarding his role in the play at hand. Morus also criticizes Raphael's undiplomatic manner ("*sermo tam insolens*"); it is neither decorous nor will it help cure the maladies afflicting the commonwealth. After he urges Raphael to adapt his speech and behavior *concinne et cum decoro* (CW4 99/12–13), Raphael responds with invective and strident rhetoric instead.

Raphael's response is unfitting from a Ciceronian perspective. Since the bond among people is forged primarily by reason and speech (*De off.* 1.16.50), virtuous persons strive to establish bonds of good will through conversation and oratory. In explaining the decorum one should observe in speech, Cicero recalls some fundamental principles which Raphael does not endorse:

> But as we have a most excellent rule for every phase of life, to avoid exhibitions of passion, that is, mental excitement that is excessive and uncontrolled by reason; so our conversation ought to be free from such emotions: let there be no exhibition of anger or inordinate desire, of indolence or indifference, or anything of the kind. We must also take the greatest care to show courtesy and consideration toward those with whom we converse. (*De off.* 1.38.136)

Perhaps in this particular instance, however, Raphael is correct in using harsh language when issues of fundamental importance are at stake. Besides, should not Cicero's emphasis on courteous and considerate speech be abandoned in administering reproof? Cicero's answer is clear:

> It may sometimes happen that there is need of administering reproof. On such occasions we should, perhaps, use a more emphatic tone of voice and more forcible and severe terms and even assume an appearance of being angry. But we shall have recourse to this sort of reproof, as we do to cautery and amputation, rarely and reluctantly—never at all, unless it is unavoidable and no other remedy can be discovered. (*De off.* 1.38.136)

This passage helps us appreciate the reaction of More's humanist contemporaries to Raphael's abrasive, even insulting, manner and speech. According to rules of decorum, one should speak as Raphael does only in the most extreme situation, not in the garden of a friendly and generous host who has asked for advice. (This will be an important principle to recall when we deal with More's polemical writings.) Yet if Raphael offends so egregiously and if Morus disagrees with him on fundamental points of the greatest philosophical and political significance, why does Morus not reprove Raphael at the end of the book? For the simple reason that decorum forbids it. Raphael is an old man, hardened and unbending in his position. What would be accomplished by confronting him with the many inconsistencies of his own account?[19] Morus explains the reasons for his decorous silence: Raphael is tired from his long and emotional tirade, and Raphael has made it clear that he will not "brook any opposition to his views" (CW4 245/27–36).

Ciceronian decorum involves a particular view of the person and of politics that differs radically from Raphael's view; for Cicero and Morus it involves a course of action that is *honestas* and *utile*. The full passage in which Morus speaks of decorum makes this clear:

> But there is another philosophy, more practical for statesmen, which knows its stage, adapts itself to the play at hand, and performs its role neatly and appropriately [*concinne et cum decoro*]. (99/13–16)

Raphael interprets this statement, as have many critics, to mean that statesmen could abandon principle in favor of expediency. This interpretation, however, goes against Cicero's consistent position that the truly expedient (*utile*) action cannot violate *honestas* and still be decorous. The just man must adapt to the ever-changing circumstances of human existence, but without ever violating moral principle. To illustrate his point, Cicero presents this tough case as an example: Should a traitor who poisons his king be rewarded by the foreign power he helps to victory? Cicero gives an unqualified "no." Since such action is not *honestas*, it cannot be *utile*.[20] What then are we to think of the Utopians who encourage and praise such action as virtuous and honorable (203/36–205/32)?

Morus explains decorum in an indirect way when he chooses the *Octavia* as an example (99/21). As John Crosset has shown, *Octavia* presents "exactly the situation about which More and Hythloday are debating: a philosopher attempting to give advice to a king" (578). Seneca, a favorite of the civic humanists, advised

Nero until that young king became an unyielding tyrant. During the five years that Nero listened to Seneca's advice, "Rome seems to have been well governed" (Crosset 578; see also A. Kinney 1986, 69–72).

Despite Morus's moderating attempts, Raphael insists that there can be no justice and no happiness without the utter abolition of private property (CW4 105/18–19). Morus once again strongly disagrees, and he sets forth the classical position in defense of private property. To understand the major differences between the Ciceronian and Hythlodaean views on this point, one would have to think deeply about the relationship between the virtue of justice and this institution of private property. For Cicero, natural justice has two parts, (1) what we commonly call justice—i.e., not harming anyone and serving the common interest (*De off.* 1.10.31)—and (2) *beneficentia*, i.e., kindness and generosity. These two natural inclinations are the foundation whereby common bonds (*communitas*) are maintained and society is established (*De off.* 1.7.20). Cicero states this clearly in *De legibus* 1.15.43, where he says that "our natural inclination to love our fellow-men" is the "foundation of Justice," or in *De amicitia* 7.23, where he says that "if you should take the bond of goodwill out of the universe no house or city could stand, nor would even the tillage of the fields abide."

Yet how do these two parts of natural justice give rise to the institution of private property? First, we must recall that Cicero defines the commonwealth itself as the property of all the people (*De re publica* 1.27.43). The political issue then becomes: how can this common property best be administered and protected? This problem is not great in the family because of the family's size and close bonds; in the family all property can be treated as common. In the state, however, the size and the nature of bonds are different, and experience has shown that common possession in a state leads to war and destroys the bonds of equity and good will (*De off.* 2.21.73, 2.23.78–79). So important is the preservation of private property that Cicero held that "the chief purpose in the establishment of constitutional states and municipal governments" was that individual property rights might be secured (*De off.* 2.21.73). Not to respect property is to subvert harmony utterly (2.22.78).[21] In arguing this position, Cicero gives the example of King Agis, a Spartan king who tried to undermine private property and was killed as a result. From that time on, "dissensions so serious ensued that tyrants arose, the nobles were sent into exile, and the state, though most admirably constituted, crumbled to pieces" (*De off.* 2.23.80). It is surely no accident that Utopia was founded in the year of King Agis's reign (CW4 120/27n, Schoeck 1956).

Aristotle, whom Cicero praises often for his study of the state (*De fin.* 4.2.3; *De leg.* 3.6.14, 1.21.55), gives a very clear and perceptive explanation of the relationship between virtue and private property, using many of the terms Cicero will borrow. Aristotle, like Cicero, distinguishes between the unity of a family and the unity of a state (*Politics* 1263b 31ff, *De off.* 1.17.53–54), a distinction Utopia eradicates (CW4 149/3–4). Trying to achieve the unity of the family in the state, Aristotle warns, leads to an inferior commonwealth because such unity destroys the plurality which the state needs in protecting the diversity of its citizens' interests and characters (1261a–b).[22] Excessive unification would also destroy private property, and without private property, political life could not succeed. Why? Aristotle gives two of the same reasons Morus presents: (1) when many people own something, each assumes someone else will care for it,[23] and (2) discontent arises because any distribution of limited goods inevitably gives rise to complaints.[24] In addition, Aristotle sets forth a reason which More implicitly uses in the invention of Utopia, a reason based on pleasure and one's intrinsic inclination towards benevolence.[25] Aristotle argues:

> How immeasurably greater is the pleasure when a man feels a thing to be his own; for surely the love of self is a feeling implanted by nature and not given in vain, although selfishness is rightly censured; this, however, is not the mere love of self, but the love of self in excess, like the miser's love of money; for all, or almost all, men love money and other such objects in measure. (1263a40–1263b4)

Because of the person's love of self, each loves to have things as his own. This love, rightly ordered, is natural and good. Aristotle then goes on to explain his justification of private property based on this good human inclination:

> And further, there is the greatest pleasure in doing a kindness or service to friends or guests or companions, which can only be rendered when a man has private property. These advantages are lost by excessive unification of the state. . . . No one, when men have all things in common, will any longer set an example of liberality or do any liberal action; for liberality consists in the use which is made of property. (1263b 5–14)

Education in the proper use of property is education in virtue. Virtues such as benevolence and liberality, kingpins in Aristotle's and Cicero's theories of ethics and politics, arise from the inclination to friendship, and friendship provides the model for the proper relations between citizens in these thinkers' view. For this reason, "the special business of the legislator is to create in men a benevolent disposition" that will incline them to use their private property for the common good (1263a 36–40). Such a statement might lead us to ask, what disposition marks the ordinary Utopian?

Aristotle shows his preoccupation first and foremost with the virtues that private property develops, not with the arbitrary laws and institutions that more or less protect private property. In fact, he criticizes those regimes that place institutional arrangements over virtue (as does Utopia), and he explicitly condemns communist institutions for undermining virtue, especially benevolence. He explains the fundamental fallacy behind the elimination of private property in a passage which I quote at length because of its special relevance to the defense Raphael gives for his utopia:

> Such legislation may have a specious appearance of benevolence; men readily listen to it, and are easily induced to believe that in some wonderful manner everybody will become everybody's friend, especially when someone is heard denouncing the evils now existing in states, suits about contracts, convictions for perjury, flatteries of rich men

and the like, which are said [by men like Raphael] to arise out of the possession of private property. These evils, however, are due to a very different cause—*the wickedness of human nature*. Indeed, we see that there is much more quarrelling among those who have all things in common. (1263b 15–26, emphasis added)

Because the most basic cause of injustice arises from human nature itself and not from institutional structures, Aristotle criticizes all political theories that look more to changes in external institutional arrangements than to arrangements that would foster virtue within (see 1263b 37–41). Of course institutions are important, but these will be fabricated and fostered by citizens of prudence and virtue. No institutional arrangement, however, could withstand a corrupt citizenry.

Raphael rejects completely Morus's traditional views on private property, not with arguments from reason but from his own uncommon experience: if only Morus had lived in Utopia, then he would believe as Raphael does. After this invocation to faith, Morus invites Raphael to tell of his unique experience in Utopia. When all has been told in the course of a long afternoon, Morus makes his final judgment in a passage that has long been a center of debate[26]:

> When Raphael had finished his story, many things came to my mind which seemed very absurdly established in the customs and laws of the people described—not only in their method of waging war, their ceremonies and religion, as well as their other institutions, but most of all in that feature which is the principal foundation of their whole structure. I mean their common life and subsistence—without any exchange of money. This latter alone utterly overthrows all the nobility, magnificence, splendor, and majesty which are, [according to commonly accepted opinions],[27] the true glories [*decora*] and ornaments of the commonwealth. (CW4 245/16–26)

Decorum, again a key term in Morus's position, refers here to what is fitting in regard to the external manifestation of the commonwealth as a whole rather than what is fitting to the words and actions of individual citizens. Taken at face value, this passage is thoroughly consistent with Morus's role as Ciceronian humanist. Cicero agrees that private property is the principal foundation of civil society.[28] He also advocates widely different policies for waging war and for conducting ceremonies and religion than those practiced in Utopia (*De leg.* 2, 3). Cicero, who greatly respected law and custom and whose own *Republic* is famous for its prudent institutional arrangement of mixed government, would never agree with Raphael's conception of the best commonwealth. Granting that this part of Morus's final judgment is consistent with Cicero, what about the last sentence, which maintains that common opinion considers nobility, magnificence, splendor, and majesty as the decorum of the commonwealth? Is that statement consistent with Cicero's philosophy?

If we consider the qualifying phrase "*ut publica est opinio*," there can be little question about this statement's consistency with Cicero's view. While certainly not agreeing with the common opinion on all political matters, Cicero insists upon the importance—indeed the political necessity—of "show[ing] what I may almost call reverence" towards men of all classes and their opinions (*De off.* 1.28.99). Cicero goes even further in his respect for public opinion: It is in the just and considerate treatment of men and their opinions that "the essence of decorum is best seen [*in quo maxime vis perspicitur decori*]" (*De off.* 1.28.99).

Yet, do not most loyal citizens think it appropriate for their leaders and institutions to be characterized as magnificent and majestic? Of course, even Raphael does. One cannot overlook Raphael's description of the Utopian cities as magnificent (CW4 112/16) and his statement that the priests of Utopia are said to possess "true majesty" (230/15). Cicero would agree that such qualities could be attributed to certain persons and things (Allen 1976, 109): he also attributes nobility and splendor to those virtuous persons who "prefer the life of service to the life of pleasure" (*De off.* 3.5.25, 1.18.61), for example, or those who are true philosophers (*De off.* 1.20.69).

There are other contrasts between Ciceronian and Utopian principles and customs. As we saw earlier, Cicero praises that commonwealth which is based on just law and universal principles. Such a foundation gives rise to institutions that foster virtues which are indeed virtues, i.e., permanent qualities of the soul that are exercised universally, not just with one's own friends or one's own state. Thus according to Cicero, the common bonds of justice establish duties to foreigners and "even to those who have wronged us." As a result, "there is a limit to retribution and to punishment," and therefore a state in its foreign relations—even in war—must strictly observe humane laws (*De off.* 1.11.33, 1.13.39–40, 3.11.47ff; *De leg.* 1.23, 2.8).

In direct opposition, the Utopians use war tactics that are understandably condemned as cruel and "of a degenerate nature" (CW4 205/23), and they use punishments so severe that their enemies will be afraid to fight again (205/23–38). Even in domestic relations, they use fear as the primary principle for control. Raphael explicitly states that fear is "the greatest and almost the only stimulus to the practice of virtue" among the Utopians (235/7–8, 221/38–223/3, 229/4–6, 233/32–36).

For the Utopians, furthermore, every action must have some pleasurable reward, even charity. Raphael explains charity as a good act done for "return of benefits" and for pleasure (164/31). Cicero, however, teaches that "virtue driven to duty by pleasure as a sort of pay is not virtue at all but a deceptive sham and pretence of virtue" (*Acad.* 2.46.140). Throughout his works, he maintains that virtue must be pursued for its own sake, i.e., for love of the good, not for any reward and certainly not for the sake of pleasure.

For Cicero, the state should give special protection to the family, granting it the freedom it needs to foster independence in its members and to foster the care and affection which are characteristic of the family. Raphael's institutions aim at destroying the family bonds (Berger 1982, 279–90).[29]

In Utopia, families can be separated for the sake of keeping numbers and trades in order (CW4 127/15–19, 137/4–6). Family meals where all would normally speak freely and enjoy one another's company are replaced by regimented sties where adults must sit in assigned places and where children stand in absolute silence, waiting for some adult to feed them from the table as one would normally feed the family dog (141–43). This scene is both humorous for its absurdity—who can imagine a room full of hungry children perfectly silent waiting for their parents to finish eating the best of the food?—and horrifying for the terror and force it would take to effect such silence.

Education in Utopia is wholly outside family direction. Instead, the state exerts the strictest possible control over what is taught. Even religious doctrines must pass state censorship, since religious beliefs must be "useful for the preservation of their commonwealth" (229/13–14). Not surprisingly, universities do not exist in Utopia (Gueguen 1983). How could they unless the free pursuit of truth were valued and encouraged?[30] As it is, most education in Utopia focuses upon the improvement of material benefits such as health, military tactics, and the preservation of the political status quo.

For Cicero, following Aristotle, magistrates determine the nature of one's regime. In Utopia, the magistrates are freely elected and are humble public servants, or so we are told. But why do these public servants get the best of everything? And why are some sent abroad "to live there in great style and to play the part of magnates" (CW4 215/31–33)? Equally disturbing are the election procedures. Candidates are preselected—only the "scholars" can hold public office—and officials are eventually elected by secret ballot. But who counts these secret ballots? In Cicero's best regime, the election procedure is both by secret ballot and by public acclaim—to prevent fraud and to let the magistrates know the true feeling of the people (*De leg.* 3.15.33–17.39).

Many other curious features come to light when *Utopia* is read as a palimpsest which juxtaposes Raphael's ideas and institutions with those proposed by Cicero. In devising this juxtaposition, More sets forth an internal measure by which Raphael and his fictitious Utopians can be judged. If weighed from a Ciceronian perspective alone, Morus wins the argument of book 1 not simply by his use of consistent Ciceronian arguments but by exercising

Ciceronian decorum and statesmanlike restraint throughout. In view of this measure, one also sees the supposed freedom and stability of Utopia in a different and less convincing light.

In weighing what Cicero and Raphael Hythlodaeus say, the attentive reader comes to see that the basic disagreement revolves upon that most central of all questions posed by political philosophers: what is the best way of life? To look at this question from another point of view,[31] we turn to the Augustinian perspective, which More examined closely before writing the *Utopia*.

7 Utopia 2: Augustinian Realist[1]

For avarice is not a fault inherent in gold, but in the man who inordinately loves gold. . . . Therefore it is not an inferior thing which has made the will evil, but it is [the will] itself which has become so by wickedly and inordinately desiring an inferior thing. . . . Evil is removed, not by removing any nature, or part of a nature . . . but by healing and correcting that which had been vitiated and depraved. (*City of God* 12.8,6; 14.11)	In Utopia *all* greed for money was *entirely* removed with the use of money. . . . Who does not know that fraud, theft, rapine, quarrels, disorders, brawls, seditions, murders, treasons, poisonings . . . die out with the destruction of money? . . . So easily might men get the necessities of life if that blessed money . . . was not in fact the only barrier to our getting what we need. (*Utopia* CW4 241–43) (emphasis added)
This heavenly city . . . [does] not scruple about diversities in the manners, laws, and institutions whereby earthly peace is secured and maintained. . . . It therefore is so far from rescinding and abolishing these diversities, that it even preserves and adapts them. (*City of God* 19.17)	To take counsel on matters of common interest outside the senate or the popular assembly is considered a capital offense. The object of these measures, they say, is to prevent it from being easy . . . to change the order of the commonwealth. (*Utopia* CW4 125)

Augustine's treatment of the best way of life in *The City of God* profoundly influenced the perspective of the medieval and Renaissance world. Since the time of Plato and Cicero, the most significant development affecting political life was the rise of Christianity. Some thought that its rise actually destroyed the traditional polis—a view prevalent and strong enough to warrant Augustine's fourteen-year, thousand-page response in *The City of God*. Others recognized that Christianity had at least changed the terms of the conversation about citizenship here on earth. If what counts is life in the next world, the view of this world necessarily changes.

With these issues in mind, we can understand why biographers and critics of More have long called for a study of the Augustinian dimension of *Utopia*.[2] To date, however, no such study has come forth.[3] Yet as I will show in this chapter, appreciating the depth of *Utopia* as well as its wit and humor depends in large measure on understanding how More incorporates the Augustinian account into his own treatment of that basic issue of political philosophy: determining the best way of life.

More scholars have frequently conjectured that *The City of God* must have played some important role in More's construction of *Utopia*. After all, More gave a well-attended series of public lectures on this work fourteen years before writing *Utopia*; he considered Augustine to be his preeminent moral authority apart from the Bible[4]; and most importantly, he recognized that *The City of God* radically altered the classical interpretations of the best way of life (Kristeller 1985, 137). As one scholar put it, "The *City of God* is an answer to Plato's *Republic,* which it eventually replaced in the West as the most authoritative account of the manner in which man should live in the city" (Fortin 4).

More gave his lectures on Augustine's *City of God* in 1501, and at that time, he seems to have studied this work in an effort to understand the nature and limits of political life. As Stapleton tells us, More's lectures were written "not . . . from the theological point of view, but from the standpoint of history and philosophy" (9). As a student of Greek and Latin classics, More would have wanted early in his civic career to think through Augustine's critique of the classical underpinnings to the civic humanism of his day. In addition, the need for lectures on this aspect of Augustine seems highly appropriate if one considers the theoretical turmoil prevalent in those years in the areas of history and political philosophy. Why this turmoil? Because, as indicated in *Utopia* itself (CW4 51/6–8), reports of newly found countries and of civilizations wholly different from Europe gave rise to a great deal of speculation—speculation about history and the causes of change as well as speculation about human nature and the nature of government and society. As Nicholas Harpsfield commented on More's "jolly invention" of *Utopia*: "[A]bout that time many strange and unknown nations and many conclusions were discovered, such as our forefathers did neither know nor believe" (110). In view of such issues, it is no wonder that More attracted large numbers of the best educated in London for these lectures.

The City of God sets forth several important principles that would clearly give direction to one's understanding of the many new discoveries in the New World: no perfect society ever will or ever can exist (19.17,20,27); no Christian can doubt that any rational creature from any country has a human nature (16.8, 19.11, 12.21, 14.1); all human beings are subject to unruly passions and the vain imaginings that arise from pride (9.3–5, 14.3); each and every soul is properly ordered only when its love is firmly anchored in the contemplation of God (11.2, 14.7); the two fundamental types of society—i.e., the City of God and the earthly city—exist everywhere (14.1,13,28; 15.1) and they intermingle throughout history (1.35, 18.54); great security is never given to any people and therefore it is folly to look for security in this world (17.13). Significantly, *Utopia* violates or denies each of these principles.

Other significant contrasts also exist between Utopia and *The City of God*: Utopia boasts of a 1,760-year history in which no civil wars have taken place and only two natural catastrophes have affected their civic life (CW4 121/30, 137/25–27, 245/9–16); *The City of God* teaches that constant war and continuous catastrophes both natural and moral will always plague human societies (19.5).[5]

Utopia is "not merely the best but the only [political order] which can rightly claim the name of a commonwealth" (CW4 237/38–39); *The City of God* denies that a truly just commonwealth is possible anywhere or at any time here on earth (19.20–21). *The City of God* argues that personal peace is attained only through a lifelong struggle with the evil forces in oneself, a struggle that involves great personal self-denial (19.4); Utopians live a life of pleasurable leisure and consider great self-denial "the extreme of madness" (CW4 163/18, 179/8). *The City of God* considers "nothing more disgraceful and monstrous" than holding pleasure as the end of life (5.20)—the very position held by the Utopians (CW4 167/6). *The City of God* is indifferent to customs if these do not directly violate the law of God (19.17); Utopia is absolutely unbending in social custom, even in such matters as arbitrary as dress, voting procedure, or choice of home. While *The City of God* considers virtue as the key to peace and is tolerant of a wide range of institutional ways of bringing about that peace (19.10,17), Utopia considers its own institutional arrangement as not only the key but the only way of bringing about peace (CW4 103/24–31, 236/31–33, 245/6–11). Lastly but most importantly from the Augustinian point of view, *The City of God* is absolutely unbending regarding teachings about God's nature and the worship due him (19.17); in contrast, Utopia officially professes the widest possible freedom about worship of God but is absolutely unbending in matters of social custom that affect the state.

Such contrasts indicate the playfully antagonistic stance which More constructs within the text of *Utopia* between Raphael's and Augustine's views on the best way of life.

Utopia raises the same question as Plato's and Cicero's earlier ideal republics: what is the best way of life?[6] In *The City of God*, Augustine discusses this theme after making a traditional distinction between three possible ways of life (19.1–4). Augustine notes that some consider the best way of life as a life of leisure passed in the contemplation or quest of truth [*in contemplatione uel inquisitione ueritatis OTIOSO*]; others, as an active engagement in human affairs [*gerendis rebus humanis NEGOTIOSO*]; and still others, as a life that combines these two (19.2, emphasis added). In setting forth this distinction in terms of *otium* and *negotium,* Augustine continues the traditional debate in the same terms as the Greeks and Romans (Cumming 1.291–92; Logan 100–103, 179, 173–75). *Utopia* carries on that same debate.

In the introductory letters to *Utopia*, Erasmus, Budé, Desmarais, and Busleyden all praise Morus for a very active involvement in *negotium* that still allows leisure (*otium*) for learning.[7] This combination of leisure-for-learning and involvement in public affairs constitutes the core of the humanist ideal. Within *Utopia* Morus shows his enthusiasm for this ideal by his frequent praise of those committed to *negotium* and by his obvious dedication to learning (e.g., CW4 39/6–41/10, 47/1–49/16). In book 1, even Raphael praises Cardinal Morton as a man of great learning who "spent his whole life in important public affairs" (*maximis in negociis,* 60/2). In addition, Raphael presents Morton as worthy of respect (59/25–27), recognizing that "the king placed the greatest confidence in [Morton's] advice" (59/39) and that "the commonwealth seemed much to depend upon him" (61/1). Of course, Morus, too, praises Morton and encourages Raphael to imitate men like Morton and Plato who counseled political leaders as part of their civic duty.

Nevertheless, Raphael refuses to give up his *otium* for *negotium*. First he argues that such involvement comprises mere *seruitus* (54/26–27), a word that acquires great significance in *Utopia* and in *The City of God*. When Morus appeals to Raphael's sense of duty, Raphael still insists that "in disturbing my own peace and quiet, I should still not promote the public interest [*tamen quam OCIO meo NEGOCIUM facesserem, publican rem nihil promoueam*]" (56/20–21, emphasis added). Raphael places the highest value on his own *otium,* and he describes his Utopians as "leisure-loving people" (179/39). This priority explains his twice-stated preference for Greek over Roman learning, since the Greeks valued *otium* more than the Romans and the Romans valued *negotium* more than the Greeks. Yet Raphael's abrupt dismissal of the Romans as having virtually no value at all conflicts with Augustine and Augustine's beloved Cicero, both of whom maintained that the Romans contributed significantly to the Greeks (8.10).

Unlike Raphael, Augustine sets forth only two principles to regulate the use of *negotium* and *otium*: do what charity demands and use part of one's leisure to contemplate God (19.19). Both principles tie the proper use of *negotium* and *otium* to Augustine's Supreme Good. These principles, when juxtaposed with Raphael's account of the best life, lead one to discover that Raphael ignores the demands of charity and that neither he nor his Utopians use their leisure to contemplate God.

Only three times in all of the *Utopia* does Raphael mention charity, and each time he misuses the term, showing his complete misunderstanding of the nature of this precise Christian concept. At 164/31, Raphael refers to charity as a good act done both for "return of benefits" and for "the actual consciousness of the good deed." This formulation stands in direct contrast to the traditional understanding of charity as a humble act done only for love of God and done without expecting a return of benefit or praise.[8] At 190/6 and 224/8, Raphael refers to charity as but one of many bonds between friends, but with no reference at all to God. Curiously, Raphael never mentions charity when recounting the major features of Christianity, and he emphatically refuses the "servitude" of serving his fellow citizens. This attitude is in marked contrast to the one More advocates for the good ruler (see chapter 3).

If Raphael misunderstands charity, he also misunderstands Christian contemplation. Giles introduces Raphael as a sailor-philosopher "eager to contemplate the WORLD [*ORBIS TERRARUM contemplandi studio*]" (CW4 50/4, emphasis added), not God. Later, Raphael seems to present the highest act of Utopian worship as the "contemplation of nature" (224/19; also compare 217/26–29 with 183/17–24 and 224/19–20). Raphael's only other references to contemplation refer either to the disordered contemplation of gold (224/19), to the pleasure derived from the contemplation of truth (172/10),[9] or to his observation that many people simply have no capacity for contemplation (128/10). In this last point, Raphael agrees with Plato and differs with Augustine on perhaps the single most important issue separating classical and Christian political philosophy: whereas Augustine held that every person could contemplate God and could thus participate in the best way of life (19.17, 22.24), Raphael and Plato maintain that contemplation is *not* possible for everyone.[10] Raphael and Augustine posit two different ends and therefore two different philosophies of life.

In books 19–22 Augustine investigates the ends of earthly and heavenly cities as well as the various philosophies which articulate and support those ends. He begins in book 19 by looking at the many ends or goods proposed by the earthly philosophers. These goods vary from the pleasure of Epicurus to the virtue of the Stoics (19.1–3). Augustine dismisses all, however, in favor of the supreme good revealed in Scripture: the eternal peace of contemplating God (19.4)—as opposed to the Utopians' temporal peace of maximized pleasure.

After establishing peace as the end of life, Augustine then shows that *lack* of peace must necessarily characterize all earthly societies, be they family (19.5), community (19.6), world (19.7), friends (19.8), or fallen angels (19.9). In the face of this perpetual conflict, man's longing for eternal peace takes on added significance, giving the citizen of the City of God more incentive to "live like a captive and a stranger in the earthly city." Therefore, this citizen does not greatly concern himself "about diversities in the manners, laws, and institutions whereby earthly peace is secured and maintained"; he realizes that conflict must necessarily arise between the two cities. Why *must* conflict arise? Because the Heavenly City "has been unable to share with the earthly city a common religious legislation, and has had no choice but to dissent on this score" (19.17). So important is right worship to Augustine that no true republic, no true justice, no true virtue, or no true peace can exist without true religion (19.26). Giving *seruitus* to the one true God is the end of the Heavenly City. Dress, manners, customs, institutions, even ways of life can change, but *seruitus* cannot.

As we have seen already, however, *seruitus* has no dignity of place in Utopia. Instead, pleasure constitutes the "end of all operations" (*operationum omnium finem,* CW4 164/11) for the Utopians. Even the exercise of virtue has pleasure as its end (166/4–6). Augustine explicitly rejects this position as "hideous," arguing that where virtue is a slave to pleasure, it no longer deserves the name of virtue (19.1). In other places, Augustine argues at length against this same position. First, he argues from history, pointing to the Romans, who exercised the arts of ruling and commanding. He shows that the more the Romans devoted themselves to perfection in these arts, the less they devoted themselves to pleasure (5.12). Augustine also ridicules the position held by the Utopians, stating there is nothing more disgraceful and monstrous than this opinion, an opinion that no good man could hold (5.21). Finally, he turns to Scripture (14.2) and philosophy (19.1,4) to refute the view of virtue which the Utopians adopt.

Opposed to Augustine, the Utopian moral philosophy rests not on a love for the good or the true, but on refined hedonism and self-interest. Apart from fear of hell, Raphael explains,

> the Utopians have no hesitation in maintaining that a person would be stupid not to realize he ought to seek pleasure by fair means or foul, but that he should only take care not to allow a lesser pleasure [to] interfere with a greater nor to follow after a pleasure that would bring pain in retaliation. (CW4 163/6–10)

The Utopians act morally, not from the love of God or their fellow man, but from fear of punishment and love for one's maximized pleasure.

Some critics, such as Edward Surtz (1957a), have tried to justify the Utopian philosophy of pleasure by arguing that the Utopians' highest pleasure is fundamentally the same as the Christians', i.e., the beatific vision. Yet as we have seen, the Utopians recognize no such contemplative end.

The greatest point of divergence between Augustine and Raphael, therefore, relates to their views of religion. In books 1–10 of *The City of God,* Augustine attacks civil religions similar to those in *Utopia.* Augustine's critique rests upon a threefold distinction of religious devotion. Of the three types, only *seruitus* renders to God an exclusive worship, a worship reserved for God alone. *Religio,* a much broader term, refers not only to one's bond with God but also to various social bonds. *Cultus* is the broadest of the three terms, going beyond social bonds to include various bonds in nature. To indicate its extreme generality, Augustine gives the etymology of *cultus*:

> It seems that [*cultus*] is not reserved for God alone. For we employ a similar word [*colere*] in reference to distinguished men whose memory or company we "cultivate." The word "cult" refers to things to which we subject ourselves in a spirit of piety and religion, but we also "cultivate" certain things that are subject to us. From the Latin word, *colere,* are derived such words as agriculturists, colonist, and *incolae,* that is, inhabitants. (10.1)

In *Utopia, cultus* is used to designate the most cherished activities while *seruitus* designates the worst of punishments. As if following Augustine's explanation of *cultus,* Raphael uses the term not only for the cultivation of land (CW4 66/10,28; 120/15,18,24), people (112/5, 134/19), and custom (154/2,5; 156/8), but also for the worship of ancestors (224/13), the god of one's choice (220/12), or Christ (128/21). *Religio* in *Utopia* has the same general and ambiguous meanings indicated by Augustine.[11] As for *servitus,* one fact becomes clear: nowhere in *Utopia* does God receive a special worship analogous to Augustine's *seruitus*.[12] This absence calls attention to the purpose of *Utopia*'s civil religions.

All religions in *Utopia,* Raphael claims, "tend to the same end, the worship of the divine nature" (*diuinae naturae CULTUM,* 232/6, emphasis added). But what is this divine nature? And do all religions in Utopia actually promote cult to God?

Regarding the first question, Utopus claims ignorance (221/13ff) and so do the Utopian priests. Despite this ignorance, they nevertheless have extremely restrictive criteria governing legitimate religions, and although Utopia may tolerate carefully selected religions, one religion alone do they and Raphael consider best and one criterion is operative in judging all religions:

> But gradually the [Utopians] are all beginning to depart from this medley of superstitions and are coming to unite in that *one* religion which seems to surpass the rest in *reasonableness*. (217/26–29, emphasis added)

"Reasonableness" constitutes the criterion whereby the Utopian priests tolerate religious beliefs and expressions. Yet reasonable according to what or whom? "Reasonable" according to the leaders of this civil religion. The priests of Utopia, those ultimate and terrifying censors of proper opinion, "take the greatest pains from the very first to instill . . . good opinions, which are also useful for the preservation of their commonwealth" (*conseruandae ipsorum reipublicae utiles,* 229/11–15), and are "of great help in watching over the condition of the commonwealth" (*ad tuendum publicae rei statum afferunt utilitatem,* 229/16–17). Notice what these statements assert: the priests of Utopia most *usefully* seek to preserve *their republic*.[13]

In other words, the Utopian priests determine the "rightness" of a religion based upon political considerations (229/10–14), not upon the worship due to God. The official religions of Utopia are definitely civil. The monthly[14] communal worship ceremonies—always followed by mandatory military exercises—seem as bland and neutral as one could imagine. The strongest form of sacrifice consists in burning incense and candles, a striking contrast to the sacrifices advocated in Augustine's *City of God,* where Augustine argues that without genuine sacrifice, a true commonwealth cannot exist (10.5,6,19; 15.17; but esp. 19.23, final paragraph).

The Utopian priests hold the greatest power in Utopia. Utopus created this religion to preserve his republic (CW4 221/10–26), arranging for his priests to control the conduct of everyone to achieve that same end. The actual status of these priests deserves careful study. They alone among the living receive veneration from the people (228/33, 230/14), a veneration expressed even in the monthly religious ceremonies (235/31–34). Yet this is no surprise, since the liturgy and the very architecture of the temples have come about through "the deliberate intention of the priests" (233/2). The priests also strive, as one of their major objectives, to instill "religious fear" throughout the country because it constitutes "the greatest and almost the only stimulus to the practice of virtues" (235/7–8). Disfavor with the Utopian priests brings about the most dreaded punishment and fear, despite Raphael's statement to the contrary (compare 229/3–8 with 229/33–36). As the ultimate interpreters of God (186/15), the priests are above any law, and no individual, official, or court can bring charges against Utopian priests, regardless of the crime they have committed (229/23–29).

Why should this class have so much power? And why the unusual criteria for truth—i.e., *utilitas* for the commonwealth? At this point, it may become clear how *Utopia* relates to the first ten books of Augustine's *City of God*. In books 1–5, Augustine argues against those who worship (*colendos*) false gods with a veneration (*seruitute*) due to God alone, and in books 6–10, Augustine proceeds with a detailed critique of mythological, natural, and civil theologies. The account of Utopia is a myth that claims to be natural and is actually civil in character, thus providing *exempla* of the civil theologies which Augustine criticizes in books 1–10 of *The City of God*.

Throughout *Utopia* More also alludes to the issues raised in books 11–18 of *The City of God*, i.e., the history of the City of God and the city of man. In the first four of these books, Augustine explores in considerable detail the origin of each city. After his complex analyses of creation, the Trinity, time, and evil, Augustine claims that the city of man arises as a consequence of man's free will. From the misuse of this free will, the city of man emerges when individuals "turn to themselves," away from the divine (12.6).

The Utopians deny free will,[15] and by choosing pleasure as the highest good, they definitely turn to themselves. Denying free will as the source of evil in the world, the Utopians consider the institutional arrangement of private property—not personal sin—as ultimately responsible for all social and personal evils:

> In Utopia *all* greed for money was *entirely* removed with the use of money.... Who does not know that fraud, theft, rapine, quarrels, disorders, brawls, seditions, murders, treasons, poisonings ... die out with the destruction of money? (CW4 241/39–243/6, emphasis added)

Not only will eliminating private property get rid of quarrels, murders, and all the other social evils listed above, it will also get rid of "fear, anxiety, worries, toils and sleepless nights" (243/6–7). "What is more, poverty forthwith would itself dwindle and *disappear* if money were entirely done away with everywhere" (243/8–9, emphasis added). Just how believable would any follower of Augustine find these claims? Augustine explicitly denies that external objects like gold or money can make the will evil (12.8,6; 14.11).

Another direct opposition between the view of history in *Utopia* and *The City of God* appears after reflecting upon books 15–18. There Augustine explains the growth and development of both the earthly and heavenly cities. Augustine repeatedly states that the heavenly and earthly cities intermingle and co-exist from the time of the first society formed by Adam and Eve. For example, through the exercise of free will, Abel chooses the Heavenly City while Cain chooses the earthly. Seth and Enos choose the Heavenly City while Enoch chooses the earthly. This intermingling of the two cities continues, according to Augustine, until the time of Noah, when God destroys everyone in the earthly city except Noah (a member of the Heavenly City) and nine others of his family. Even at this time, however, the City of God does not exist alone, since some members of Noah's family freely choose the city of man while others remain faithful to the City of God.

Throughout books 15–18, Augustine points out that the earthly and heavenly cities will continue in perpetual conflict until the end of the world. To look for lasting peace in this world is sheer folly (17.13; also 19.4,20; 22.22). Since the citizens of the City of God are pilgrims, they must prepare themselves for persecution and suffering, not peace on earth.

In contrast, the Utopians do not suffer from the normal cycles of war and peace. Utopia claims a history of 1,760 years of unbroken peace and prosperity (CW4 121/30).[16] As Raphael reports, the Utopians

> have adopted such institutions of life as have laid the foundations of the commonwealth not only most happily, but also *to last forever*. At home they have extirpated the roots of ambition and factionalism along with all the other vices. Hence there is *no danger of trouble* from domestic discord. (245/6–11, emphasis added)

Utopia, indeed, epitomizes Enoch's earthly city: "a city of earth, at home and not in exile in the world, a city satisfied with such temporal peace and joy as is possible here" (15.17).

In direct contrast to Utopia's lasting peace and prosperity, Augustine argues that no such peace can exist on earth and that even the most just cities are essentially other Babylons, cities of contention and confusion (18.41; 23.22; 15.4; 16.4; 17.4,16). Hence, no state on earth can rightly use the name commonwealth (19.23–24). When, therefore, Raphael boasts that Utopia is "not merely the best [commonwealth] but the only one which can rightly claim the name of commonwealth" (236/31–33), he directly opposes the main argument underlying *The City of God*.[17]

Because the citizens of the City of God are pilgrims, Augustine advises them to adapt as best they can to wherever they might be. For example, in 19.19 Augustine argues that these pilgrims should not care at all what kind of dress or social manners another has, so long as these do not contradict the divine law. In striking contrast, Utopian civil law imposes drab uniformity in dress on everyone and strictly regulates every aspect of social life. In 19.17, Augustine states that the City of God finds no fault with diversity in customs, laws, and traditions; it actually works to preserve and follow them. The Utopians, however, have rigid and unchanging customs and traditions. Such contrasts between *The City of God* and *Utopia* are so direct and pointed that More has obviously juxtaposed them in order to stimulate our reflection and reaction.

It is important to remember that the story of Utopia arises from a conversation in which Raphael Hythlodaeus has set out to defend what he considers his own virtuous way of life. "*Vivo ut volo* [I live as I wish]," Raphael proudly and emphatically tells Morus (CW4 56/1), and throughout books 1 and 2 Raphael tries to persuade Morus of the superiority of his view of the virtuous life.

Vivo ut volo. Augustine uses the same phrase, but with an important qualification. Augustine insists that *no* one can live as he wishes in this life, not even the just and virtuous:

> No one lives as he wishes but the blessed [*nisi beatus non vivit ut vult*], and no one is blessed but the just. But even the just man does not live as he wishes, until he has arrived where he cannot die, be deceived, or injured. (*City of God* 14.25)

Raphael expects a degree of worldly happiness, peace, and freedom that Augustine considers impossible. The root of this difference goes deep.

Augustine defines virtue as the "order of love" whereby a person is attached first and foremost to God (15.22) and does everything else for the love of God—a definition identical to the one given in More's earlier writings (see chapter 2). In Utopia, we discover that virtue is "living according to [nature's] prescription" (CW4 165/14–15). The important question is: what does nature prescribe and how does one find out? As we have seen, in Utopia the prescription of nature is authoritatively interpreted by the Utopian priests, who surprisingly teach that not only is life ordered to "pleasure as the end of all our operations" (163/20–21); they also teach only those opinions about nature "which are also useful for the preservation of their commonwealth" (229/11–15). With this politically motivated interpretation of virtue, we are less surprised to discover that "religious fear towards the gods [is] the greatest, almost the only, stimulus to the practice of virtues" (235/7–8). In contrast, love of God is the greatest stimulus to virtue for Augustine.

Therefore, what Augustine would call true virtue—action based on genuine love of God—plays no official part in Utopia.[18] Granted, one of the two official games in Utopia (both are war games) consists in "a pitched battle between virtues and vices" (129/21–29; Berger 1982, 290). Yet, what parents usually encourage their children to imitate vice and practice it in their play? As unusual as these official games may appear, they constitute an integral part in teaching the machiavellian tactics which the Utopians proudly use in their foreign wars. A closer look at Utopian foreign policy and their attitude towards war reveals more clearly the Utopians' inadequate notion of virtue and their dehumanizing way of life (Weiner 20–21, Dorsch 354–56).

Raphael opens the section on military affairs by reporting that the Utopians utterly loathe wars as subhuman behavior. Nonetheless, all citizens—men, women, and children—constantly and assiduously train for war after their religious ceremonies. Next Raphael states that Utopians do not readily go to war. However, he then gives a long list of exceptions, which implies a constant readiness and perhaps an eagerness for war, especially since the Utopians see war as a game of wits (CW4 203/18,27; 129/19–29). Utopians go to war, not only for self-defense, but also "in *pity* for a people oppressed by tyranny" or "to requite and avenge injuries *previously* done" to their friends (201/7,11–12, emphasis added). Even more broadly, they consider it just to go to war "when the merchants among their friends undergo unjust persecution under the color of justice in any other country, either on the pretext of laws in themselves unjust or by the distortion of laws in themselves good" (201/17–20). With this list of reasons, the Utopians could declare war on any nation at any time, simply because their sense of pity or commercial justice warrants it.

Lest one miss the degree of license the Utopians employ, a revealing example follows, an example worthy of Lucian. After giving the "exceptional" reasons for going to war, Raphael explains why the Utopians recently helped the Nephelogetes in waging war against the Alaopolitans: "The Nephelogetic traders suffered a wrong, *as they thought,* under pretense of law, but *whether right or wrong,* it was avenged by a fierce war" (201/23–25, emphasis added).[19] Although the Utopians do not know the issues of justice involved, they readily ignore the established laws which justified the Alaopolitans' course of action.[20] Instead, force and partisan prejudice conquer law and reason. To reveal the degree of this violent injustice, Raphael continues with his Lucianic description:

> Into this war the neighboring nations brought their energies and resources to assist the power and to intensify the rancor of both sides. Most flourishing nations were either shaken to their foundations or grievously afflicted. The troubles upon troubles that arose were ended only by the enslavement and surrender of the Alaopolitans. Since the Utopians were not fighting in their own interest, they yielded them into the power of the Nephelogetes, a people who, when the Alaopolitans were prosperous, were not in the least comparable to them. (201/25–33)

The Utopians do not hesitate to enslave a whole people and to "shake to their foundations" the most flourishing nations surrounding them.

Yet the Utopians go further still in their injustice: they are willing to exterminate an entire people such as the Zapoletans. Since Utopians consider Zapoletans subhuman, the Utopians "do not care in the least how many Zapoletans they lose, thinking that they would be the greatest benefactors to the human race if they could relieve the world of all the dregs of this abominable and impious people" (209/12–15).

Augustine argues explicitly against such genocide. In book 19.12 he suggests that his readers imagine a nation of wild men, quite similar to the one the Utopians wish to eliminate. Augustine rejects the possibility, however, that any nation could be so thoroughly corrupt; only in fiction could such a nation exist.

As a general policy, the Utopians "require such severe punishments of those on whom they lay the blame that for the future they may be afraid to attempt anything of the same sort" (CW4 203/30–32). This policy seems incongruous for a people who claim to recognize mercy as a primary virtue (139/20, 205/26). Yet, once the Utopians declare war, they will use tactics "elsewhere condemned as the cruel deed of a degenerate nature" (205/23). The Utopians, for example, actively "sow the seeds of dissension broadcast," turning brother against brother and neighbor against neighbor (205/33–38). How would such tactics be judged according to traditional Christian ethics? Augustine clearly condemns such tactics (see book 19 especially), thus drawing our attention again to the divergent ways of life depicted in *The City of God* and *Utopia*.

Given this divergence, we cannot leave the topic of Utopian virtue without investigating more deeply the underlying motive of Raphael in defending his "virtuous" way of life and that of the Utopians, which Raphael presents as the best proof for the justice of his own.

Anyone who has struggled with and pondered the long history of debate on the nature of the highest good and the respective roles played by pleasure and virtue sees immediately that the Utopian position is philosophically untenable. Of course, the Utopians themselves recognize this, as their unusual amalgam of "religion" and philosophy indicates:

> They never have a discussion of happiness without uniting certain principles taken from religion as well as from philosophy.... Without these principles they think reason insufficient and weak by itself for the investigation of true happiness. (CW4 161/32–35)

Religion alone grasps the nature of happiness for the Utopians, a truth that Augustine too maintains. But what end do the Utopians advocate? An end which culminates in pleasure and is achieved through fear. In contrast, Augustine advocates an end which culminates in contemplation and is achieved through love.

The indefensible character of Raphael's notion of virtue becomes clear by comparing two passages in book 2. At 173/12, as we have seen, Raphael leads us to believe that the genuine pleasure and therefore the true end of life is the pleasure of contemplation. Yet one page later, Raphael concludes the section with this apparently contradictory statement:

> To sum up, they [the Utopians] cling above all to mental pleasures, which they value as the first and foremost of all pleasures. Of these the principal part they hold to arises from the practice of the virtues and the consciousness of a good life. (175/34–37)

In commenting on this passage, the editors of the Yale edition of *Utopia* ask: "What significance is to be attached to the omission of mental pleasures [contemplation] mentioned previously: '*intellectum, eamque dulcedinem quam veri contemplatio pepererit*' (172/10–11)?" In answering their own question, the editors speculate that "[i]t may reveal the essentially moralistic and voluntaristic cast of mind of More and his fellow humanists" (460n). The above passage does indeed reveal an essentially moralistic and voluntaristic cast of mind, but the cast of mind is Raphael's and the Utopians', not More's.

The indefensible character of Raphael's position is also seen in Raphael's statement about the "sole object" of the Utopian commonwealth: "that for all the citizens, as far as the public need permit, as much time as possible should be withdrawn from the service [*servitio*] of the body and devoted to the freedom and culture of the mind [*animi libertatem cultumque*]" (135/20–24). The difficulty with this statement is that it actually applies to very few people in Utopia. It applies primarily to Raphael and to the heads of church and state; the rest of the Utopians live in virtual slavery and in constant fear. In fact, no one in Utopia has real freedom of mind about the highest questions—except for Raphael, who has made up this story. Even in the story of Utopia itself, Raphael recognizes that a good percentage of the population could care less about this "cult of the mind" (129/8–12, 225/26–29, 115/20–21).

At most, 500 of a population of 108,000 to 156,000 are exempt from menial labor to pursue this cult of the mind (CW4 410, 415);

to provide these few with their life of leisure, an extraordinarily repressive regime is necessary. True, we are told that a few of the nonelect may work their way into the ranks of the 500, but why would the most gifted and inquisitive even try when they are prohibited from pursuing the truth under pain of forfeiting their status of citizenship? As we learn, those who disagree with the prescribed beliefs are not even considered human, lose all rights, and can hold no office or position (221/34–35, 223/4–6).

Another way of trying to understand the "virtue" advocated in Utopia is to consider the type of activities that are honored and praised. All honored activities relate directly to service to the Utopian state; no one can give honor for independent excellences such as art, philosophy, or music. For example, the types of "philosophy" honored in Utopia are restricted to medicine and mathematics (183/10–12, 159/22ff) and to what they call moral philosophy (161/17). No independent thought is allowed, however, in this latter field because questioning the basis of the Utopian civil religion can lead one to be considered—and treated—as a beast. The terms of highest praise in all of book 2 go to the priests (229–31) and to the strategic war planners, who use cleverness and calculation to crush their enemies (203/20–21).

What then is the strongest motive for virtue in *Utopia*? As we have seen, fear motivates the majority of oppressed citizens. But what about the motive of those who rule? It seems to be what Augustine calls the lust for rule and Aristotle, despotism (*City of God* 1.Preface, 1.30, 4.6, 5.19, 14.15, 18.2; *Politics* 1333b29–1334a11; CW3.2, no. 243). This motive is hinted at in the new names of the rulers: whereas the old household leaders were known as syphogrants ("old men of the sty"), under the new regime they are known as phylarchs ("fond of power"). In the old regime, the leaders seemed content with good food and honor of place; in the new regime, however, the lust for dominion—which originally led Utopus to invade and conquer Utopia—now motivates those in power. This lust for dominion is evident in virtually everything done on this island. The leaders require every man, woman, and child to train regularly for war; they direct all commercial enterprises to gain the various kinds of wealth needed to sustain their wars or at least to bargain for victory—whether that be paying off mercenaries or bribing traitors. Even their agricultural policy makes most sense if one realizes this is a warring state. Why else would the entire citizenry (except of course the 500 elect who alone share the privileges of power) be forced to learn and be engaged in farming? This is a society whose life is focused on the exigencies of war, and all of Utopia is ordered to martial conquest.

The dominant passion of the Utopian rulers may well be the most vicious possible for human beings. As Augustine explains, those who desire dominion yet despise glory are crueler than beasts (5.19), and the Utopian rulers do not seem the least concerned with glory. They prefer pleasures more tangible and immediate; some even retire for a year or more to palatial estates outside of Utopia "to live there in great style and to play the part of magnates" (CW4 215/33).

Utopus, that conquering prince who overthrew the "rude and rustic" inhabitants (113/5), began his reign by completing fortifications of the island to make it virtually invincible to outside forces (113/8–11, 111/19–33). So thorough were his fortifications that even the water sources of each city were protected "lest in case of hostile attack the water might be cut off and diverted or polluted" (119/28–30).

The rulers of Utopia exercise tyrannous control over their subjects, and they wage expansionist wars which have brought them extraordinary wealth. But who controls the armies and who coordinates military plans and efforts? Raphael never raises these issues, just as he never indicates if Utopus had an official successor. Such practical issues are not Raphael's concern. He is interested primarily in the final results of this communist state, which serves the will of the 500 elect, among whom Raphael imagines himself. Ultimately, as we have seen, Raphael is interested in justifying his own way of life.

If More alludes throughout *Utopia* to the great historical and philosophic issues examined in *The City of God*, how does the presence of this Augustinian subtext affect the way we read *Utopia*? It provides another level for dialectic weighing and consideration; it also provides an important level of Lucianic play.

As we have seen, More loved Lucian's comic dialogues, and he translated three from Greek to Latin in 1506, ten years before *Utopia*'s publication. More praises Lucian's "very honest" and "very entertaining wit" in reprimanding human frailties (CW3.1 3/10–11) such as the "fruitless contentions of philosophers" and the "inordinate passion for lying" (5/8–25). The *philosophus gloriosus* is one of Lucian's favorite objects of satire and one of More's favorites as well, judging from the dialogues he chose to translate (Wooden 1972, 43–57).

In Lucian's *Lover of Lies,* for example, Eucrates and his fellow "philosophers" discuss the various charms, animal skins, and incantations they use to cure diseases. At one point they argue whether the cure for rheumatism involves wrapping the tooth of a weasel in the skin of a lion just flayed or in that of a hind still immature and unmated (CW3.1 7). Having scornfully laughed at the narrator for disbelieving these superstitions, Eucrates and his companions ask with dramatic irony: "Do you consider it *incredible* that any alleviation of ailments are effected by such means?" (8, emphasis added). Of course, both the narrator and the reader do consider these claims incredible, and much of Lucian's humor involves such unconscious revelation by the main characters (Dorsch 345–63; Wooden 1972, 43–57).

Such revelation also takes place throughout *Utopia*. As a dramatic dialogue, *Utopia* constantly calls upon the reader to make judgments about the claims of each character. Raphael Hythlodaeus makes many incredible claims, especially the claim that complete communism eliminates *all* vices and lays the foundation of a commonwealth that would live *forever,* or the claim that a country could enjoy 1,760 years of internal peace and prosperity. There are other claims less dramatic, but equally incredible. Even today with vastly improved technology we cannot transplant an entire forest of grown trees (CW4 179/31–33). Nor could we transform a peninsula into an island by removing fifteen miles of land with a pick and shovel (113/8–18). Although subtler than Lucian's, More's irony belongs to a humor of the same kind.

The overall effect of the Augustinian allusions that pervade book 2 of *Utopia* is to cause one to question Raphael's credibility and motivation in telling the tale he presents. Raphael originally introduced his tale in order to justify his way of life to Morus and Giles. In this, he clearly fails, since neither Morus nor Giles changes his way of life or lessens his involvement in what Raphael considers a thoroughly corrupt state. Nevertheless, many aspects of Raphael's ideal republic deserve praise and even implementation, despite his lack of credibility on other points. Just as Cardinal Morton discriminately adopts certain suggestions of Raphael (81/7–18), so will the discriminate reader of *Utopia*, and once the reader begins discriminating, he enters the dialectical game More has constructed.

These Augustinian allusions point to yet another internal measure for our consideration: the charity dramatized in the character of Morus as opposed to the proud railing exhibited by Raphael. *Utopia* begins with Morus's descending from Christian worship, eager to serve those in need. Morus warmly greets his friend Giles and not only welcomes Raphael Hythlodaeus but feeds him twice and uses a rhetoric designed to gain his good will and to avoid unnecessary offense. In contrast, Raphael seems to worship a god of his own making. He speaks bluntly and offensively, and he exhibits the same pride he condemns by placing himself in the only privileged position that can save Europe from her corrupt ways—without giving up the leisure he values most highly. *Vivo ut volo,* Raphael insists. Yet, as Augustine reminded us, no Christian humanist could claim such freedom.

Part Three

Issues in More's Career
as Statesman

8 The Limits of Reason and the Need for Law

In the early years of his theoretical and practical preparation, More learned many important lessons about the limits of personal reason and the necessity of enforcing law through public authority.

In 1506, for example, a minor incident occurred that More would remember and comment upon later at great length. It was an incident that revealed in a dramatic and personal way the limits of reason and the need for lawful intervention by public authority.

This incident involved a friar at Coventry who "taught that anyone who daily recited the Psalter of the Blessed Virgin could not lose his soul" (SL15 132). This friar attracted a substantial following since, as More observed, his assurance of salvation "opened up an easy way to heaven" (132). Not surprisingly, comments More, "the very worst sinners" became "the most pious in the recitation of the Psalter, only because they had assured themselves of the permission to do anything at all," without suffering the consequences (133). When the local pastor warned his people about this senseless doctrine, the friar denounced him as a fool and a blasphemer, and the people "stormed upon him with violent indignation; they hissed and booed him out of the pulpit, and exposed him everywhere to public ridicule as the enemy of Mary" (133–34). Without realizing the intensity of the conflict that was brewing, More was personally drawn into this argument while visiting his sister in Coventry in 1506.

This Coventry friar may well have served as a model for the intolerant and revolutionary character More created in *Utopia*'s Raphael Hythlodaeus seven years later. It may also have been an example More remembered when confronted with Luther's simplified doctrine of salvation, especially since both denied the personal responsibility of individuals for their actions. In any case, the event deserves special note because More presented it as a clear example of the harm that could be done when seditious ideas are left unchecked.

More vividly told the story of his encounter with this Coventry monk:

> Just when the situation was red hot, I happened to go to Coventry to visit my sister there. I had hardly dismounted when the question was put to me, "Could a person who daily recited the Psalter of the Blessed Virgin lose his soul?" My answer to the silly question was a laugh. I was promptly warned, that sort of answer was a dangerous thing, for a very holy and learned Father was preaching quite the opposite. I shrugged off the whole affair as none of my business. (CW15 134)

In response to this "dangerous thing," More reacted in his customary manner of humor and disengagement. Yet no easy disengagement was to be possible:

> I was at once invited to dinner; I accepted and went. And, of all things, in came an old friar, cadaverous, stern, and gloomy; a boy behind him was carrying a stack of books. I saw at a glance I was in for a battle. We sat down at table, and, so as not to lose a moment, the topic was promptly broached by the host. The friar put forth exactly what he had been preaching. I did not say a word myself. I do not like to get involved in arguments that are unpleasant and sterile. (134)

More's next response showed a diplomatic style that he would use often in the future:

> At last they asked for my opinion too. Since I now had to say something, I gave a statement of my views; but I was brief and casual. Then

the friar launched out on a speech that was carefully prepared and tedious; for the length of almost two sermons he babbled on and on at table.... Then I calmly remarked, there was not in his entire lecture a single convincing argument for those who would deny the miracles he had recounted, and such denial was reconcilable with the Christian Faith; and even if those miracles were authentic, they were not sufficient proof for the point at hand; true, one could readily find a sovereign who on occasion would pardon even an enemy in answer to his mother's pleas; but no one is so foolhardy as to promulgate a law that would challenge his subjects to insolent disobedience by the promise of impunity to all disloyal citizens who obliged his mother by a specific act of homage. Much was said on both sides, but the final result of my efforts was that he was lauded to the skies and I was laughed at as a fool. (134–35)

What is significant in this episode is that no amount of reason was able to affect the prejudices of this friar and his loyal band—just as Raphael Hythlodaeus would be unaffected by the reasons given by Giles and Morus, and just as Luther would be unaffected by the reasons given by theologians such as Erasmus. As More then went on to point out,

Thanks to the misguided zeal of men who gaze through the mask of piety with a kindly eye upon their own sins, the situation eventually became so bad that it was brought under control only through the most strenuous efforts of the bishop. (135)

Where reason proved powerless, law and public authority had to step in.

From 1510 to 1517, More witnessed many other incidents in which law and public authority had to intervene in an effort to maintain or restore civic harmony. During these years, More served as a judge for virtually every type of civic disorder, from ordinary acts of violence like physical assault to more subtle forms of violence like slander (Guy 1980, 6).

More pointed out that slander causes such grave harm that "every well ordered region has by plain laws prohibited and forbidden" it (CW8 590). In England, "slanderous railing words" were not only "by the common laws of this realm upon great pain forbidden," but also by statutory laws which applied to the written as well as the spoken word (CW8 592).

In 1515, More found it necessary to explain the difference between slander and satire to his learned colleague Martin Dorp, who had severely criticized Erasmus's *Praise of Folly* in ways that were slanderous (CW15 42/3, 44/5).[1] Erasmus had simply written good satire: i.e., he had used "cutting words" in jest against classes of foolish and corrupt people with the intent of discouraging vice and folly. Dorp, however, used cutting words in earnest against easily recognized individuals, with the intent to destroy (112/22–114/1). The difference between these two approaches, More noted, is immense: "[V]irtually no one refuses to laugh at a jocular saying aimed at him; no one stands for a serious one" (111; see also 107–21).

Even before publishing *Folly*, Erasmus knew that his book would be misunderstood and would need defense. For that reason he dedicated the book to More and asked him to come to his protection. In this same letter prefaced to the first edition of *Folly*, Erasmus also set forth the nature and limits of satire:[2]

> If someone censures the lives men live in such a way that he does not denounce a single person by name, tell me if he appears to bite and worry mankind, or rather to teach and admonish them? . . . One who leaves no class of human beings unscathed appears angry not with any person in particular but with every kind of vice. So, if anyone arises to cry out that he is hurt [by Folly], he shows either that his conscience is pricking him or at least that he is afraid. (CWE2 164)

More expressed a similar view of satire when he praised Lucian's ability to reprimand and censure human frailties "with very honest and at the same time very entertaining wit" (CW3.1 3). More considered him first-rate in satire because he censured "so cleverly and effectively that although no one pricks more deeply, nobody resents his stinging words" (3). To achieve this effect, Lucian used literary figures and never attacked individuals by name.

In the next few years, More faced numerous incidents of public unrest arising from the flagrant misuse of reason, especially from slander.

In 1517, for example, More was commissioned to discover the cause of the Evil May Day Riots. He had been personally involved, having been asked to help stop the rioting once it had begun. As Edward Hall reports, More "almost brought them to a stay" (1.159) when another group of rioters began to "throw out stones and bats and hurt diverse honest persons" (1.159). Later, after investigating the causes of this riot, More found that two young apprentices used lies to stir up other disgruntled apprentices and journeymen against foreigners living in London (CW9 156). Their slanders developed into sedition, i.e., into "fighting words" intent on inciting rebellion. As a result, a thousand angry youths took to the streets, and the danger to public safety was considered so great that the city was placed under royal military control, the rioters were charged with treason, and several leaders were tried and "executed in most rigorous manner" (Hall 1.159ff). This was another incident in which law and public authority had to intervene once slander had prevailed.

Civil unrest caused by slander occurred even among the dons of Oxford. In 1518, as one of his first official actions after joining the royal council, More wrote to the directors of Oxford to express his amazement at their negligence in letting the campus become factionalized by the "Trojans," who were set on eradicating "Greeks." Certain professors, "either because they despised Greek or were simply devoted to other disciplines, or most likely because they possessed a perverse sense of humor," formed a society "named after the Trojans" (SL 96, CW15 133). By publicly denouncing Greek students as "little devils" and Greek teachers as the "chief devils" (SL 100, CW15 143), these slanderous attackers caused such animosity on campus that More warned the Oxford directors that "no situation has . . . arisen in recent years, which . . . more urgently requires your serious attention" (SL 96, CW15 133). After giving a strong defense of Greek studies, including the New Testament (SL 100ff, CW15 139ff), and after appealing to their sense of duty and prudence (SL 101, CW15 145), More reminded these university officials that their university would "go to ruin" if "the foolish and slothful were allowed to flout sound learning" with impunity (CW15 147, SL 101–2). More not only reminded them of their duty, he gave an ominous warning that if they did not rule in this important matter, the King would step in and do so. By the end of the letter, he made clear that law and public authority would step in, if reason at Oxford was lacking.

Another incident occurred in 1519 where More found himself defending one friend against the slander of another. In his "Letter to a Monk," More wrote in an unusually blunt and straightforward way, although he suppressed the name of the person he addressed. He used extremely strong language because the Monk should have known better than to misuse his position as a religious to spread slander about a fellow priest of Erasmus's proven reputation. With clear evidence of lies and deliberate misrepresentations, More reminded him forcibly of his first principles as a monk, of his limited education, and of his serious offense in misusing Scripture and his position "for slandering some other person as you do" (CW15 273).

In 1520 yet another philippic came from More's pen, also motivated by knowledge of the serious harm slander could do. This thunderbolt was occasioned by what More saw as a sustained and calculated lie designed to bring an end to his career and even his life. More's spirited self-defense[3] arose in light of Brixius's accusations that More was disloyal to his king (CW3.2 649, 641). More explained that if these accusations "were any less widely appreciated and our prince were as ignorant as [Brixius] ma[d]e him out to be," then More would have been in "dire peril" (CW3.2 649). Not only did Brixius print lies, More wrote, he also had "taken secret steps to secure my undoing so far as it was in his power" (CWE7 252). The calculated character of this "dire peril" was what led More to call Brixius's slanders "criminal" and "pernicious" (CW3.2 649). More responded in this way because he had been advised by others "to protect [him]self against the man's perfectly ludicrous calumnies." He insisted to Erasmus that self-defense was his "sole object" and that he was not willing to let

Brixius be "victorious without a battle" (CWE7 252, 239). Although More quickly withdrew this letter from publication, he did so only after he had written a detailed response to Brixius's charges. Good lawyer that he was, he continued to follow this tactic in the future.[4] In his "Letter to Brixius," More stayed within the bounds of satire except that he had no other choice than to address his attacker directly and by name. This situation was unavoidable, More pointed out, because Brixius attacked first and his attacks were public, with the intent to destroy.

As we will see in the next chapter, the same was true when More turned his pen against Luther, Tyndale, and the others calling for social and ecclesiastical revolution. More had long been an advocate of reform, but he supported reform that would not endanger the peaceful progress of society. Legitimate reform, therefore, had to rely on the progressive implementation of reason and law. Instead of using these traditional methods, Luther and his English followers attacked reason and law, and even put them at odds with the Christian faith. They also did not hesitate to distort the truth in their efforts to topple institutions, laws, and traditions that were centuries old.

In other words, from 1506 to 1523, More had plenty of evidence that "fighting words," if left unrestrained, would make civic harmony impossible. During this same period of time, Henry VIII also had ample evidence of More's extraordinary rhetorical and legal abilities in dealing with ideas that threatened civic harmony. It was not surprising, therefore, that Henry asked More to use the full force of those skills against what he considered to be the major danger to England's peace: Luther's violent attack upon the legitimacy of all civil and ecclesiastical law. Not only the King and his counselors considered Luther a danger to peace; by this time, all the principal rulers of Christendom also agreed. Within a year, even Erasmus denounced Luther for using tactics and advocating doctrines that were sure to destroy the unity and peace of Christendom.

But why did More attack Luther and Tyndale personally? For the same reason he attacked Brixius personally. Brixius attacked first, with slander, and with intent to destroy. This situation was analogous to a just war, undertaken for self-defense. Even in this situation, however, More recognized that limits had to be observed, and he conscientiously respected them. As we will now see, More devised a rhetoric that was designed to expose what Luther and his fellow revolutionaries were actually proposing. Hence, More's polemic is unusual in that it took his opponents' arguments paragraph by paragraph, often sentence by sentence, and held them up to rational inspection and to satire. Throughout, he appealed to reason as did those classical satirists and comedians whom he imitated. He never appealed to the anger by which Luther set fire to the world.

Long before 1523, when he reluctantly[5] wrote his polemic against Luther, More strongly defended the need for law and public authority to step in when reason and rhetoric were flagrantly misused. He did not, as some have claimed, suddenly become a political reactionary in the 1520s, thus throwing off his compassionate sentiments for reform evidenced in the *Utopia*. For More, reform was necessarily tied to the advancement of good letters—and hence, to reason, diplomacy, and law.

9 Reform over Revolution: In Defense of Free Will and a United Christendom

> Peace cannot long endure . . . unless it be directed by the decisions of prudent men. *Erasmus, in praise of More* (EE 2750, To Faber, 1532)
>
> There was but one soul between us. *Erasmus about More* (EE 3049, August 31, 1535)
>
> Like very beasts did [they] also violate the wives in the sight of their husbands, slew the children in the sight of the fathers, and, to extort the discovering of more money, when men had brought out all that ever they had to save themselves from death or further pain, . . . then the wretched tyrants and cruel tormentors, as though all that stood for nothing, ceased not to put them afterwards to intolerable torments. . . . And some failed not to take the child and bind it to a spit and lay it to the fire to roast, the father and mother looking on. (CW6 370–71)

Seasoned judge and longtime student of history that he was, More knew well the potential for cruelty that resides in the human heart. For this reason, More ardently defended the rule of law and the maintenance of peace. As G. R. Elton put it, "Because he thought that he understood the dark heart of man, More, it would seem, was exceptionally conscious of the thinness of the crust upon which civilization rests, a conclusion which our age has no cause to doubt" (1983, 349). And yet, oddly enough, Elton then proceeds to doubt this very conclusion, a conclusion manifest in all that More wrote.

G. R. Elton, preeminent prophet of "The Real Thomas More," holds that More was not a voice of reason asking for the rule of law, but a man of such "helpless fury" that his "interminable, high-pitched scream of rage and disgust . . . at times border[ed] on hysteria" (1983, 348). Elton faults More for losing "all sense of proportion when faced with the new heresies" (349), descending to "ruthless" and unfair tactics (345). Apart from his "manifest psychological problems" (345), Elton points to More's "essentially conservative temperament" to explain why More considered that human beings "simply could not be trusted to command their own fate" and that, therefore, the existing institutions had to be preserved "at all costs" (350). Contrary to Elton's claims, this entire book has demonstrated More's unchanged position that each human being is genuinely free and can alone command his or her own fate. It was this very point that Luther and Tyndale denied and that More predicted would lead to political chaos and disaster.

The soul More and Erasmus shared was that of Christian humanism. Ardent reformers for many years before Martin Luther and William Tyndale came into prominence, they sought reform through education, law, and international diplomacy. Once it became clear that Luther gravely endangered this project, both More and Erasmus opposed him in the same year about the same central issue. In 1523, when More wrote *Responsio ad Lutherum* and Erasmus decided to write his *De libero arbitrio,* neither doubted that the ecclesiastical and political orders greatly needed reform, yet both opposed what they considered to be the revolutionary action Luther proposed.

Luther and his followers frequently invoked Erasmus's authority and sought his support during the early years of their reform movement. They claimed to seek the same reform that he had advocated for more than a decade. Erasmus, however, withheld his support and finally rejected the legitimacy of their methods. Well aware of the abuses that needed correction, he initially hoped that Luther and his followers could help bring about a genuine and peaceful reform; instead, he eventually saw them as responsible for violence and unrest.

Erasmus's first outright challenge to the legitimacy of Luther's teaching came in his 1524 *Discourse on Free Will*. Using the mildest possible rhetoric, Erasmus proposed to Luther a friendly discussion about the grounds and implications of this one fundamental issue of free will.

Luther's response was anything but friendly, and it was not a deliberative examination of the grounds and implications of his denial of free will. Rather, it was a hostile and defamatory frontal attack, accusing Erasmus of atheism, ill will, and cowardice; it became one of Luther's loudest calls to arms. Luther's tract was immediately translated into German, and it was reprinted six times in the first two months. If Luther really wished to clarify and remove misunderstandings, Erasmus asked, why did he not confront the issues on the plain of reason? Erasmus judged that Luther, by using incendiary language and by having his response translated into German, intended to "violently excite against me weavers and farmers, whom once having been agitated I am not able to placate, since I am ignorant of their language" (*Hyperaspistes,* Boyle 110). Once again, Erasmus complained, Luther chose to denounce and rail and not to reason. For example, in response to Erasmus's caution that Luther's inflammatory rhetoric would spark uprisings and bloodshed, Luther replied:

> For myself, if I did not see these tumults I should say that the Word of God was not in the world; but now, when I do see them, I heartily rejoice and have no fear, because I am quite certain that the kingdom of the pope, with all his followers, is going to collapse. (*Bondage of the Will* 52–53)

Violence did come, but it came first to Luther's own Germany with the bloody massacre of the Peasants' Revolt in 1525, followed by the extreme cruelty of the Germans during the invasion of Rome in 1527. These events Erasmus saw, like More, as a consequence of Luther's teaching and inflammatory rhetoric. In his *Hyperaspistes* of 1526, for example, Erasmus condemned Luther's unbridled and violent rhetoric, stating that "no one has written more stark raving madly than Luther" (Boyle 100). Throughout, he points to Luther's incivility as encouraging sedition rather than reform or virtuous cooperation.

Also opposed to Erasmian humanism was Luther's rejection of international debate and discussion. At first, Luther agreed to present his views at a council of Christendom, but he soon refused. Erasmus then invited him to argue his position in print by responding to his *Discourse on Free Will*. Once again Luther refused to enter the council of reason; instead he called for a field of war. As Erasmus wrote to Elector John of Saxony in March 1526,

> Luther could not have wanted a more courteous opponent for debate. If his teaching is true, he had the opportunity of establishing his position; if not, he could not be admonished more courteously. In short, there was nothing in my treatise that could offend anybody, no matter how irritable he might be. . . . How can his teasing taunts, his silly mockery, his barbed guffaws, his slanders, threats, and tricks, be in conformity with such a serious and perilous business that has shattered almost the whole world? . . . What good can come from all those sneering remarks, from that derisive laughter and maligning? The only purpose it can serve is to stir up widespread sedition and bring down the worst ill will upon the gospel and also upon good learning. (EE 1670, Hillerbrand 191)

Here Erasmus draws attention to the political upheaval caused by Luther's seditious speech, and he concludes by explaining why he thinks it necessary to restrain Luther's destructive rage with the force of law:

> I am writing this, renowned Prince, not out of any desire for revenge, but because it is a matter of general public interest that Luther be forcibly reminded by law and your authority that he is not to rage with like insolence against anyone; for such conduct does no good to

anybody but tends to destroy all good things. (EE 1670, Hillerbrand 193)

So fiery is Luther's attack that Erasmus compares him to an Achilles (EE 1523) who "has shattered almost the whole world" (EE 1670). "The only purpose [this hostility] can serve," Erasmus complains, "is to stir up widespread sedition" (EE 1670).

Thomas More agreed with Erasmus's position that public authority had a duty to restrain seditious behavior, but he came to his conclusion several years before his scholarly friend.

As we have seen in the early chapters of this book, More was well aware of the human propensity to take a good idea, exaggerate it, wrench it from its context, and become obsessed with it. As with the Trojans at Oxford in 1518 and the Monk at Coventry in 1506, More knew that it was sometimes necessary for authorities to step in and prevent the civil unrest caused by uncivil behavior. Although Luther was correct in pointing out abuses that needed reform, More strongly opposed what appeared to him as a highly dangerous disregard for law, authority, and tradition.

In opposition to Luther's revolutionary program, More undertook a writing campaign that was unparalleled in the medieval or Renaissance world. One would have to go back to Cicero's voluminous verbal warfare to find a head of government who relied so heavily upon the pen rather than the sword to bring about his objectives. In the five years between 1529 and More's arrest in 1534, Sir Thomas wrote and published more than he had in his previous fifty years. Was this the work of uncontrolled fury as Elton, Fox, Trapp, and Marius have suggested? Or was it, as Brendan Bradshaw proposed, a brilliant and courageous "strategic military operation" (Bradshaw 549, 554ff), a strategy aimed at preventing a method of change that went counter to England's and Christendom's time-tested methods of reform—public deliberation and the subsequent legal change? Before answering one way or the other, one must carefully consider the rhetorical character of the works involved.

It was Luther's most learned contemporary and one favorably

disposed to his initial project who eventually criticized Luther for his inflammatory rhetoric, a rhetoric calling progressively louder for righteous anger and definitive action against agents of evil. Erasmus was not alone in this evaluation of Luther's dangerous rhetoric. In contrast, contemporaries never criticized Thomas More for anger and fury (as do his reconstructionist critics today); instead, his opponents accused him of an unbecoming mockery that did not take the issues seriously enough. One of those opponents called him "Master Mock" (CW11 339, 12), and even a generation later John Foxe complained that More was "full of imaginations" and "too much given to mocking" (Foxe 4.610). In using this approach, More consciously imitates the great satirists of the past, especially Horace; in so doing, he appeals—not to anger as Luther commonly did—but to the intellect, as all the classical satirists and comedians had done.

When pressed, however, today's proponents of the theory that More was out of control and driven by fury do not try to prove their accusation on the basis of rhetorical analysis. Instead, they base their accusations on the length of his polemic and the frequent repetition of the same criticisms.

Yet repetition can be a highly effective rhetorical strategy, even though much of More's repetition undoubtedly arose from not having time to revise. In these controversial works, More was not attempting to write great literature; he tried and in fact succeeded in writing a highly effective polemic. It was so effective that his opponents expended great effort in trying to refute his criticisms. John Frith returned to England in 1531 to hearten the Protestant effort in the face of More's opposition (CW7 cxxx), and even a generation later John Foxe complained that More's "books be not yet dead, but remain alive to the hurt of many" (4.645).

To deny that More was driven by fury, however, is not to deny that More was indeed "driven"—i.e., highly motivated and passionately committed. He had to be to write as much as he did in such a short time. Yet he was driven by what he considered his responsibility to safeguard the survival of an entire cultural movement—Christian humanism—that was just promising to come to fruition. More also felt his responsibility as a government leader for the well-being of his country and for the survival of a united Christendom.

More foresaw that decades of war could result from the tactics proposed by Luther and his followers. As R. W. Chambers put it:

> More did not need to have the *Cambridge Modern History* on the shelves before him to know that the volume on *The Reformation* would be followed by the volume on *The Wars of Religion,* and that by the volume on *The Thirty Years' War.* He had said so: "After that it were once come to that point, and the world once ruffled and fallen in a wildness, how long would it be, and what heaps of heavy mischiefs would there fall, ere the way were founden to set the world in order and peace again." (165, quoting CW6 405)

For present-day critics like Elton, Fox, and Marius to pretend that More should use the polite language of scholarly circles to counter individuals set upon tearing down all that he judged necessary for a civilization's survival seems utopian indeed, mistaking harsh political realities for the school room. These critics level the very same charge against More that was leveled by Christopher St. German, whom More called "the Pacifier."

More answered the Pacifier's criticism (that he did not write kindly about his opponents), and his response shows that he carefully deliberated over the rhetorical design of his polemics. After all, rhetorical invention was the first and, in some ways, most important part of rhetoric (Cicero's *Orator* 43–49), in which one analyzes the particular issues and the specific audience at hand. The greatest problem More faced in his invention was that his opponents refused to argue the issues on the plain of reason. They "rail rather than reason," More repeatedly points out. But, then, how is one to argue? Erasmus tried; he was scornfully abused and slandered; and he finally recommended that the law step in. More, as chancellor, ordered that the law step in as well, but he also took up the pen to write one million words in defense of the humanist methods of reform: collective reason, progressively improved laws, and the artful use of rhetoric.

More's rhetoric in the polemical works was both masterful and highly effective, even though he often sacrificed literary form in the process of hasty composition. More was using all the acceptable rhetorical means at his disposal to prevent war and bloodshed by steadfastly appealing to the consciences of his fellow English citizens. If Henry and Cromwell had not decided to manipulate England's political process, misusing the full force of the king's power, More's rhetorical and political strategies might well have been successful.

Again and again More tried to show that Luther and Tyndale "rail"—i.e., they use verbal violence instead of rational deliberation. Instead of pointing out and trying to correct specific abuses, for example, More's opponents denounced "*all* the whole catholic church"; "they say that during these eight hundred years *all* the corps of Christendom have been led out of the right way from God and have lived *all* in idolatry" (CW9 44, emphasis added). Worse than exaggerating, such statements were slander, malicious lies designed to bring about the destruction of persons and institutions unquestionably flawed but legitimately protected by law (Boyle 138).

As More points out, every country has found it necessary to pass laws to protect its citizens, rulers, and institutions from just such slander (CW8 590). More says that he would gladly speak fair words and bear all patiently if they would agree to speak villainously against only himself (44/36). "But surely their railing against all other, I purpose not to bear so patiently, [but] to let them hear some part of like language as they speak" (45/6–8). More returns "some part of like language as they speak," but he indicates that he does not intend to exceed the bounds of honest rebuke (45/10–11). He will not lie, and he uses the technique of extensive quoting to insure as fair a representation of his opponents' views as possible. He considers this the most honest means of investigating the truthfulness of claims:

There cannot be a more level plain for the struggle, or one less exposed to ambush, than a controversy carried on by means of published books.... Whatever he is able to bring forward at his leisure in accordance with the merits of the case—that will with honest fidelity appear in public. (CW5 45–47; see also 19–21)

There is an obvious rhetorical problem with this heavily rational approach, however: it is far less appealing than a rhetoric which is emotionally inflammatory and slanderously mocking.

What rhetorical invention, therefore, does the master rhetorician use on such an unlevel field of verbal battle where the opposition slanders? Given this battlefield, More decided upon his own version of railing and mockery, but without appealing to anger or using slander; the railing and mockery he chose was actually classical satire that was intended to stay within the bounds recognized by the humanist tradition.

In a prefatory letter to his first polemic, *Responsio ad Lutherum*, More explained in an indirect way his rhetorical strategy. His fictional narrator recounts how he was urged to respond to Luther's brawling and raving by a noble friend, "a most honorable man and the glory of his country," a man of "remarkable learning and outstanding virtues" (CW5 7/6–7, 13/17–18). The narrator, a university man, insists that he normally would never have agreed to contend with a person like Luther, who has abandoned reason and turned "wholly to wrangling" (7/10–12). Nonetheless, this noble friend, "to whom I owed almost more than to my whole family," presses the narrator to respond to Luther in order to "benefit and profit all good men" (9/30–31). The narrator still resists, however. He is aware that such an "encounter will cast the stain of wantonness" on himself, and he argues, invoking Horace's satires, that it would be a useless battle, as if one fool were to enter battle with another fool (*Satires* 1.5.51ff, CW5 11/20–35). But the noble friend insists. He wants the narrator to "expose and restrain with [his] pen the madness of the shameless fellow" in such a way that "what many find their sole pleasure in him may come to delight them on the other hand when it is read about him" (CW5 9/15–16, 11/28–32). Still reluctant, the narrator nonetheless agrees, "at his [friend's] urging and for the sake of the common good" (11/18). What the narrator will write is a satire that is frequently Juvenalian.

Even Horace, however, milder by far than many like Juvenal, had to justify himself for giving offense through his satire. In defense of his art, Horace argues that satire has a constructive purpose: it enables the young and innocent "to steer clear of follies" by "branding" those follies "one by one" with humorous and unforgettable examples (*Satires* 1.4.105–6). The satirist is thus able to "uphold the rule our fathers have handed down" and to keep the youths' and innocents' "health and name from harm" (116–20).

The problem, as Horace explains, is that every age presents many foolish ideas as wisdom; therefore, the young will often be misled. By ridiculing the foolish, satire serves to keep the inexperienced "from vices which bring disaster" because "the tender mind is oft deterred from vice by another's shame" (128–31). In this way the satirist serves the common good pleasantly and effectively, even if causing discomfort or embarrassment to the foolish themselves.

In *Satire* 1.4, Horace explains how such writing goes back to "Aristophanes, true poets, and the other good men to whom Old Comedy belongs." They were witty men "of keen-scented nostrils" who knew their work: "If there was anyone deserving to be drawn as a rogue and thief, as a rake or cut-throat, or as scandalous in any other way, [they] set their mark upon him with great freedom" (1.4.1–10). All satirists are accused of giving pain and doing so "with spiteful intent" (78–79), but they do so for the sake of the common good.

This satiric dimension of More's polemical writings has not received the serious attention it deserves. What must be remembered is that More was not intending in his polemics to change the minds of Luther, Tyndale, and their followers. He wrote to deter the common Englishman from accepting the ideas of those who would subvert the methods of social change which More considered necessary for peace and justice. The chief deterrent he used was satire, focusing on those actions and beliefs widely considered shameful in England. In general, More's intended audience consisted of hardy, clear-thinking, salt-of-the-earth English men and women devoted to self-rule, intent on making up their own minds and deeply committed to their traditions.

This explains the persona of *Responsio ad Lutherum,* More's first polemical work. William Ross is an ordinary, commonsensical Englishman who is astonished and frequently angered by Luther's Thrasonic character and his refusal to be bound by consistent reasoning. Drawing heavily from Roman literature, Ross identifies Luther throughout with Thraso, Terence's pretentious braggart who prides himself on his wit and intelligence (CW5 817ff). He also refers to Luther as Cerberus and "Tosspot" to emphasize what he considers to be Luther's major intellectual strategy: an "excess of virulent railing and mad brawling" rather than rational disputation (65)—the same strategy that Erasmus identified.

Ross frequently satirizes what he sees as Luther's presumptuous assertions:

> "By what reason, father, do you prove that you alone must be believed?"
>
> To this he returns this cause: "Because I am certain," he says, "that I have my teachings from heaven."
>
> Again we ask: "By what reason are you certain that you have your teachings from heaven?"
>
> "Because God has seized me unawares," he says, "and carried me into the midst of these turmoils."
>
> Again there we demand: "How do you know that God has seized you?"
>
> "Because I am certain," he says, "that my teaching is from God."
> "How do you know that?"
> "Because God has seized me."
> "How do you know this?"
> "Because I am certain."
> "How are you certain?"

"Because I know."
"But how do you know?"
"Because I am certain." (CW5 305–7, quoted in Greenblatt's *Renaissance Self-Fashioning* 59)

Here, as he does throughout, Ross insists on proof. By so insisting, he reveals a concern that is fundamental to all Erasmians of this period, a concern even more fundamental than law, tradition, and peace; it is the concern for intelligibility (Greenblatt 63). As such, it involves the fundamental assumption of the entire humanist project: that reason is strong enough to direct the collective lives of human beings. By revealing that Luther does not proceed according to reason and that he sets himself up as the criterion for interpreting Scripture, Ross seeks to discredit him.

Ross also imitates the Roman satirists in drawing attention to Luther's vulgar and pretentious statements and by appealing to the type of humor found in Terence and Chaucer, a humor highly popular in England at the time. In one section, for example, Ross quotes an intemperate and vulgar passage which Luther wrote about King Henry:

> [King Henry] would have to be forgiven if humanly he erred. Now, since he knowingly and consciously fabricates lies against the majesty of my king in heaven, this damnable rottenness and worm, I will have the right, on behalf of my king, to bespatter his English majesty with muck and shit and to trample underfoot that crown of his which blasphemes against Christ. (CW5 311/6–12)

Angered by such disrespectful words to his king, loyal Ross answers vulgarity with heightened vulgarity, yet immediately apologizes to his "gentle readers" if he has offended.

Luther's disrespect for King Henry is just one example of the "evangelical freedom" which he claims for himself and his followers. Later Ross indicates that the great attraction of Luther's project is the lure of a freedom often dreamt of, but never possible because of laws and customs which restrained such "evangelical freedom." Concerned with the effects of such an appeal to false freedom, Ross concludes with a warning and a prediction that civil chaos will surely follow (691–93).

This prediction seemed to come true very quickly, as More noted in his next polemical work, *A Dialogue Concerning Heresies*. There he argued that the Peasants' Revolt in Germany (1525), the Lutheran mercenaries' sack of Rome (1527), and the growing unrest in England all stemmed from Luther's inflammatory teachings and especially the lure of false freedom:

> And one special thing with which he spiced all the poison was the liberty that he so highly commended unto the people, bringing them in belief that, having faith, they needed nothing else. . . . He taught them . . . that, being faithful Christians, they were so near cousins to Christ that they are in a full freedom and liberty discharged of all governors and all manner of laws spiritual or temporal except the gospel only. And although he said that of a special perfection it would be well done to suffer and bear the rule and authority of popes, princes, and other governors—which rule and authority he calls but only tyranny—yet he says that the people are so free by faith that they are no more bound to them than they are bound to suffer wrong. And this doctrine Tyndale also teaches as the special matter of his holy book of disobedience. (CW6 368–69)

To tempt people with "full freedom and liberty" while equating legitimate law with tyranny was, in More's view, a call to revolution.

More judged that such doctrines had blinded the common people of Germany and eventually led to open force and violence. So great was this violence that the German rulers ended up slaying "seventy thousand Lutherans in one summer, and subdued the remnant in that part of [Germany] to a right miserable servitude" (CW6 369). What happened in Germany could also happen in England, More warned. The German lords allowed an irresponsible element to disregard laws and customs which protected the clergy (369/19–20). Why? Because these temporal lords had begun seriously "gaping after the lands of the spirituality."[1] Once such irresponsible forces had been unleashed, however, they would "burst out and fall to open force and violence" against spiritual and temporal lords indiscriminately (369). Such violence would inevitably result once the habitual respect and fear of law were broken. Then, once the thin crust of civilization was rent, the worst of atrocities would occur, allowing people to act like "abominable beasts" (370). Such beastly actions did result, and More describes them in vivid and dramatic detail (370–72).

More insisted throughout these polemical writings that violence was the natural outcome of Luther's widely advocated theory that says no one is responsible for his actions and that each one's moral obligations proceed only from the private "feeling" faith that arises from personal inspiration. Like Erasmus, More wondered how one then decides if some supposed inspiration might not be a mad imagination, instead of a true inspiration. Before the time of Luther and Tyndale, private inspirations had to pass the tests meted out by the common corps of Christendom. For More, refusing to acknowledge such authority was inherently seditious, leading inevitably to violence and civil unrest.

In the Preface of *The Confutation of Tyndale's Answer*, for example, More explains that he, following King Henry's own example (CW8 28), is "deeply bounden" in duty as chancellor to address books that are seditious causes of destruction and manslaughter (29–33) and which undermine law (30–33). He writes so people can "plainly perceive" the true face of these seditious teachings, which More describes as a dangerously infectious disease (27, 38–39). "The very breast of all this battle" (34) was whether there could be an unknown congregation of pure and spotless individuals, each of whom received direct inspiration from God himself, or whether God worked through the collective means of Christendom. So important to More was this "battle" that he wrote nine books, comprising 1,034 pages, to argue for the danger and absurdity of an elect congregation as opposed to a common church of sinners.

More argued strongly that it was not enough to *say* one has been inspired by God. If Christ and all the great saints used exterior signs (especially miracles) to *prove* such inspiration, then Luther and Tyndale should do the same. How else is one to tell the difference between false imaginings and what is true and enduring? As More puts it:

> For where as Tyndale would have us suppose, that he feels it written in his own heart with the very hand of God, that friars may lawfully wed nuns, God has himself so plainly told the contrary to all the old holy saints this fifteen hundred years before, and by all the same space to all Christian people besides, that now there is no good man in all Christendom, but he feels and finds written by God's hand in his own heart, that Tyndale feels not that foul filthy heresy written in his heart by the hand of God. But if he feel it written there in deed as he says he does then he feels it scribbled and scraped in his heart by the crooked cloven claws of the devil. (816–17)

In our own day, the most controversial part of More's polemic seems to be the "rude refrain" that calls Friar Luther lecherous for marrying Sister Kat. More states clearly that he repeats this refrain "like a blind harper who harps all on one string" (727). However, despite the fact that he says he uses it consciously "almost a thousand times" (713/17–18), the reconstructionists insist that it arises from an irrational and out-of-control hatred, motivated by sexual obsessions and repressions (e.g., Elton 1983, Marius, Fox 1983).

Yet seen in the light of satire and rhetoric, this refrain serves to summarize and to remind the reader of a question of fundamental importance to More and Erasmus: why should all of Christendom believe Luther's "feeling faith" against all the councils of Christendom? Any lawyer or practiced rhetorician will appreciate the power of such a refrain, especially since the common opinion of Englishmen was strongly opposed to the marriage of monks and nuns.

This refrain actually culminates at the end of the work in a fictional council of Christendom set in the reign of Saint Gregory the Great (590–604), a pope dedicated to reform in a time preceding the wholesale corruption claimed by Tyndale and Luther.

Before "this full general council of the whole universal church assembled," Friar Luther is accompanied by Sister "Kit Cate" in order to defend and even boast about their marriage, arguing "that vows of chastity could bind no man, for no man ought to make them since it were sin and presumption for any man to make them" (CW8 925). This scene is a *tour de force* of comic irony and of satire. Throughout, More invites the reader to weigh Luther's actions and beliefs from a broad perspective of history and to judge Luther's claims in that light.

Once again, the great question in this long debate was how one distinguishes between private imaginings and verifiable knowledge. This issue acquired all the more urgency when these private interpretations called for the public disregard of laws and traditions on one hand, and the blind obedience to a ruler's tyrannical actions on the other (Carlyle 290–91). More was convinced that such teaching "set[s] the people in sedition" (CW8 57) and leads to the kind of bloodshed seen in Germany of 1525 (126–27) and in Rome of 1527 (370–71).

In book 1 of *Confutation*, therefore, More defines his task as revealing the "foul feet" of these "new spiritual men" who appeal to "an evangelical and in manner angelical liberty to do what they wish so that they give the law some cause that may serve their lust" (CW8 121). As More pointed out in his earlier polemical works, the greatest attraction of these new spiritual men was the lure of a freedom never before justified by Scripture or society. The assumption of this new theory is, as we have shown, the denial of free will. More, like Erasmus, insists that the most blasphemous and socially destructive feature of this teaching was that "by the taking away of man's free will [Luther and Tyndale] would make us think that God alone works all our sin, and then damns his creatures in perpetual torments for his own deed" (72).

Books 2 and 3 of *Confutation* devote some 250 pages to analyzing the scriptural foundations for Tyndale's and Luther's theory. The whole point of this analysis is to show their departure from the text of Scripture itself as well as from the accepted interpretation of 1,500 years. Should one trust the private inspiration of one or a few who appeal to feeling faith? Or should one trust the consensus of the common corps of Christendom based on public miracles and 1,500 years of written international agreement? Throughout his writings, More emphasized the importance of an international tribunal that would not show favoritism to a particular nation or time in judging the merits of various claims. In the same spirit, More submits his own writings to the judgment of others and acknowledges the advisability of doing so (e.g., CW6 23–24, CW8 39).

In book 4, More emphasizes what he calls "the secret seed of Tyndale's chief poison": the denial of man's free will (CW8 498). To show the highly dangerous political implications of this theory, More invents the memorable character "Jack Slouch" to offset Tyndale's school-marm example of a pious child's sinless character. With his characteristic irony, More ridicules Tyndale for "play[ing] the master and set[ting] all the Catholic Church again to school" with such an unrealistic example (491). Instead of the good child Tyndale proposed, the child who "loves his father and all his commandments" (489), More proposes wily Jack, who is "twenty winter stept into his knavish age" (492). Instead of slight oversights of love, hardened Jack falls into such horrible deeds as "adultery with his mother, poisoning his father and murdering his brother, in sacrilege, and incest" (493). With this example, More then proceeds to consider Tyndale's claim that such a man cannot freely sin "because of his feeling faith which so lies hid in his heart that he feels nothing; thereof he consents not in his mind to none of those deeds, nor doth none of them willingly nor of purpose" (493). To counter this "fairy tale of a tub" (495/25), More invites his reader to "take testimony and witness of his own wit" (494/26).

Another effective passage that questions Tyndale's rejection of free will is More's close analysis of King David's adultery with Bathsheba and the consequent murder of her husband Uriah. In this example, More aims to show the absurdity and outright deceitfulness of Tyndale's position that God's elect can commit no deadly sin.

The comic irony More employs in recounting Tyndale's interpretation of the incident with David and Bathsheba is characteristic of his approach throughout the *Confutation*. After a lengthy quotation of Tyndale's account, More comments sarcastically:

> Lo good readers, here you see that by Tyndale's doctrine, David did no deadly sin but was ever out of fault and not blameworthy, neither by impatience drawing near to despair in persecution, nor by the purpose of much manslaughter at an angry word, nor by adultery conceived at the sight of another man's wife, nor by the traitorous destruction of his friendly servant in recompense of truth and amends of his misdeed. All this was no deadly sin in him, because he was an elect. (530)

More then proceeds to go through scriptural texts showing that Tyndale misrepresents the story and the texts involved. More's strongest and most memorable passages, however, are those where he appeals to the common sense of his audience. In response to Tyndale's statement that David was "hard in sleep [while he was] in the adultery of Bathsheba, and in the murder of her husband Uriah" (533), More writes satirically:

> David was here in a very long slumber and a very deep deep sleep in deed, if he did all those devilish deeds in his sleep. Tyndale of likelihood lay near him and heard him all the while snort and snore. And if he so say that he did then is his tale as full proved as is any part of all his heresies. And except he say it of his own certain knowledge, he shall else never make me believe, that David did spy her, and sent for her, and talk with her, and get her with child, and sent for her husband, and devise the murder, and write the letter, and sent the man to his death, and all these deeds in divers days, and all this while still asleep. (534)

Such carefully designed rhetoric serves to lead the "good Christian reader" to see the problems and contradictions in Tyndale's account, and at the same time works up to this climax:

> Did David in all this while among all these evil thoughts, all these ungracious words, all these abominable deeds, never fall from the love of the law of God but was all this while asleep, and never consented

to sin, nor did none of all these things willingly? No says Tyndale. I say no more but it is likely yes. And therefore let Tyndale tell us whereby he proves the contrary. (537)

In this context of David's deliberate sin, More gives perhaps the clearest definition of malice in all of his works. It is the "contempt and despising of God's law," and it is a trait he attributes to both Luther and Tyndale. For example, More sees malice in Tyndale's interpretation that David "could not sin deadly because he was an elect for which cause God kept him through feeling faith from consenting to the service of sin and from the malicious casting off of the yoke of God's commandments from his neck" (539). To prove malice, More attempts to show that Tyndale's interpretation goes directly against the very words and claims of Scripture. More maintains that David's and God's own words—"in plain and evident Scripture"—show that David did act with malice, i.e., "contempt and despising" of a law recognized as good and proper (539). In denying Scripture's evident sense, Tyndale—following Luther's example—acts with just such malice, More argues. Otherwise Tyndale would not have deliberately changed the words of Scripture and would not refuse to meet More's objections straight on.

Here as throughout the *Confutation,* More adopts the voice of a reasonable lawyer who asks the jury to consider the proof, while challenging Tyndale to give evidence for his own position. This challenge is a recurring refrain throughout his polemical works. After presenting many such passages to undermine Tyndale's credibility on the level of reason alone, More continues to question Tyndale's grounding in Scripture. More analyzes, for example, the text of 2 Kings 12, where "God here says that David did those horrible deeds despite both his law and himself" (540/21–22). To make this point, More gives his own translation of the crucial passage involved, citing the words which God ordered the prophet Nathan to say to David:

Why have you then set my word at nought, and done evil in my sight? You have killed with sword Uriah Hetheus, and his wife have you taken as your wife, and him have you slain with the sword of the sons of Ammon. And therefore the sword shall never be taken away from your house, because you have despised me. (540/5-9)

At this point, More gives no commentary; he simply addresses his good readers: "here see you very clearly" that Tyndale's views are "reproved by the very plain words of Scripture" (540-41).

More uses the same procedure to counter Tyndale's claim that Judas and Peter and the rest of the apostles did not sin in rejecting Christ. But in these new examples, More's attacks upon Tyndale become stronger and stronger as he claims that Tyndale invents facts (e.g., 549/32ff), changes the words of Scripture (e.g., 555/17ff), and deliberately mistranslates key terms to support his position (e.g., 559/12ff). This section concludes with More's insistence once again that Tyndale give proof.

More's attack on Tyndale in book 5 continues with the charge that Tyndale misrepresents More's position, confuses issues, and disregards clear passages of Scripture while taking refuge in the darkest and most obscure sections of the Bible. How, More wonders, can Tyndale disregard all law in the name of "evangelical liberty" (585)? Or how can Tyndale exaggerate and emotionally slander *all* Church leaders? It is precisely for such malicious behavior, More observes, that the protection of law is needed and why all countries outlaw such slander as Tyndale's (590-92, 596). Such malicious lying has no place in civil society. Nor is it possible to "reckon railing for reason and shameless open lies for good and sufficient proofs" (598/17-18). As we will see in the next chapter, More criticizes St. German for using the same arsenal of slander to destroy England's traditional separation of church and state.

Book 6 continues to accuse Tyndale of deliberate confusion of issues (e.g., 599), repeated lies, failure to establish proof, and offhandedly rejecting the past eight hundred years—without explaining why he accepts the previous seven hundred years, which also argues against his positions denouncing free will and a known church.

Reform over Revolution 181

By book 7, More characterizes Tyndale as a "wild goose" because of his frantic lies, railing, mocking, and falsification of Scripture in his attempt to defend the "feeling faith" which is the ultimate foundation of his theoretical enterprise. Throughout this book, More insists upon exterior proof to verify the existence of Tyndale's interior faith. Christ and the saints performed miracles, More argues. Why should Tyndale and Luther expect to be believed by reasonable people without similar proof? In book 8, More turns from Tyndale to Friar Barnes, but we learn that Barnes is but one more example that More chooses in order to illustrate the fundamental error in Tyndale, Luther, and all of their friends: each claims that his own unknown church is the highest tribunal, thus ignoring the international and historically continuous corps of Christendom. As in the case of Tyndale, More asks his good readers to assess for themselves the credibility of Barnes's claims, the central one being that Barnes's church is pure, spotless, and unknown. As in each of the preceding books, More takes long portions of his opponent's written argument and analyzes it in detail. In doing so, he insists upon respect for the humanists' international and historically continuous tribunal of reason.

In contrast, Tyndale and Luther accepted a radically new theory which replaced public deliberations that had been carried on for centuries. Instead, Tyndale and Luther gave first place to personal opinion based on private and unverified inspiration. By so diminishing the role of collective reason, these reformers seemed to insist that each of them alone—through a personal and unverifiable inspiration—understood Scripture and the moral law. Because of this predilection for private experience over verifiable proofs, both More and Erasmus characterized these reformers as the new gnostics (CW7 21, Boyle 142ff)—acting, perhaps, as another Raphael Hythlodaeus. These new gnostics were bent on revolution, not reform, and they violently rejected the ordinary means of reform used for twenty centuries: collective deliberation and progressively improved laws (CW9 100). Alistair Fox eloquently summarized Thomas More's position in this way:

More entered into controversy with Luther, Tyndale, Fish, Frith, and St. German in the late fifteen-twenties and early thirties because, in their wish to reform English civil and ecclesiastical polity, they sought to use means which would destroy responsible corporate order and reduce English society to chaos. Not only would these means prove less constructive than the processes already in existence, but the reformers' expectations were also mistaken, because they failed to perceive the painful realities of the human situation. Their complete repudiation of the past history of English regenerative impulses meant a negation of the possibilities offered in the contemporary renaissance. To More the tree of history needed to be pruned and developed, not cut down. The most immediate danger to him was that all his opponents were seeking to transform the machinery of the state into an instrument of their purpose. (1975, 45)

10 The Limits of Government and the Domain of Conscience

> As for the law of the land, though every man being born and inhabiting therein is bound to the keeping in every case upon some temporal pain, and in many cases upon pain of God's displeasure too, yet is there no man bound to swear that every law is well made, nor bound upon the pain of God's displeasure to perform any such point of the law, as were indeed unlawful. (Corr 524)

> I do nobody harm, I say none harm, I think none harm, but wish everybody good. And if this be not enough to keep a man alive in good faith I long not to live. (Corr 553)

> Every true and good subject is more bound to have respect to his said conscience and to his soul than to any other thing in all the world besides. (Harpsfield 157)

> If a lion knew his own strength, hard were it for any man to rule him. (More about King Henry, Roper 28)

So important was conscience in More's understanding that he considered all education to be ordered to its formation (SL 106), and he maintained that allegiance to one's conscience takes precedence over allegiance to any state law. Conscience is a power of reason that operates in every individual, even the most hardened tyrant (CW2 87) and the most embittered traitor (CW14 427–65). So powerful is it that it caused Richard III at the height of his power to awake screaming at night, and it brought Judas such distress that he hanged himself after achieving all he had so carefully planned. Because conscience is the faculty by which fundamental issues of good and evil are manifest to all human beings, even the most corrupt, More considered it to be the metaphysical foundation for law and justice.

"That I should perceive mine own conscience should serve me, and that I should first look unto God and after God unto [King Henry]" was the "first lesson . . . that ever his Grace gave me at my first coming into his service," More recalls several times (SL 229, 209, 250–51). He considered this teaching about conscience "the most virtuous lesson that ever prince taught his servant" (SL 250–51). Yet as is well known, Henry did not live up to that promise.

When More entered King Henry's service at the age of forty-one, did he anticipate such a change of mind? Having known the Tudors all his life, did he consider Henry to be the good shepherd protecting the English flock or a potential wolf seeking his own advantage? Seventeen years later when he mounted the scaffold to his death, did he judge Henry to be a goodwilled but mistaken monarch or a hardened tyrant beyond help?

More certainly had good reasons for not wanting to serve under the Tudors. His experience with Henry VII as well as his own study of history were strong reasons to anticipate future dangers. In addition, he undoubtedly hesitated because of the significant losses involved: independence, leisure to write, time with his growing family, and the large income from his successful law practice. On this last point, More waited ten years in public office before he could match the income he made in private practice. Of far greater importance, he would never again have the leisure to write another book like *Utopia*, which he wrote just before going to court. Why would a person of More's unquestioned contemplative and literary bent choose a position that effectively meant depriving himself of the intellectual and cultural goods he enjoyed most greatly? It is the very question debated in book 1 of the *Utopia*.

In 1513, after the first of Henry's wars in France, More went on record—subtly, of course—expressing his concern that Henry was leaning towards tyranny in his lust for honor and French lands while neglecting to rule well his own country (CW3.2, nos. 243–44). Even years before, from the very beginning of Henry's reign, More warned him about the dangers of tyranny by pointing out in his coronation ode that "unlimited power" could corrupt even the best (no. 19/90–91). More never seemed to have illusions about the "kings' games . . . played upon scaffolds" (CW2 81/6–7, cii), nor about the insecurity of a courtier's life (CW3.2, no. 162; CW2 cii).

In 1518 More formally entered the King's service despite these concerns, but only after observing Henry's manner of rule for nine years.[1] But why enter the royal service at all? Answering this question, most of the reconstructionists postulate lust for power, the very motive More condemned ever since his earliest writings. Motives more consistent with his character and convictions would be the sense of duty and love for his country, motives dear to any Ciceronian humanist. This appeal would have been powerfully made by More's closest friends in England. John Colet, Cuthbert Tunstall, and Thomas Linacre were already serving Henry VIII—and with remarkably promising results. The young monarch seemed to identify himself closely with the major objectives of these humanists, except for his position on war. Yet even here Henry showed himself open to opinions differing from his own, as evidenced by his surprising exchanges with John Colet in 1512 and 1513 (Adams 65–71, CWE8 242–43). Furthermore, as of January of 1518, England was pursuing a course of universal peace (Scarisbrick 71–74, Gwyn 98–102).

In accepting to serve as a royal counselor, More was putting into practice his own theory about good government under a monarch. More firmly believed, with Seneca and many others, that the most effective check upon a monarch was the quality of the counselors whom the king freely chose to consult about his actions and opinions. How else could a lion be controlled?

What Morus says in *Utopia* to persuade Hythlodaeus to enter the king's service could well have been said to More by any of his humanist friends in England:

> If you could persuade yourself not to shun the courts of kings, you could do the greatest good to the common weal by your [counsel]. The latter is the most important part of your duty as it is the duty of every good man. (CW4 87)

> If you cannot pluck up wrongheaded opinions by the root, if you cannot cure according to your heart's desire vices of long standing, yet you must not on that account desert the commonwealth. You must not abandon the ship in a storm because you cannot control the winds. (CW4 99)

More's fellow humanists were strongly devoted to improving the life of the commonwealth. His Greek teacher Thomas Linacre, for example, was royal physician at the time, a founder and first president of the Royal Academy of Physicians in London and the one who endowed the first chairs of medicine at both Oxford and Cambridge. More's close friend and spiritual confidant John Colet began the first public school in London, served as a royal counselor, and preached zealously about reform to king, clergy, and laity. Cuthbert Tunstall, accomplished scholar and diplomat who was to become one of More's closest associates, had also joined the King's service and is highly praised in the opening of *Utopia*. Most importantly, however, Thomas Wolsey and Henry were committed to a program of peace by the beginning of 1518. Therefore, given the times and the players, More's entry to public service is not surprising, even though the personal cost to him was great.

Between 1518 and 1524, More played "a strategic part" in Henry's court and possessed "a position of extreme trust" with both

Henry and Catherine (Guy 1980, 16, 18). Already in 1519, More had helped convince Henry to take a more active role in government reform (Scarisbrick 117–19). In 1521, More must have been especially heartened with Henry's vigorous defense of the Church's traditions against Luther, although he disagreed with the strength of the King's submission to papal authority in secular matters (SL 212). This apparently small disagreement would, in the next eight years, reveal a fundamentally different conception of the very nature of civil government: More saw the power of the king and his ministers as coming from God through the people, while Henry saw his power coming from God through the divine authority of the papacy—up until 1529. To understand this difference is to understand why Henry defended the papacy so strongly during the early part of his reign, even over More's objections. While More acknowledged the people as the intermediary source of the king's temporal authority, Henry never adopted that position.[2] In an effort to justify his unchecked monarchy after 1529, Henry resorted to legends from the past (Scarisbrick 271-72) and to a spurious theory of divine right that was so repugnant to English tradition that violence, manipulation, and intrigue were needed to force its acceptance. Within a few generations, however, the English people would destroy that unchecked monarchy with even greater force.

This larger issue of legitimate sovereignty lay behind More's cautioning Henry in 1521 about his relationship with the pope. More's position on this point was the traditional one held, for example, by William the Conqueror. William clearly understood there to be two orders, temporal and spiritual, whose governments were necessarily separate and distinct but, ideally, complementary and mutually supportive. When, therefore, Gregory VII commanded fealty and allegiance, William offered allegiance gladly but refused fealty adamantly (Brooke 225ff). More was well aware that the papacy, in the difficult effort to maintain its spiritual independence, frequently became involved in imprudent temporal entanglements and overstepped its bounds. As More often commented, no individual or institution is without fault;

therefore, each is in need of constant correction and reform. He advocated the traditional "two swords" theory whereby distinct and separate authorities existed to rule over separate jurisdictions: the church over matters religious, the state over matters temporal. These two authorities, having their own laws and courts, served as effective checks to the all-too-human limitations inherent in each and served to strengthen a particular country as well as Christendom at large. Since corruption would always exist in both church and state, the vigilant members of one would support the vigilant members of the other, especially through their legal and judicial systems (CW9 53–54, 108).[3]

The year 1523 was auspicious for developments that More favored, but foreboding as well of the troubles to come. As Speaker of the House that year, he made a formal petition that King Henry allow freedom of speech within the House so political issues could be better deliberated. More had been in Parliament before, and he had been painfully aware that freedom of speech was not the rule in those assemblies, which were called, dismissed, and carefully monitored by the king. More was undoubtedly relieved and encouraged that Henry VIII granted immunity to all to speak their minds freely in 1523. Yet the Parliament of 1523 had a dark side as well, since it was called to raise money for an unpopular war. In an effort to browbeat the Commons into accepting his tax bill, Wolsey broke the traditional liberty of the House by coming himself with his impressive retinue to argue for the bill. After his speech, Wolsey demanded a reply.

What occurred next points to a fundamental difference between More's theory of government and that of Henry and Wolsey. Both Henry and Wolsey were despotic at heart and greatly disliked Parliament. More, however, as we have seen, considered Parliament not only a good and necessary check to centralized power, but a form of government potentially superior to monarchy. Dramatized in this encounter with Wolsey was the old struggle between independent-minded citizens jealous of self-rule on one side and monarchical or ecclesiastical despots on the other. This drama was nothing new in England. But one must appreciate that More always considered himself part of those independent-minded Englishmen, even when serving as a royal counselor.

More's sympathy with Parliament against Wolsey's despotic ways can be seen in how More handled Wolsey's intrusion upon the independence of the House. After Wolsey gave his speech, all the members of the House followed what More had subtly suggested beforehand: they remained silent, a silence Wolsey called marvelously obstinate. Roper reports the conclusion of this incident:

> And thereupon [Wolsey] required an answer of Master Speaker, who first reverently upon his knees excusing the silence of the House, abashed at the presence of so noble a personage, able to amaze the wisest and best learned in a Realm, and after by many probable arguments proving that for them to make answer was it neither expedient nor agreeable with the ancient liberty of the House, in conclusion for himself showed that though they had all with their voices trusted him, yet except every one of them could put into his one head all their several wits, he alone in so weighty a matter was unmeet to make his Grace answer.
>
> Whereupon the Cardinal, displeased with Sir Thomas More, that had not in this Parliament in all things satisfied his desire, suddenly arose and departed. (11)

Such shrewd speech and courageous action in the face of the second most powerful person in England suggests why the commoners loved and respected More and why Wolsey would come to fear him; it also foretold the courageous actions to come in the face of Henry himself.

After 1525, More's concern about the character of Henry's rule increased steadily. As Robert Adams put it, More "wrote no more epigrams on tyranny; he had begun to breathe it distinctly with the daily air" (188). In that year Henry's infatuation with Anne Boleyn began, but Anne was certainly not the first woman to catch Henry's fancy. There were far more troubling signs long before this development. In 1519 Henry had made a bid for the imperial crown of Germany, an action that would have gravely endangered England's future independence if he had succeeded. In 1521 he executed Buckingham, who supposedly threatened the security of his crown. In 1522 he initiated another senseless war with France. By 1524, More registered his concern with Henry's vaulting *libido dominandi* when he told Roper that "if my head could win him a castle in France . . . it should not fail to go" (Roper 12). These developments simply followed the pattern More identified in his early poems about the dangers of monarchical powers: "A king in his first year is always very mild indeed. . . . Over a long time a greedy king will gnaw away at his people. . . . It is a mistake to believe that a greedy king can be satisfied; such a leech never leaves flesh until it is drained" (CW3.2, no. 198). Henry VIII certainly would leave England drained. Despite the wealth left by Henry VII and the enormous increase that came with the dissolution of the monasteries and from unprecedented taxes, Henry VIII nevertheless left the country in grave economic condition at the time of his death. As G. R. Elton put it:

> Left to himself, King Henry VIII turned his hand to the search for personal glory and national aggrandizement, playing a part he had always fancied and never been fit for either in his personal capacities or the resources of his realms. His achievement must strike the reflective mind as remarkable: a grave threat of invasion from France, an uncured canker of war in Scotland, the wasting away of the crown's recently enlarged resources, a country drained by the heaviest taxation for centuries (some of it dubiously legal), and a major economic crisis in what had been the least crisis-prone of the economies of western Europe. That his achievement did not destroy the monarchy . . . nor produce a real collapse and a class war in England, was none of his doing. (1977, 316)

Another major concern in 1526 and 1527 was Henry's indifference to the grave dangers posed by the "relentlessly advancing Turkish armies" (Adams 258–68). By pursuing wars that actually weakened Christendom, he proved himself to be more concerned with his own chivalric exploits than with the survival of a united Europe. In these years, Henry also continued the practice of relying progressively more on Wolsey's eager talent for rule than upon his own involvement in the difficult concerns of good government. What was said of his youth developed even more as he approached middle age:

> The King was young and lusty, disposed all to mirth and pleasure and to follow his desire and appetite, nothing minding to travail in the busy affairs of the realm. . . . That knew [Wolsey] very well, . . . and so fast as the other counsellors advised the King to leave his pleasure and to attend to the affairs of the realm, so busily did [Wolsey] persuade him to the contrary. (Cavendish 12–13; see also CSPS 44, 45)

In 1527 the sky continued darkening, foretelling the storm that would soon break. Henry was vigorously pursuing his divorce from Catherine, and despite the expectations of many, Henry's infatuation with Anne was not assuaged with time as it had with others.

This same year Henry first asked More about the divorce, and More's response reveals a great deal about his thought and character. Knowing the danger of giving advice to a king that was "disagreeable with his desire" (Roper 18), More at first declined to comment, on the grounds that he "had never professed the study of divinity" (17). When pressed, he agreed to ponder the scriptural passages the King showed him, to confer with the people recommended, and to study the matter carefully. Having done so, More then returned to the King. Throughout his reply, More shows that he is fully aware of the difficulties involved in advising a lion who is proud, prosperous, and practiced in achieving his own will:

> To be plain with Your Grace, neither my Lord of Durham, nor my Lord of Bath, though I know them both to be wise, virtuous, learned and honorable prelates, nor myself, with the rest of your Council, being all Your Grace's own servants, for your manifold benefits daily bestowed on us so most bounded to you, be, in my judgment, meet counselors for Your Grace herein. (Roper 17)

In this first part of his reply, More diplomatically points out the conflict of interest involved in asking servants for advice on an issue of such personal interest. Servants, often too prone to please the one who feeds them, do not make the best counselors. This, of course, is just the difficulty that would continue to plague Henry throughout his reign.

More continues administering the medicine his patient is not about to like:

> But if Your Grace mind to understand the truth, such counselors may you have devised, as neither for respect of their own worldly commodity, nor for fear of your princely authority, will be inclined to deceive you. (17)

Here More draws attention to the same point again, clearly indicating to Henry the danger he faces: the deception of those who fear his authority or those (like Wolsey) who wish to benefit from it. Having disqualified himself and the others Henry originally mentioned as counselors, More gives his own list of those Henry should consult:

> To whom he named then St. Jerome, St. Augustine and divers other old Holy Doctors, both Greeks and Latins, and moreover showed him what authorities he had gathered out of them, which although the King (as disagreeable with his desire) did not very well like of, yet were they by Sir Thomas More, who in all his communications with the King in that matter had always most discreetly behaved himself, so wisely tempered, that he both presently took them in good part, and ofttimes had thereof conference with him again. (17–18)

This passage is of great importance in understanding More's relationship with Henry. Even in this first conversation about the marriage, Henry did not like what More told him. Yet, because of the diplomatic way in which More prepared and then administered the bitter medicine, Henry "ofttimes" came back for advice (Roper 18). Nonetheless, it is still surprising that Henry would choose More for his chancellor since More's opposition to his divorce was unquestionably strong. That he would choose More is further evidence of More's ability to administer counsel skillfully and effectively.

This diplomacy was not based on flattery and manipulation as the reconstructionists maintain; it was based on a profound understanding of human nature, of pride, and of the particular moral and psychological difficulties facing the advisor of someone who has it in his power to do whatever he wills or merely wishes. All that More studied and pondered as a youth (see chapter 1) was now being brought into play.

In 1528 and early in 1529, two books of major importance were published which would play significant roles in the great struggle for Henry's conscience. That Henry was a man of conscience who needed justifications for his actions is misunderstood by those who wonder at his long delays and indecisiveness in bringing about his much-sought divorce. But Henry was raised in a nation of strong laws and deep traditions, and he firmly believed in their importance. Nonetheless, his passions were also strong, and he was not practiced in ruling them. The interior war for virtue, that central theme of More's early literature, was the same war Henry now faced within himself.

There was no legitimate way to acquire a divorce at that time, but Henry wanted one. To achieve it, Henry would eventually have to sever his ties with Christendom by declaring himself an emperor who held in his hands the reins of all temporal and spiritual authority. This meant schism from the Christendom he had revered and strongly defended throughout his life. Before taking such drastic action, Henry would have to justify it before the tribunal of his conscience. Not until Henry read the book Anne Boleyn recommended in 1528 did he find that justification. Nevertheless, it would take four more years of intrigue by the Boleyn faction before Henry forced through their radical solution, in a fit of anger and desperation. Although Alistair Fox would have us believe that More played Iago to Henry (1983, 186, 198), other actors we are now to see may be better candidates for that role.

From 1528 on, Anne Boleyn and her family actively played upon Henry's imperial ambitions, using what would normally have been a most unlikely lure, William Tyndale's *Obedience of a Christian Man*. This book, published in 1528, presented a theory of divine right that would serve to legitimize Henry's deepest imperial ambitions (Carlyle 287ff). According to Pollard, Schuster, and Guy, "the inspiration of Tyndale's *Obedience* may be traced in every act of parliament that led up to the royal supremacy" (CW8 1182; Guy 1980, 108). Nevertheless, this book posed a significant difficulty for Henry: although he loved the theory, he absolutely rejected the author for his heretical beliefs. Subsequently, part of More's strategy was to encourage Henry to confront and resolve this contradiction and to see that the theory of divine right was also built on unacceptable principles. Cromwell and Cranmer had the opposite strategy; they worked to gloss over the contradiction by finding more respectable sources for the same theory. As Cranmer and Cromwell clearly realized, neither Henry nor the English people were prepared for such a radical departure from English tradition in 1528. Hence such a change could not be made either overtly or at once. For this reason, they would soon begin an extensive and carefully calculated propaganda campaign to create a better climate of opinion for breaking the independence of the English Church and for severing England's unity with Christendom.

In the first months of 1529, Anne Boleyn gave Henry another important book, Simon Fish's *A Supplication for the Beggars*. If Tyndale's *Obedience* provided the theory to allow Henry to proclaim himself supreme head of the spiritual and temporal orders of England, Fish's *Supplication* provided the practical means by which the independence of that spiritual order was to be toppled.

At first glance, Fish's pamphlet appears to be just one more virulent attack upon the clergy. It defended Lutheran doctrines but took on the face of a philanthropic defense of English interests, especially the interests of the poor and of the king. What danger could there possibly be in such a work, especially given the long history of anticlerical sentiment in England and the Lutheran elements of the pamphlet that previously had been wholly inadmissible to Henry? Henry's perspective was changing rapidly, however, and by the end of 1529, he would give his first qualified defense of Luther (CSPS 4.349). Another critical circumstance was the timing of Fish's pamphlet. Published and circulated just months before the Commons would discuss the Grievances against the Ordinaries, Fish's *Supplication* was subsequently used as part of the orchestrated campaign to destroy the Church's independence in England.

Fish's artful pamphlet begins by crying out to King Henry for relief from the many ills affecting England. And what is the source of *all* these ills? The clergy. Beggars, whores, poverty, lack of obedience to the king—*all* are caused by the "holy idle thieves" who have formed a kingdom within Henry's kingdom, a kingdom that is close to becoming and will indeed become more powerful than Henry's unless Henry takes action soon.

Henry's favorable reaction to Fish's sixteen-page diatribe and then to Fish himself (CW8 1187) readily explains why More published such a lengthy response (more than ten times as long) with surprising rapidity and rhetorical force. More was undoubtedly aware that this pamphlet had won the King's favor; undeterred, however, he fulfilled what he considered his duty as king's counselor and as one officially entrusted with the Church's defense.

More's rapid response, *Supplication of Souls,* gave a strong defense of the clergy as well as an accurate assessment of the strategy his opponents were employing: since they were unable to undermine England's confidence in the Church, they were now attempting to heighten anticlerical sentiment with Fish's *Supplication for the Beggars* and similar polemics. By so attacking real faults of the clergy and then by grossly exaggerating these and by making up wholly false crimes, they would be able to destroy the independence of the English Church. This is just what eventually took place.

Before responding to Fish's *Supplication,* however, More first replied to Tyndale's *Obedience of a Christian Man,* but subtly. This prudent approach was necessary, since Henry had entered upon a dangerous new infatuation, an infatuation with imperial and despotic power. To counter this, More appealed to what remained strong in Henry: his orthodox convictions. In his *Dialogue Concerning Heresies,* for example, More explicitly objects eight times to the lack of orthodoxy in Tyndale's *Obedience*. Seven times he shows Tyndale's rejection of views which Henry himself supported (CW6 289, 291, 303, 349–50, 388, 424–25, 431). The eighth time, however, occurs with a forceful attack upon tyrants, one of the strongest in all of More's writings (369–72). Here he gives a stern and ominous reminder that, without the restraint and guidance of law, human beings can act like "abominable beasts . . . wretched tyrants and cruel tormentors" (370).

Early October 1529 brought Wolsey's fall, another hopeful sign for More and his humanist friends. As they saw it, the greatest responsibility for Henry's change of character lay with this counselor who was closest to Henry throughout the previous fifteen years. He encouraged Henry's ambitions and wars. Many even believed Wolsey, based on his own boasts, was the one who first suggested a divorce from Catherine to make way for a politically more expedient marriage alliance with France (Roper 16–17, Harpsfield 76–77, Stapleton 178). Wolsey also embodied all that the Erasmians were trying to reform. While Wolsey could have used his administrative genius to bring about the much-needed reforms in the English Church and to have counseled Henry to greater moderation, he used that power to amass a grand fortune, to wage wars, and to further his ambitions to become pope, playing all the while upon Henry's weaknesses to bring about these objectives (Cavendish 12–13). There can be no surprise, then, that More denounced Wolsey so forcefully before the Parliament in November 1529. In addition to believing that Wolsey deserved such a strong rebuke, More was aware that Henry was still considering Wolsey's restoration in order to gain control over the likes of Bishops John Fisher and William Warham, who were not showing any signs of relinquishing the Church's independent status to bring about his imperial aims.

To replace Wolsey as chancellor, Henry selected More, despite his known opposition to the divorce. After accepting, More wrote to Erasmus saying he did so for the good he might do for Christendom (SL 172).

In this same year of 1529, Cranmer began to play an important part in shaping the forces that would bear heavily on Henry's conscience. He was the first to suggest that Henry enhance the respectability of his cause by enlisting the support of distinguished university dons. But of far greater importance, Cranmer was soon to begin compiling a theological defense of Henry's supposed imperial status. Encouraged by the Boleyns and perhaps by Cromwell, Cranmer developed the ideas presented in Tyndale's *Obedience,* but gave it the appearance of greater respectability. This manuscript, the *Collectanea satis copiosa,* was ready in September 1530. Henry studied it with uncommon care, making over forty marginal comments expressing his enthusiasm and occasional surprise (Fox and Guy 157). From then on, he strongly sought to establish this imperial status, a status that would soon mean the destruction of the Church's independence.

Already by September 19 Henry used his royal prerogative to forbid exercise of foreign authority in England. He also asked key counselors about the power and disposition of Parliament; when they advised him that Parliament would not look favorably upon his plans, he angrily prorogued it until he could find a way to exert his will (CSPS 2.460; Guy 1980, 130). During this period Eustace Chapuys reported that More was nearly dismissed for his staunch opposition (CSPS 2.433; Guy 1980, 139).

More's opposition continued throughout 1531. So effective and vigorous was this action that Charles V sent him a letter of appreciation in March, but More refused to accept it lest it compromise his action in any way (LP 5.171).

Despite Henry's efforts to intimidate the leading clergy throughout 1531, there were no signs of Henry's success in their Convocation. Even under the strong pressure Henry exerted in February, Convocation conceded to him the title of Supreme Head of the Church in England, but only after Fisher added the deadening qualifier "as far as Christ's law allows" (Hughes 122). Neither was Henry any more successful in Parliament in 1531 and early 1532. As late as mid-April of 1532 Henry had to rebuke the Commons for discussing the adverse effects of his intended divorce (Guy 1980, 194). This situation changed dramatically, however, once Henry decided to skirt the parliamentary process and use the full force of his powers to intimidate and break the resistance of his opponents.

The plain truth of the matter was that, despite slanderous materials like Fish's *Supplication* and despite Henry's clear and insistent desire to obtain a divorce, Parliament and Convocation considered it legally and politically impossible to enact the radical changes which were entailed. Even Henry himself was unprepared to follow through until late April of 1532, and then he went ahead only in a fit of rage and desperation. In these months Henry's tyrannical desires won over his kingly prudence.

Changes accelerated when Cromwell took charge of Henry's legislative initiatives to obtain a divorce, early in 1532. By this time Henry had decided to adopt Cranmer's suggestion of 1529: to bypass Rome and to obtain the divorce through the English Convocation and Parliament. But with Wolsey now gone and Warham staunchly refusing to go along, Henry did not know what to do apart from his usual strategy of bullying threats. Cromwell, however, fabricated a strategy that eventually succeeded (Guy 1980, 183ff). He shrewdly began with a modest bill that sought to stop certain payments to Rome; this bill had wide support, especially given the high anticlerical sentiment of the time. By changing the wording, Cromwell submitted what amounted to a legal revolution, proposing that Parliament renounce the papacy's very jurisdiction in England. Hence, he cleverly used an existing grievance (the loss of money) to conceal a legal revolution—a strategy that he would continue to use in the future.

Understandably, this Restraint of Annates Act met the strongest resistance in both the House of Lords and the House of Commons. Warham went so far as to dissociate himself formally from the statutes of that Parliament in late February. Henry personally went to the House of Lords to force its narrow victory, with the bishops unanimously opposed. Even with this pressure, Henry had to make the enormous concession that the act was to be conditional and therefore had to be confirmed at a later time. Since resistance in the House of Commons was also strenuous, Henry forced a division of Commons, a flagrant violation of Par-

The Limits of Government   199

liament's traditional liberty rarely seen before that time (Guy 1980, 184–85).

Although the Conditional Restraint of Annates Act was not a legislative victory for Henry and Cromwell, it did provide them with an important list of Parliament members who would stand for and against their manipulative designs. This occurred at the end of March, and thus gave Cromwell all of April and half of May to try to get the needed support for his next, more radical bill, the Submission of the Clergy. The Restraint of Annates Act was intended to break England's unity with Christendom; the Submission of the Clergy was to destroy the Church's independent status. If the first did not succeed, why did the second succeed when it proved to have even less support than the first?

By May 10 Cromwell must have seen clearly that he did not have the needed votes in Parliament to support his bill for Submission. Furthermore, on May 13, More openly led the opposition in Parliament (LP 5.1013; Guy 1980, 200). Because Henry and Cromwell could not succeed in this legal forum, Henry prorogued Parliament abruptly the next day and focused his intimidation tactics on the Convocation of the clergy. Hence, since Parliament steadfastly resisted, Convocation became the scene of the last battle for the Church's independence. More believed that this battle could and should have been won: if the bishops had been statesmen, they need not have been vanquished.

What actually occurred, however, began on May 10, when Henry sent the articles of Submission to Convocation. The bishops' reaction "closely approached panic," but they showed their resolve to resist by sending that same day a delegation of ten from both houses to confer with Fisher, who was ill at Rochester (Kelly 113). The next day, however, Henry increased his coercion by declaring that the clergy was "but half our subjects, yea, and scarce our subjects."

With his oft-repeated "the king's anger means death" undoubtedly ringing in his ears, Warham sent a reply on May 13 that offered compromise instead of resistance. In light of this capitulation, Henry's demands increased, once on May 13 and twice on

May 15. In addition, Henry prorogued Convocation, thus demanding an immediate answer; he also took the unusual but highly intimidating step of sending six high-ranking nobles to Convocation to show he meant business (Kelly 114–15).

Given this level of intimidation, Warham devised a strategy that probably aimed at buying time to allow Henry's anger to subside. But for whatever reason, Warham did not resist in May of 1532—nor did he allow the rest of Convocation to do so. He dismissed the lower house before it could vote, and perhaps as few as three bishops in the upper house gave their full consent to the Submission. Whatever the exact numbers, however, this "rump Convocation" could not legitimately speak for the English Church (Kelly 108–9). And the old and politically shrewd Warham knew this. Since Henry's actions showed clearly that he was not disposed to respect the law, Warham was prepared to use a strategy learned from England's most popular saint, Thomas Becket.[4]

Warham died that summer, however, and, with Fisher still sick, no other bishop arose to oppose Henry's caesaropapist designs. Fisher and More both expressed reproach towards these ecclesiastical leaders for cowardice in deserting their post in the moment of greatest need. Fisher lamented that "the fort is betrayed even of them that should have defended it" (Hughes 162). More expressed a similar rebuke in his last work, *The Sadness of Christ*. In one section he laments the apostles' falling asleep while "Judas the traitor at the same time was so wide awake and intent on betraying the Lord that the very idea of sleep never entered his head" (CW14 259). Then follows one of the most severe reproaches in all of More's writings, but the reproach is directed not only to the ecclesiastical rulers of his own place and time, but to all rulers of all times. As More puts it, no amount of sadness, weariness, or fear that arises from the weight of public office is an excuse for falling asleep on one's responsibilities:

> If a bishop . . . neglects to do what the duty of his office requires for the salvation of his flock—[he is] like a cowardly ship's captain who is so disheartened by the furious din of a storm that he deserts the

helm, hides away cowering in some cranny, and abandons the ship to the waves. (CW14 265)

Within hours of the May 16th ceremony of the clergy's submission, Thomas More resigned as chancellor. John Guy describes that scene well:

> At 3 P.M. in the garden at York Place, Westminster, More came into the royal presence and watched by the duke of Norfolk, handed back the white leather bag containing the great seal to Henry VIII. . . . The ironical inflexion of More's voice, the piercing gaze of his eyes, and the nobility of his composure all gave the lie to his excuse that he was "not equal to the work." . . . Cromwell's victory of 15 May was "narrow, blundering and legally suspect." More's gaze in the garden told Henry so, and the king averted his eyes. (1980, 201)

If Henry averted More's eyes, it was because More had again touched his conscience. For that reason, More had good reasons to continue his appeals to Henry's better judgment.

After his resignation and up to his very execution, More continued these appeals in the hopes that Henry would change. That More would take such risks shows that he did not consider Henry hardened in his ways. Like Catherine of Aragon and others close to Henry, More thought the King was temporarily deluded by his passion for Anne and by the flattery and intrigue of false advisors (Guy 1988, 131). More continued his opposition to Cromwell's and Henry's policies—but as always, he did so subtly, acting under the public charge he had received in 1529 to defend the Church.

After 1532, More knew that the most dangerous attacks were no longer the external ones from Luther and Tyndale, but rather the internal ones from Cromwell, Cranmer, and their legal counsel, Christopher St. German. This experienced lawyer and scholar posed a threat that More considered equal to or even greater than that of any other opponent. St. German's tactic was the same as Fish's: to play upon anticlerical sentiment. St. German was, however, far subtler and far more masterful in execution. In writing his *Division between the Spirituality and Temporality,* for example, St. German adopted not the strident tone of Fish, but the reasonable voice of one seeking peace and lamenting division. Yet, as More would show, St. German wrote precisely for the opposite reason, to create greater division between the clerical and temporal estates. In addition, St. German had also worked out a highly influential legal theory that would gain ascendancy for generations to come. The major thrust of his argument was that common law was the chief law of the land and that all canon and ecclesiastical law should be submitted to its review. Eventually he would argue that even Scripture and one's conscience should be submitted to English common law as determined by the king in Parliament (Fox and Guy 179–220). Although his theories would be used to bring about Henry's supremacy over the English Church, St. German was undoubtedly displeased to see Henry's caesaropapism replacing what he envisioned to be Parliament's proper role (Guy 1988, 133; Fox and Guy 119).

More's assessment of the danger involved in St. German's project can be partially seen in the speed and urgency of his reply. St. German's *Division* was published by the king's printer in February of 1533; More's response in his *Apology* was out in April. St. German's *Division*—printed five times by the government press between February 1533 and the end of 1537—blamed the clergy for the growing unrest in England because of their undue harshness towards the laity and their unfair partiality towards fellow clergy. In response, More strongly denied that such a division actually existed, and he defended "the very good old and long approved laws, both of this realm and of the whole corps of Christendom" (CW10 9/16–18, CW9 53). Throughout, he calls his opponent "the Pacifier"—a masterful use of irony to suggest gradually, as with Shakespeare's "honorable" Brutus, that something quite different was actually involved.

St. German's reply to More, *Salem and Bizance,* came in September; More's lengthy and detailed rebuttal, *The Debellation of Salem and Bizance,* appeared in October. Six months later More would be imprisoned—largely, as John Guy has suggested, because of his active and continuous opposition to Henry's and Cromwell's designs (Fox and Guy 112–19).

The Limits of Government   203

Yet even in prison, from April 1534 until his death, More continued to write, always it seems with the conscience of his king in mind. More knew that his writings were heavily scrutinized; after all, they were searched diligently for any bit of evidence to use against him. Although it was unlikely that Henry read any of More's writings, he received reports from those who did. Besides, More was not writing for Henry and his time alone; he knew well that the motives and forces he faced were the same that faced every generation. Hence, the subtle counsels to Henry within these last works were addressed not only to him but also to all the "other caesars and their governors" who would betray the flocks entrusted to their care (CW14 547). In his last work occurs the strongest statement of this warning. There More seems to suggest that Henry is another Caiphas betraying Christ while the apostles (the bishops) were asleep (259–61, 341, 371–75, 619).

How is one to assess the success or failure of More's war of words? As long as More stayed within the bounds of what was politically acceptable to Henry VIII, he was judged to be extremely successful. The King approved of his forceful style; indeed he had been the one to ask More to write against Luther's harsh attack. Because of More's rhetorical skill and success, the English bishops later asked him to take up the Church's defense in the face of attacks from Tyndale and others. More's first measured response in 1529 has been recognized as a masterful Platonic dialogue,[5] and it was reprinted in More's lifetime. More's later contributions to this debate were so successful that by 1531 Frith returned to England to hearten the Protestant effort (CW7 cxxx), and in recognition of his accomplishment, the bishops later offered More the exceptional sum of 4,000 to 5,000 pounds, which More refused (Roper 23–24).[6]

The dread power of kings crushed More's war of words, however, as soon as More went beyond what Henry was prepared to accept. Yet crushed is the wrong word, for it took several years to defeat an opponent as legally shrewd and rhetorically powerful as More.

Once King Henry became convinced that the separation of

church and state must end, More became the principal obstacle. With the bishops' capitulation and Fisher's ill health, More's voice had the single-most influence with the English. More's rhetorical effectiveness made him dangerous to Henry's and Cromwell's plan. So strong and effective was More's written and political opposition that Henry found it necessary to manipulate an unwilling Parliament to remove this last obstacle from his path and from his conscience. Yet as long as the battle of words took place on the plain of reason, More was not defeated. It took all the king's power of manipulation and force to crush More's discreet and respectful appeal to law and tradition.

At his trial, More respectfully but forcefully expressed his fundamental disagreement with Henry's personal despotism. There More stated his convictions about the sovereign position of law and of limited government, which is derived from the best deliberations of the people, not from an individual's will or pleasure (Roper 42, 45–46; Fox and Guy 164). He also expressed his conviction about the separate jurisdictions of the spiritual and temporal orders, a conviction Henry fully shared until 1529, when he began to claim an absolute imperial jurisdiction based on his alleged divine right. More was to die for his respectful but unyielding opposition to Henry's imperial tyranny.

In this great contest over legitimate sovereignty, More's life was cut short, but history has prolonged his memory. Whereas Thomas More has become a standard-bearer of justice and an example of serene and courageous statesmanship, Henry VIII has become the pitiful example of a gifted man who fell prey to his passions, introduced one of the bloodiest periods in English history, and set back England's political reformation by generations (Scarisbrick 21, 506–26; Guy 1988, 133–34, 156ff; Adams 301).

Conclusion

> Cicero is said to be the only wit that the people of Rome had equalled to their empire. . . . We have had many, and . . . Sir Thomas More [was one]. . . . Nothing is worthier the study of the statesman than that part of the republic which we call the advancement of letters.—Ben Jonson, *Discoveries*

Cicero was the statesman most admired by civic humanists of the Renaissance (Baron 1.94–133, esp. 113–14, 121ff). He was also an accomplished lawyer, a master rhetorician, a lifelong student of philosophy, and a political martyr who died in defense of the Roman republic. That Thomas More soon became known as the "Christian English Cicero" has, therefore, considerable significance (Harpsfield 174, CW7 6, Jonson 11.591).

Like Cicero, More carefully prepared himself for a career of civic leadership. For fifteen years after his formal education in law, he studied political philosophy, history, and theology; he learned Greek, practiced rhetoric, and gathered experience in the practical workings of the city. Like Cicero, he was convinced that the advancement of good letters was the best way to promote civic justice, since they were the best time-proven means to reinforce the power of reason.

Like Cicero, More recognized the importance of humor and

irony, but More gave comic irony a centrality unlike any other statesman before him.[1] In devising his distinctive approach, More learned from such diverse predecessors as Aristophanes, Socrates, Lucian, Plutarch, Horace, Juvenal, Martial, Plautus, Terence, Aquinas, and Chaucer.[2] Like them, he saw the power of comic irony in both strengthening and enabling reason to break the hold of passion and prejudice. From them he learned that one can tell the "full truth in jest" (CW9 170/36). From the Bible, he learned in a special way the power of irony in appealing to conscience.

Unlike Cicero, More drew upon biblical revelation to answer questions which Cicero considered unanswerable by human reason alone. More accepted the biblical account that each person is free and has access to a transcendent ground for virtuous action. That ground was not an idea of the good, but a person who can be known, loved, and contemplated. Hence, genuine human virtue can be acquired regardless of one's intellectual or cultural endowments.

As a free creature, every person exercises will and intellect to choose goods, actions, and a whole way of life. Before the Fall, in the "natural state," the best way of life was clearly known and fervently desired; it was a contemplative life, "a life good, quiet and restful, with spiritual delight, in such knowledge of God and his wonderful works, as reason at the least without revelation might attain unto" (CW13 37/2–4,9). Despite this satisfying knowledge and love of a personal God, the first man and woman indulged a "foolish proud affection" to be like a god and goddess (CW13 16–19, 7/12–16), thus delighting in their godlike powers rather than in God.[3]

This free choice led to the destruction of the harmony and power of man's intellect and will, and it resulted in war, pain, and death (CW13 13/22–27). The root cause was pride, a condition that now describes the permanent disposition of the soul in its fallen state. As such, the soul of every person has the tendency to become enamored with an image of the good, a "worldly fantasy" of its own creation. Or, to put it in another way, pride is the disordered love of one's "own private pursuits to the detriment of the common cause" (SL 130). Given the universal power of this inherent quality, no one is simply virtuous (CW13 7/17ff, 9/24ff), and everyone is capable of rebelling against the dictates of the good in exercising this fundamental freedom. Anyone can, however, live a contemplative life, despite the tendency to mistake temporal pleasures for true goods. In this light, More understood well Aristotle's statement that "the whole concern both of virtue and of political science is with pleasures and pains."[4]

Because of this tendency to err, all human beings have a special need for government after the Fall, although the authority to govern was present, especially in the family, before the Fall (CW13 13/16). The family is a natural society that conforms with our nature as free beings ordered to love and care for others (CW13 21/19–22/4; CW3.2, no. 264, lines 20–25; CW6 415/6–28). Here are learned the virtues and habits that will be exercised in the larger civil society.

Regarding the extent and source of political authority, More took guidance, as always, from his understanding of the person as free though fallen (CW13 3–25). Since no one is perfect, no one can be invested with unqualified and absolute authority—either by inheritance or election or divine right. Everyone needs advice; in fact, all sound minds seek and love good advice.[5] Just as England consults and ponders issues in Parliament and inns of court, so too must each person do the same with wise and well-chosen friends.[6]

Furthermore, since authority exists in order to give reliable guidance in the proper exercise of freedom, the good ruler is presented as a devoted father towards his children, not as a master towards his subjects (CW3.2, nos. 111, 109; Aristotle's *Politics* 1285b 31–33); he serves as a watchdog and guardian, not as a tyrant and wolf ravaging the flock (CW3.2, nos. 133, 109, 115; CW2 24/30); he considers himself the head of a people whom he sees as part of his own body (CW3.2, no. 112).[7] This conception of authority leads him to conceive of himself as a chosen ruler of a free people, not a master of slaves (CW3.2, nos. 121, 198, 120, 201, 206); as one humble enough to do "lowly service," not as a lord lusting for power (CW3.2, no. 243; CW13 111/30–31).[8] Of notable importance, however, More does not compare the good ruler to a physician.[9] This omission is a significant break with the classical authors he usually follows, and it reflects his understanding of the distinct though complementary roles of church and state.

Church and state each has its proper sphere of jurisdiction (CW7 129–31). More thought the state violated its legitimate sphere of authority when, for example, it sought to appoint bishops (CW13 73), and he thought the church violated its legitimate authority by claiming too much temporal power (Gogan 261–62). The church's proper authority extends to the care of souls, primarily through the administration of the sacraments and the preaching of Scripture. Its temporal authority comes largely from the state (CW9 98–99). More approved of the two systems of laws, ecclesiastical and civil, an arrangement which had a long tradition in England and throughout Christendom. In fact, he strongly defended the independence of the ecclesiastical courts and laws throughout the last years of his life. Because of the "dregs" in both church and state (54), the existence of two systems provided better protection for the innocent. The ecclesiastical privilege of sanctuary (CW2 28–31, 115–19; CW9 244 n.57), for example, existed to counter those known instances when "the state itself turn[ed] thief and murderer" (Fenlon 457). In such ways the church helped "to keep the crown responsible to God and man" (460), and the state could help the church in like manner.

In seeing the governed as free citizens and not slavish subjects, More shows his theory of government to be characteristically English. This view explains More's distaste for unchecked monarchy and his defense of free speech.[10] In Epigram 121, More articulates most clearly what he considered to be the true nature of authority:

The Consent of the People both Bestows and Withdraws Sovereignty
Any man who has command of many men owes his authority to those whom he commands: he ought to have command not one instant

longer than his [people] wish. Why are impotent kings so proud? Because they rule merely on sufferance? (CW3.2)

Such a view explains why More would prefer a representative form of government to monarchy.[11] The reasons which More gives for preferring elected officials to an hereditary monarch are similar to Aristotle's:[12] elected officials are more receptive to reasonable advice than are kings; their choice is more likely to be based on a reasonable agreement among the people; they are more mild and responsive to the people; and there is a hope for a change if they are evil (CW3.2, no. 198). More's distrust of kings arose from his understanding of human nature and of history, a perspective which supported the need to limit power because "unlimited power has a tendency to weaken good minds, and that even in case of very gifted men" (no. 19/90-91).

Although More discreetly indicated his preference for a representative form of government,[13] he also recognized that rarely can one choose (no. 198). Regardless of the form of government, however, More considered law the fundamental criterion of a government's justice. Human laws, "which truly are the traditions of men," arise naturally from the work of prudent citizens concerned for the common good (CW5 281/14-15). More agreed with Aristotle that laws are necessary because even the best persons can be "so much influenced by feelings of friendship or hatred or self-interest that they lose any clear vision of the truth and have their judgment obscured by considerations of personal pleasure or pain" (*Rhetoric* 1354b, CW6 262). Law also serves as a "sure and substantial shield" to protect the judge "from the hatred and obloquy" that would otherwise follow even the most just sentence since "men are so partial always to themselves that our hearts ever think the judgment wrong that brings us to the worse" (CW6 262). Law is absolutely necessary for true freedom and a relatively just society (368-72, 403-5). Although no law is perfect (CW10 164), "people without law would rush forth into every kind of crime" (CW5 279).

More advocated respect for all laws, even unjust ones. In the face of an unjust law, More advised waiting for a "place and time convenient" to advocate change, and he disapproved of "open reproof and refutation" (CW9 96–97; CW10 193, 228–30). This More showed in his own life by his manner of respectful resistance and acceptance of death when confronted with a law he could not obey.

Given the important function of law in offering a stable and disinterested standard of justice, More insisted that he would give even the devil justice, for the sake of the common good (Roper 21–22). More recognized an objective law of nature written in the human heart (CW6 141), which anyone can know by reason. Since all have free will, however, all can ignore this law as made known by conscience in order to follow the "foolish fantasy" of one's own imagination—but only for a limited period of time. Why? Because violation of conscience always causes grief (EW 461–62, CW13 258, SL 237), even in the most hardened and cruel tyrant (CW2 87/8–21, CW14 457). Conscience, then, provides the metaphysical foundation and the ultimate binding force of law, arising from the very structure of one's being and not merely (as Raphael implies in *Utopia*) as the result of threatened punishment.

In the letter that I would call his "Dialogue on Conscience,"[14] the imprisoned More discusses with his daughter Meg the relationship between law and conscience. Margaret has obeyed the Parliament's law by taking the oath which More has refused. Meg argues that More has a duty to conform his conscience to a law which has been widely debated and agreed upon:

> You well ought and have good cause to change your own conscience, in confirming your own conscience to the conscience of so many others, namely being such as you know they be. And since it is also by a law made by parliament commanded, they think that you be, upon peril of your soul, bound to change and reform your conscience, and confirm your own as I said to other men's. (Corr 524/379–85)

More forcefully rejoins that "yet is there no man bound to swear that every law is well made, nor bound upon the pain of God's displeasure, to perform any such point of law, as were indeed lawful" (Corr 524/391–93). More argues that positive law must be judged by the well-formed conscience. To emphasize this point, More insists to Margaret: "I never intend (God being my good lord) to pin my soul at another man's back, not even the best man that I know this day living; for I know not whither he may hap to carry it" (521). Here More expresses the traditional Christian view that each person is radically free—and responsible—before God, and that one is therefore bound to obey the dictates of his conscience. Of course, the first responsibility is to form one's conscience well, and More repeatedly makes the point that he has spent years of study and many sleepless nights thinking through the issues involved in his present case (528, 530); his conscience is sure and not in doubt (SL 221–23, 235, 250–53).

To summarize, the whole of More's understanding of statesmanship revolves upon his conviction that human beings are free and therefore responsible. Since human persons participate in God's highest powers, each person is capable of genuinely free action—so free that each one can accept or reject one's own good.

As a practical consequence of this position, the statesman's primary responsibility as the wise and skillful counselor to self-governing persons is to appeal to that nation's conscience in every available way, thus encouraging these self-governing citizens to work freely and generously for the common good. To encourage his fellow citizens to obey law, the statesman would appeal first to reason and good will, but would not fail to use lawful compulsion when persuasion did not bring compliance with the common good.

In drawing out the implications of a statesmanship based on freedom, law, and conscience, More presented a consistent defense of institutional arrangements now taken as basic to all democratic government: rule of law, division of power, separation of church and state, elected representation, and protected forms of free and public deliberation. Nonetheless, More considered these institutional arrangements to be a work of prudence and tradition, a work that could always be undermined if it was not protected by virtuous political leaders. Without virtue and the support of tradition, no laws and no customary institutions could long stand. Why? Because tyrants—the very opposite of statesmen—would rise up unless virtuous and sharp-sighted statesmen remain courageously vigilant.

More differs from Cicero in presenting law and education as more important than rhetoric in this task. Cicero's statesman was, first and foremost, the wise rhetor;[15] More's is the wise minister of law who sees law as the nation's second greatest educator.[16] Although an accomplished rhetorician himself,[17] More did not even include rhetoric in the education he devised for his children. Nor did he write about it in any notable passage. He was undoubtedly aware of the difficulties with rhetoric that Plato and Aristotle indicated.[18] He was also keenly aware of pride's power in moving individuals to obtain victory rather than truth (CW15 75).

To implement, interpret, and improve a nation's laws, the wise statesman must have a thorough knowledge of his nation's laws, traditions, and literature as well as a thorough knowledge of human nature. By knowing these well, he can draw upon the nation's longest-standing experience and deepest consensus to help him govern with the people's consent. In this role, he first advises and reminds his fellow citizens of their most cherished convictions, laws, and customs; only then does he execute the laws which they have agreed upon.[19] More was convinced that law, not individual persons, should rule, since law represented the best reasoning devised over many generations of experience and reflection. Laws, therefore, were not to be changed lightly, and all laws deserved respect—even unjust ones. When Luther (at least in his early writings) undercut the importance and the authority of secular laws, More ridiculed his position as absurd and urgently warned that chaos and bloodshed would necessarily follow. More consistently faulted Luther and his followers for neglecting the most ordinary and effective means of reform: public deliberation ordered to legal reform. Similarly, when Henry, Cranmer, and Cromwell worked to put the king above the laws of England and of Christendom, More respectfully and staunchly resisted.

Despite the importance given to law, More's expectations were modest: no law would be perfect and even the best laws could not protect every innocent person.[20] More learned from Plutarch, from Richard III, and from his own experience that often laws "are just like spiders' webs; they would hold the weak and the delicate who might be caught in their meshes, but would be torn in pieces by the rich and powerful."[21] He was acutely aware from his earliest days that even the best laws could be manipulated if learned and prudent statesmen did not exercise vigilant diligence.

Law alone, therefore, will never be enough to insure justice. More was convinced that statesmen will always be needed, good people whose words and good living persuasively teach the spirit of the laws (CW6 142/5–9, CW8 794/6–8). Without diligent statesmen, the thickets of law could be easily torn down and, then, who "could stand upright in the winds that would blow?"[22]

This theme of diligence was one that More stressed throughout his writings, but especially at the beginning and end of his life. In his earliest poems and prose works, More insisted on the need for vigilant diligence and warned about the dangers of negligence.[23] In his final works, More speculated that a fundamental cause of the Fall was negligence;[24] he also made clear that any leader would lose those entrusted to him "all for his negligence."[25]

A statesman's diligence, therefore, must lead him to exercise uncommon patience and ingenuity in appealing to the conscience of individuals and the nation at large. In this enterprise, the statesman would draw upon the best of that nation's laws and literature[26] and would use the best educational and diplomatic skills he could devise. A statesman's diligence would also lead him to execute just law in his effort to bring about the common good. At times this would mean using just punishment, legitimate force, and as a last resort, just war (CW6 415). Such diligence is the statesman's most difficult and most praiseworthy exercise of freedom, a diligence that requires heroic courage (CW14 559/10).

In his last work, written just before his death, More addresses himself to future statesmen. After a full life of experience, both theoretical and practical, More warns that the weight and difficulties of public office can "so grip the mind that its strength is sapped and reason gives up the reins" (CW14 263). At such times, the weight of these burdens can lead anyone[27] to "neglect to do what the duty of his office requires . . . like a cowardly ship's captain who is so disheartened by the furious din of a storm that he deserts the helm, hides away cowering in some cranny, and abandons the ship to the waves" (265).

Yet if the statesman, like the skillful captain, rides out the storm, the ship of state can once again embark upon its course. Even if his particular ship were to go down and the captain were lost, future generations could learn from that captain's courage and skill. Here the poet enters to see beyond the present and beyond appearances and reminds us that powers exist that can prevail over the wisest and most heroic—but only briefly.[28] Because "time tries truth,"[29] a wise and brave person can "lose his head and have no harm."[30] Indeed, by such a loss, a true statesman can be of greater help to his nation and can therefore achieve greater glory.

Notes

Introduction

1. Jonson, volume 8, page 325, lines 440–52, emphasis added.
2. More himself never uses the word "statesman," but he uses the concept throughout his writings, even from the earliest. As Plato does, More carefully distinguishes the good ruler from the tyrant. The good ruler is the statesman, the one who is concerned for the good of the state and not for his own self-interest. Jonson and Shakespeare seem to be the first major writers to use the English word "statesman."
3. Erasmus and More use similar terms, except that More never compares the political ruler to a physician (see chap. 3, n. 5 below). For example, Erasmus uses these terms in CWE27 206, 223, 227, 229, 242–43, 274.
4. Jacob Klein's illuminating commentary on these dialogues points out the active role the attentive reader must play in considering, comparing, weighing, and finally judging the statements of each speaker. Klein remarks, for example, that the drama of the dialogue "compels *us*, the listeners, to 'mend' the 'disorderly' account of the Stranger" about statesmanship in light of the remarks that Socrates has made in the first dialogue (171).
5. More wrote this history while studying "with avidity all the historical works he could find" (Stapleton 14). He would have especially studied Sallust, Tacitus, and Suetonius, but also Plutarch, Thucydides, and Augustine (CW2 lxxx–civ). Such a diversity of perspectives would have given More a significant range of measures in assessing the forces of his own time.
6. More was actively involved with this school of law throughout his professional life. As a young lawyer, he lectured there in the autumn of 1511 and was chosen to be the "Lenten Reader" in 1515. This lectureship was the highest honor conferred by the inns of court, one reserved for the best and most experienced practitioners of law. From 1510 to at least 1515 he served as an officer or governor of Lincoln's Inn,

and throughout the 1520s he attended lectures and legal discussions (Roper 22).

7. The undersheriff "was a permanent legal official who advised the sheriffs and sat as a judge in the Sheriff's Court" (Guy 1980, 5). In these positions, More would have dealt with the widest possible range of people and issues throughout London. This position would have made him ineligible for the Parliaments of 1512, 1514, and 1515. In the next Parliament of 1523, he was chosen Speaker of the House of Commons.

8. More makes clear that statesmen must possess and exercise virtue, but not that the statesman's primary concern is to develop virtue in others. Throughout his writings, More seems to indicate that the development of virtue belongs primarily to those most immediately involved in education: family, church, and schools. Of course law and tradition would recognize the primary importance of virtue and would encourage it.

9. More's earliest recorded memory was about Richard and occurred in 1483 when he was six years old. A conversation about Richard's rise to power probably produced such a look of horror on John More's face that Thomas could recall the incident thirty years later in writing his *History of King Richard III* (CW15 327/19–329/3, Chambers 55).

10. Thomas praised his father as an "affable man, charming, irreproachable, gentle, sympathetic, honest, and upright" (SL 181–82).

11. This and the following few paragraphs are largely taken from my biography, *Thomas More: A Portrait of Courage* (1995), pp. 7–8.

12. As Schoeck points out, Morton was a doctor of both civil and canon law (1963, 139 n.42).

13. J. C. David points to these in his analysis of *Richard III*, pp. 43–46.

14. Other assessments of Morton's character in *Utopia* are given by New 17, 24–25, 81; Berger 1965, 64–65; Branham 33.

15. A major point of Augustine's work is indicated clearly in the opening of one of More's last works: "We have not here a dwelling city, but we seek the city that is to come" [Hebrews 13:14] (CW13 3).

16. See chap. 7 below.

17. The best account of More's training as a rhetorician is still Nelson's study of 1943. Daniel Kinney contributes perceptively in CW15 lxii ff.

18. For the importance of rhetoric, see Jerrold E. Seigel's *Rhetoric and Philosophy in Renaissance Humanism*.

19. When applied to More or Erasmus, the phrase "humanist scholar" will be used interchangeably with "Christian humanist" or "civic humanist." As Paul Kristeller has shown, a humanist was "a highly trained classical scholar and a student . . . of the *Studia humanitatis*, the humanities, that is, of a cycle of studies that are described as containing grammar, rhetoric, poetry, history and moral philosophy" (1980, 5). Men like Erasmus and More added the study of the Bible and the Church Fathers.

20. John Guy gives the best account of More's political activity (1980, 1988).

21. Publication of the last volume is expected in 1996.
22. Fox 1983, 9, 15, 27 n.58; Marius xxi–xxiv, 12, 38–39, 290–91. Elton depicts More as a man of "helpless fury," but he does not present him as melancholy (1983, 348–49).
23. Erasmus concentrates on the same topics in his book *The Education of a Christian Prince* (CWE27).
24. Literature is here used in the broad sense (as it was used in the Renaissance) to include rhetoric, history, poetry, and philosophy. See, for example, Hardison 36–37; Davis 252; Vickers 1988, 715ff.
25. To facilitate reading, I have modernized the spelling and punctuation whenever possible.
26. *American Heritage Dictionary*, second college edition, 1982, pp. 1191–92; *Webster's New International Dictionary*, 2d ed., 1959, p. 2461.
27. We have no word in English that easily reflects the dual sense captured in Plato's "*Politeia*." By using this word, Plato implies—as does the whole of the *Republic*—that the best order or constitution of the state depends upon one's conception of the proper constitution of the soul.

1. Can Reason Rule the Free?

1. CW3.2 62; CW2 xlix; Grace 1985, 116; Fenlon 453ff.
2. Erasmus explains this view of literature in his life of St. Jerome: "Very many of the ancients thought it a pious and dutiful practice to make use of suitable stories, which they invented out of concern for the common weal. Their aim in fact was either to offer precepts for the proper and virtuous conduct of life or to arouse and inflame the minds of laggards to the pursuit of goodness or to give support to the weakness of individuals or to put fear into the wicked, whom neither reason reforms nor love moves" (CWE61 19). Earlier in the same work, Erasmus presented the importance of literature in his own artful way: "So great was the veneration always accorded to literature even by pagans, . . . that they supposed the origins of all the liberal arts should be ascribed to the gods alone as their inventors. . . . Further, [the greatest rulers] had the maxims of great authors inscribed everywhere in marble or bronze and set them up for all men to see; they bought their works at vast expense and had them faithfully and almost religiously copied, enclosed them in chests of cedar wood and rubbed them with cedar oil, then laid them up in their temples" (3).
3. A. C. Cousins presents a particularly good reading of this poem, pp. 48ff.
4. Rebhorn gives a perceptive assessment of the garden imagery used in *Utopia*.
5. For example, one of the major themes in *The Four Last Things* is that "sin is painful and our virtue pleasant" (EW 495). See Donner 1952, 348; Doyle-Davidson 372–73; Rodgers 214–15, 235–37.

6. To grasp the centrality of pride in *Utopia,* consider CW4 243–45, ci; Grace 1989, 277–78; New 76ff; White 1982; Hexter 1952, 73–81.

7. More's preference for the word "fantasy" illustrates how pride involves a movement of both powers of the soul: it signifies rational desire based on a deliberate act of the intellect. See the editor's note on this word at CW12 61/27.

8. Although the Queen knows that man's laws, nature's laws, and God's laws are on her side (CW2 38–39), she never takes any steps to invoke those laws to protect her son, her relatives, or her friends. That More wanted his readers to consider this avenue of defense can be seen in the many references to law throughout this *History*. Consider, for example, the references to due process (CW2 32/4, 33/14, 57/30–58/1), the importance of lawyers (81/25, 45/25), and the central role of law (81/21–22, 70/15, 8/3).

9. In several places More seems to invite his readers to reflect on Edward's personal responsibility. The first appears in the opening sentence, which contains "errors" so glaring as to make any reader knowledgeable of the period stop short. This sentence, however, from a literary point of view, serves the same function as More's title of *Utopia*: both serve to warn the attentive reader of the literary game at play. In this opening sentence of *Richard III,* for example, More claims that King Edward lived fifty-three years; actually he lived only forty—a fact that More tells us later in the same work. The same sentence goes on to say that King Edward died in 1443; actually he died in 1483. These errors stand out all the more vividly when one realizes that the entire *History* covers only four consecutive months (April through July 1483). Most importantly, they draw attention to the cause of the war following Edward's death. If Edward *had* lived to be fifty-three, his children would have been old enough to rule; given that he in fact died thirteen years earlier because of his own wanton living, Edward seems doubly responsible for the civil discord that followed. More could not have made these errors inadvertently. In fact, More simply imitates his classical ancestors in using a standard literary device to warn careful readers that he does not intend to write either a chronological account of Richard's life or a mere listing of known dates and events. He intends to tell the truth, not of the historical accidents of time and place, but of Richard's "essence"—i.e., his nature as a tyrant. As More states early in the work, "the duke's demeanor ministreth in effect all the whole matter whereof this book shall entreat" (CW2 6/8–10).

In short, More's *History of King Richard III* does not claim historical accuracy as understood today (Grace 1977, Dean, Kincaid, Hanham, Grant, CW2 lxxx ff). More intends to relate not the accuracy of individual details but the truth of three lessons which he summarizes at the end of his *History*:

> Which things [leading to the murder of the princes] on every part well pondered, God never gave this world a more notable example

[1] neither in what unsurety stands this worldly welfare,
[2] or what mischief works the proud enterprise of a high heart
[3] or finally, what wretched end ensues such pitiless cruelty.
(CW2 86/21–24)

By calling Richard the most notable *exemplum* God has ever given the world, More again indicates the literary character of his *History*. Furthermore, in setting forth the facts of his *History*, More indicates the reliability of his sources. Some items, he tells us, derive from rumor; other accounts come from what "wise men say" or are "for truth reported"; and still others vary according to the source. All of these qualifications show More's concern for truth-telling, and they also ingeniously convey the impression of secrecy and deceitfulness which so characterized Richard's nature (CW2 xcvi). Early on, More takes care to caution his readers not to jump to conclusions based on insufficient evidence, because "whoso divineth upon conjectures may as well shoot too far as too short" (9/6–7). In contrast to the qualifications made in introducing individual facts or events in his story, however, More unqualifiedly sets forth his judgment about Richard's essential character from the very beginning of his *History*:

> For Richard, Duke of Gloucester, by nature the uncle [of the princes], by office their protector, to their father beholden, to them by oath and allegiance bound, all the bands broken that bind man and man together, without respect of God or the world, unnaturally contrived to bereave them, not only their dignity, but also their lives. (6/2–8)

Throughout his *History,* More never doubts Richard's essential tyranny, and the four months dramatized in More's account simply manifest Richard's tyrannical nature most in act.

After seeing Richard break all the bonds of nature and society to satisfy his beastly appetite for power, More's audience comes to see both the limits to reason's power and the needed guidance offered by laws and by strong, sharp-sighted statesmen.

10. Through both theory and experience, More knew that human beings could be malicious (CW8 514, 539, 1007; CW10 88; CW13 77; CW14 407; Elton 1983, 349; Billingsley 10–11).

2. First, Self-Rule

1. Lehmberg 1956 and Gabrieli give helpful analyses of these omissions and additions.

2. For example, in reference to fear, consider CW11 94 and CW13 13; in reference to love, consider CW13 82–85.

3. More repeats this same point at the end of his life at CW14 217.

4. The beginning of Richard III is another significant instance of supposedly mistaken dates. See chap. 1, n. 9.

5. Francis Zapatka makes a comparative study of Pico's and More's versions of these twelve rules.
6. Significantly, More uses this very phrase later in life when closing letters to his children. See SL 226, 253, and 223.
7. As CW12 309 indicates, Vincent's name means "one who has conquered."

3. Ruling Citizens: What Is Needed?

1. Aristotle expresses this classical and Renaissance commonplace at, for example, *Nicomachean Ethics* 1102a.
2. The word More uses to describe the effect of Christ's irony is *percelluit*, which literally means "knock down" or "hit hard." To defend the use of such verbal force, More also points out similar hard-hitting uses of irony in Scripture: the "pungent" (*salsius*) way that St. Paul ironically "polishes off" (*perstringit*) the Corinthians (CW14 294–95); or the "forceful and biting" irony (*Ironia fortius aut mordatius*) "with which God's prophet ridiculed the prophets of Baal as they called upon the deaf statue of their god" (295). Even God the Father uses sharp irony to "scorn" Adam in an effort to get him to see and admit his grave error in considering himself "a God as we be" (CW13 19). Hosington interprets More's and Christ's tone to be somewhat sarcastic (63–64), but the element of contempt does not seem to be present in either of these cases.
3. Brenda Hosington gives a perceptive analysis both of Christ's use of irony (63–65) and of "sleep" as a metaphor.
4. How thoroughly the medicinal character of language can be misunderstood is manifest in G. R. Elton's complaint that More's "wit, which so enchanted his friends, nearly always had a sharp edge to it: he often, and knowingly, wounded his targets" (1983, 345). Elton interprets this "consistently ambiguous" "front" as hiding "manifest psychological problems" (345). Yet such remarks overlook More's intent to wound in order to heal. This has nothing to do with psychological problems and everything to do with the traditional understanding of rhetoric's nature and power. More learned his technique from Socrates, from the great satirists and comedians of the ancient world, and from Christ.
5. More seemed to assume that the care of the soul was, primarily but not exclusively, the concern of the church. Even in the example given earlier in this chapter about the skilled physician who can treat the vices of the city, More is referring to a priest (SL 4–5). I have not been able to find any clear uses of the statesman-as-physician metaphor in More's writings. Raphael Hythlodaeus uses it (e.g., CW4 101/6, 105/35ff), claiming Plato's authority, but Raphael cannot be said to represent More's own views. At CW6 261–62 (also seen earlier in this chapter) More does compare the judge to the physician, but the comparison hinges upon the many contingent factors each must weigh. Finally, More makes an explicit comparison between his work as chancellor and medicine (e.g., CW8 28/17ff), but it arises in the context of his "duty deeply bounded" to help

prelates in dealing with heresy. More explains that this duty arises "by mine office in virtue of mine oath," not by the nature of the office itself. If this observation is correct, then More differs with Erasmus on this point (compare Erasmus's position, for example, at CWE27 274).

6. More does, of course, use the conventional language of the day in his rhetorical addresses, and he recognizes that the king has a special role in society that must be reverenced. He uses biblical language in at least two important passages referring to the king as ordained and consecrated by God (CW8 595/10–20, CW9 50/31). But these passages are few and they stand in contrast to More's customary practice.

7. Erasmus agrees. See, for example, CWE27 265, 269, 271, 273.

8. One of the greatest examples of such a judge in all of More's writings is Chief Justice Markham (CW15 459; CW 2 70, 143), who resigns his office rather than give approval to his king's tyranny. Twenty years after he wrote *Richard III,* More resigned his office for similar reasons.

9. Of all the kings presented, More does seem to favor humble and courageous David. In general, David does rule well; he makes mistakes, but admits them and tries to make amends.

10. Despite these failures, however, Morton does appear as a ruler generally worthy of imitation. Consider how well he rules the cross-section of English society that is assembled at his court in *Utopia*—an event that takes place later than those in *Richard III*.

11. This poems gives a fairly comprehensive account of issues to be addressed by the statesman: respect for his people's freedom (lines 12–25, 50–53, 86–89), respect for ancient rights and customs (26–29, 102–3), respect for laws (32–33, 96–99, 108–15, 138–42), encouragement of trade (30–33, 100–101), freedom to speak and assemble (42–49), protection of property (36–42), public authority based on virtue and learning (144–49, 104–7, 116–33, 70–96), peace at home (134–37). Throughout, the emphasis in this poem is upon virtue, law, and freedom.

12. This ideal is present in More's literature. I agree with Leonard Dean's position, for example, that More's ideal king can be discerned "by translating More's ironic characterization of Richard" (323).

13. See chapter 8 for an assessment of More's "Letter to Dorp" and his "Letter to a Monk."

14. More indicates his support for just war on several occasions. He argues that

> nature, reason, and God's behest bind first the prince to safeguard his people with the peril of himself . . . and after [God] binds every man to the help and defence of his good and harmless neighbor against the malice and cruelty of the wrongdoer. For as the holy scripture says, . . . "God has given every man charge of his neighbor to keep him from harm of body and soul as much as may lie in his power [Eccl. 17:12]." (CW6 415/1–6; see also 414/33–36)

Only the secular magistrate who has received the "legitimate authority to fight" can, however, use that sword against evildoers (CW14 495, 477–79).

15. Notice, for example, how Raphael uses conscience at CW4 222/23 and 78/8. He makes clear that fear is the ultimate basis for obeying law (CW4 221–23).

4. Literature and the Acquisition of Political Prudence

1. See Klein's commentary on Plato's *Statesman, Theaetetus,* and *Sophist.*

2. As we have seen (p. 18), More reminds us that "by neglecting the figures of speech," people "very often miss the real sense" of what they read (CW14 295–97). This fundamental principle of interpretation is essential when analyzing More's own writings. Any attempt to deal with his writings must take into account the epistemology that lies beneath the literary forms he chose.

As Brendan Bradshaw points out, by ignoring More's Platonic influences, revisionists such as Alistair Fox ignore More's "most characteristic rhetorical devices, adapted from classical antiquity," such as antithesis (540), irony, and dialectic. Yet, throughout his writings, More makes clear his indebtedness to Plato; early biographers such as Stapleton note that he "read especially Plato" (15). Erasmus draws attention to More's special study of Plato, and Harpsfield calls his school a Christian version of Plato's Academy (CWE7 23, Harpsfield 104–5). During his lifetime More was even criticized by one fellow poet for holding that what "the poet ought rather to look to is sense, quarried out of the Socratic texts, than to strain for fine wording" (CW3.2 493). Why did More value Plato and Socrates so highly?

To ponder this question is to ponder the very reason that the Renaissance found such excitement in the rebirth of classical literature—and why, consequently, irony came to mark much of Renaissance literature. As Norman Knox rightly observes, "The central fact about the history of irony in Greek use is its inseparability from Socrates' personality and influence" (3).

The earliest recorded use of the Greek word for "irony" occurs in Plato's *Republic,* where it is used to describe Socrates's characteristic stance of feigned ignorance. Even today irony is often defined by reference to Socrates. Webster, for example, defines it as "a pretense of ignorance and of willingness to learn from another, assumed in order to make the other's false conceptions conspicuous by adroit questioning" (*Webster's Seventh Collegiate Dictionary* 448). Irony thus constitutes a necessary part of Socrates's strategy for engaging willing interlocutors in serious conversation or dialectics.

To appreciate the strategic need for irony that More shared with Socrates, one must first reflect on the difficult philosophic project Socrates undertook: examining another's innermost thoughts and dispositions; indeed, examining his very soul. For such an investigation to take place, Socrates had to induce individuals to reveal themselves freely and honestly. By using irony, he was actually inviting individuals to participate in such self-revelation. Yet Socrates was not investigating the mere opinions of another. First and foremost, he wanted to learn something about the soul of that specific person *through* the particular line of conversation he established. From a literary point of view, Socrates was a master of what we now call dramatic irony. Hence, the attentive reader of the Platonic dialogue needs to be "sharp-sighted," aware of the irony constantly employed whereby the deepest traits of character are revealed through the subtlest actions and lines of conversation.

From this perspective, Douglas Duncan rightly explains the effect of Socrates's and More's irony:

> The challenge of ironic speech is that it forces the hearer to gauge sense and implication by intellectual tact, by a matching of minds with the speaker, taking clues "from the subject-matter or the circumstances" and without relying on the normal guidance of facial expression and tone of voice. (60)

Irony invites dialectical inquiry, and dialectics involves a careful weighing of all factors in an effort to "see" what is behind these figures of speech.

3. Surtz pointed out many years ago that this letter "indirectly discloses . . . the literary principles according to which More writes" *Utopia* (1958, 319).

4. W. J. Barnes's treatment of irony also deserves careful consideration. He argues that "irony is closely associated with contexts involving conflict, confrontation, dialectic, dialogue" (363).

5. The greatest challenge to the poet's wit and yet the greatest source of revelation for the reader is the literary structure or underlying conceit of the work as a whole. A well-devised structure allows perceptive readers to go beyond a simple reading to a dialectical participation designed to reveal the essential characteristics of the subject at hand. Plato calls such a structure an "organic" one.

In certain dialogues and letters (esp. Letter 7), Plato indicates the importance of the organic unity of his writings. In the *Phaedrus,* for example, Socrates speaks of good writing as a carefully ordered, living entity:

> Every discourse must be organized like a living being with a body of its own, as it were, so as not to be headless or footless, but to have a middle and members, composed in fitting relation to each other and to the whole. (264c)

In explaining the meaning and importance of this organic unity, the Platonic scholar Allan Bloom observes:

> Every argument must be interpreted dramatically, for every argument is incomplete in itself and only the context can supply the missing links. And every dramatic detail must be interpreted philosophically, because these details contain the images of the problems which complete the arguments. Separately these two aspects are meaningless; together they are an invitation to the philosophic quest. (Bloom xvi)

Dramatic detail and philosophy constitute, in other words, organic or inseparable parts of the living structure of the Socratic dialogue. As we will see, More creates this same living structure in the *Utopia*.

5. *Utopia 1* and *2*: Dramatizing Competing Philosophies of Life

1. An earlier version of this chapter appeared in *Philosophy and Rhetoric* 23.4 (Winter 1990): 288–306, under the title "The Rhetoric of Opposition in Thomas More's *Utopia*: Giving Form to Competing Philosophies."

2. The views on Morus noted in this paragraph belong to: Sylvester 1968, 296; Altman 87; Schaeffer 18; Skinner 1987, 153; McCutcheon 1983, 52; Elliott 332–33; Wooden 1972, 56. The articles pertaining to Raphael's character are: Rudat 47, 61; Schaeffer 11; Berger 1965, 63; Logan 35; Skinner 1987, 149; Marius 152ff; A. Kinney 1979, 9–10, 23. Another prevalent view is the one articulated in its most classic form by David Bevington, who interprets *Utopia* as "the impartial presentation of two points of view, as a dialogue of the mind with itself" (497); see also A. Kinney 1986, 86 and Grace 1989.

3. What we would call the stereotype or stock character, Erasmus calls the "general type of person"—whether "an old man, a young man, a slave, the head of the house, or a pimp" (CWE24 584).

4. Some references to this important biblical theme are: 1 Cor 1:17–30, Isaiah 29:14, and Ecclesiastes 7:1–7. Erasmus treats this theme extensively in his *Praise of Folly* and his *Enchiridion*. See also Erasmus's "Letter to Dorp" (1515), CWE3 111ff.

5. Germain Marc'hadour gives the significance and a brief history of the puns on More's name in EA 549–57.

6. CW4 48/31n sets forth a brief summary of the scholarly opinion on Raphael's name.

7. That More opposed a decadent form of scholasticism in favor of humanistic scholarship, see Kristeller 1980, 12, as well as More's own letters, especially numbers 15, 60, 75, 83 in SL. Warren Wooden argues that the first of these presents "a vehement indictment of the schoolmen and their methods" (1977a, 31ff). However, More had great respect for the best of the scholastics. For example, he considered Thomas Aquinas "the very flower of theology" (CW8 713/24) and a "most learned and also most holy man" (CW5 355).

8. Compare Raphael's argument with Pico della Mirandola's at EW 369–70.

9. McCutcheon's 1971 article gives an excellent study on More's use of litotes.

10. For the significance of the stage metaphor in More's writings and thought, see Kincaid 377–78, 380, 386.

11. This word was undoubtedly selected for both its literal and metaphoric meanings: "scene" and "public."

12. Sylvester questions the credibility of both Raphael and Morus. He

sees Morus as a naive persona similar to the "Chaucer" in *Canterbury Tales*. I argue, in contrast, that Morus acts quite differently, that he charitably and wisely adapts his rhetoric according to the person with whom he speaks, a hardened and intolerant sophist.

13. Raphael has even longer "conversational" exchanges with Morus. See Schaeffer's comments on Raphael's 464-word and 924-word sentences at 83/31ff and 90/22ff. Schaeffer concludes, "By carrying rhetorical *copia* to these absurd lengths, Raphael is revealed as a burlesque of the humanist" (14).

14. W. Kennedy gives a perceptive analysis of Raphael's manipulative and unreliable manner of speaking (96–100). See also Blaim 9–10; Schaeffer 11–13; Berger 1965, 63–65; Altman 82. Compare these analyses with Logan's statement that "Hythloday is a completely attractive, if completely stock, figure" (33).

15. Raphael's ultimate "proof" consists in a belief very similar to religious faith. After Morus has refuted each of the arguments Raphael uses to justify abstention from political counseling, Raphael appeals to evidence that Morus has never seen. Raphael's ultimate proof is: "If you had seen Utopia . . ."

16. As Wooden explains this same point: "Utopia is Hythloday's universal and, as in the scholastic method, he posits it as true and judges everything else accordingly" (1977a, 37).

17. One could argue that Raphael uses a prophetic rhetoric that is characteristic of the Old Testament prophets or the rhetoric of plain speech. Such rhetoric, however, became associated with the sixteenth-century misanthrope, not the sixteenth-century humanist. For the early humanists, a courtly manner and a pleasing rhetoric formed a part of their way of life. See Seigel; Berger 1982, 279–90. More "spoke respectfully . . . even when addressing those with whom he disagreed" (Byron 75). For evidence of the effectiveness of More's approach, consider how More's "genuine good will, powers of argument, and gentle chiding and ridicule appear to have helped win Dorp back over to Erasmus's side" (Guerlac 158).

18. Neither are actually sailors, but both are known for their ability and willingness to lie. In Lucian's *Philopseudes* Tychiades argues that the lies of Ulysses are not only pardonable but even praiseworthy since Ulysses lies "to win his own life and the return of his companions." In Plato's *Republic* Socrates argues that the "noble lie" is a necessary foundation of the city of speech.

19. Palinurus is a sailor who resists the lies of a god and dies in loyal and heroic service to Aeneas. Cf. Virgil's *Aeneid* 5.837–71.

20. In another literary work, More refers to Martin Luther as "a Ulysses indeed of consummate shrewdness" (CW5 51/6–7). Even Logan, who regards Raphael as a "completely reliable commentator," must admit that "More presumably does not mean us to forget entirely that Ulysses is a notorious liar" (33n).

21. In the early Renaissance, "Ulysses" carried a pejorative connotation, such as Erasmus describes. Later in the Renaissance, the connotation became ambiguous and, in some cases, highly favorable. See Stanford, esp. pp. 137, 299. As Stanford reports, in the medieval and early Renaissance view, Ulysses was a "symbol of sinful desire for forbidden knowledge" (181). By the time of Eliot and Ascham, "Ulysses formerly decried as a hostile treacherous Greek is now built up as a prudent, proto-Protestant, nationalistic gentleman" (299).

22. Compare Morus's response here to More's response to Pico at EW 368–69. See also chap. 2, pp. 66ff above.

23. Many critics have pointed out Raphael's misjudgment here. See Sylvester 1968, 298; Schaeffer 12–13; Fox 1983, 62–63 for examples. Logan also recognized this misperception, but blames More, not Hythlodaeus: "One may, however, feel that it is likelier that More, trying to do too much at once simply lost track of one of the implications of the passage" (47).

24. More expresses similar views at CW12 180/2–13 and CW5 275/31–277/17.

25. Ward Allen gives a partial listing of the gnostic terms, allusions, and symbols which occur throughout *Utopia* (1967, 157, 160–62, 165; 1971, 57). A comparative study with Irenaeus's *Against Heresies* may also prove illuminating. Irenaeus argues extensively against the gnostics in this work, and More may well have been familiar with it through Erasmus. Erasmus published an edition of this book in 1526, but he had read Irenaeus before 1516, the year More wrote *Utopia* (see Erasmus's 1516 letter to Warham, CWE3 252–66). Compare, for example, the Utopians' practice of marking the ears of criminals with Irenaeus's report that "the followers of [the gnostic] Carpocrates . . . had branding marks on the back of the right ear-lobe" (1.25,6).

26. See Peter New's analysis, which also concludes that Raphael Hythlodaeus ultimately "is to be taken as a false ideal" (19).

6. *Utopia 1*: Ciceronian Statesmanship

1. An earlier version of this chapter was presented at the Renaissance Society of America, Harvard University, March 31, 1989, and was subsequently published in *Moreana*, no. 104 (December 1990): 5–26.

2. Allusion plays an important role in More's poetic. He explicitly recognizes the importance of this literary principle in his "Letter to Brixius," where he writes of the poet's obligation to consider context and original meaning when making an allusion (CW3.2 551ff). In that letter, More severely criticizes Brixius, a French poet, for randomly alluding to classical sources without careful selection and control of those sources in terms of their original context and in view of their connotation in a new literary and historical context. Alistair Fox explains well More's artistic ideal:

More typically adumbrates classical and scriptural allusions or echoes within the text of his narrative in order to illuminate the significance of what is taking place.... The effect of such adumbrations is to present the occasions as archetypal. (1978a, 14)

Arthur F. Kinney has also shown that "the patterns in the sources and ideas behind *Utopia*" are a deliberate part of More's artistry, "requiring [the reader's] active interpretation and judgment" while at the same time pointing the way in forming that interpretation (1986, 80, 78).

By alluding to previous great thinkers, More deepens and broadens his own dialectic about the best way of life and the best state of the republic. In doing so, More invites his humanist audience to think through the same issues, considering what was said before in light of the new perspectives which he brings to bear, thus playing upon well-known themes and terms.

3. More chose the active life of the civic humanist years before writing *Utopia*. He had already served in Parliament, was an undersheriff of London, and had one of the largest law practices in England. He writes *Utopia* while representing the king, and he was trade representative of the London merchants on at least two other embassies prior to this one (Guy 1980, 7). See Mermel.

4. For example, Neal Wood maintains that Cicero was "a mediocre philosopher, unoriginal and eclectic" (11). Walter Nicgorski argues for a positive assessment of Cicero's political philosophy in two articles which shed new light on the integrity of Cicero's philosophy and therefore provide an important contribution to Ciceronian scholarship (1978, 1984).

5. *Utopia* 246/2, emphasis added, my translation. The last five words of *Utopia* are "*ciuitatibus optarim uerius quam sperarim.*" Cicero's formulation in *De re publica* 2.30.52 is "*civitatemque optandam magis quam sperandam.*"

6. More did not have access to the full text of *De re publica,* but he knew it through Augustine's *City of God* and through commentaries. The distinction Morus repeats is also significant, since Cicero habitually distinguishes between *optare* and *sperare* throughout his works. He uses *optare* to express a desire for the impossible and *sperare* for the fulfillment of a possible wish. (See James Reid, ed., *Academica of Cicero,* London: MacMillan & Co., 1885, p. 319n.) For example, Cicero uses *optare* in referring to someone who propounds wild theories (*Acad.* 2.121, *Tusc.* 2.30, *De fat.* 20.46, *Verr.* 1.1), while using *sperare* in referring to someone hoping for the possible (*Balbo* 59, *Verr.* 2–1.19, *Milo.* 78; Morus also uses *sperare* in this sense at 40/18). See also Aristotle's *Politics* 1265a 17, 1325b 39, 1288b35–1289a8.

7. Already in 1963, however, R. S. Sylvester put forth an account of More's use of allusion and showed how it operated in *The History of King Richard III* (CW2 lxxx–civ).

8. More, a great student of literature, explicitly recognizes the "imitator's obligation to consider context and historicity" when using and

alluding to classical sources (CW 3.2, 551ff and Epigrams 188–95, but especially no. 193; Corr 218–21; Greene 2, 243–44, 332–33 especially; Sylvester 1977, 468). For a perceptive overview of the Renaissance practice of imitating and alluding to earlier authors, see Pigman 1–32. See also McCutcheon 1985 and notes 2 and 7 above.

9. Cicero's admiration for Socrates and Plato is seen throughout his writings. For example, see *De leg.* 3.2.5, 3.6.14, 3.14.32, and 3.1.1; *Brutus* 12e; *De or.* 3.3.15; *Orator* 3.10.

10. *Academica, De finibus bonorum et malorum, Tusculanae disputationes, De natura deorum, De officiis.*

11. For the importance of pleasure in *Utopia*, see Grace 1989, 279–80; New 32–51; Jones 1971; Surtz 1957a.

12. As Logan explains well, the first step in what he calls the best-commonwealth exercise is explaining the nature of a person and what leads to happiness; determination of the best commonwealth follows (136). By appreciating this progression, one can understand why politics proceeded from ethics for classical and humanist thinkers (Logan 87), despite Logan's ultimate conclusion to the contrary.

13. *Acad.* 1.8.30ff, 2.20.65ff, 2.23.74.

14. At *De off.* 1.27.94, Cicero states that "in everything to discern the truth and to uphold it—that is [decorum]," for "what is proper is morally right, and what is morally right is [decorum] (*nam et, quod decet, honestum est et, quod honestum est, decet*)." Throughout book 3, Cicero insists that *utile* and *honestas* cannot be separated. See 3.34 as an example.

15. Here Cicero shows the ground of his philosophical reasoning. He does not ground his moral theory on a system of logic or of physics as the Epicureans and the Stoics do. His ultimate ground and test is the ability of a way of life to satisfy the full complement of natural inclinations manifest in real, not logical or speculative, human beings. As Nicgorski suggests, Cicero does have an ontological basis for his theory of ethics and politics, a basis similar to Socrates's and Plato's (1984, 575, 561ff, 572–73).

16. Robert Coogan's article "*Nunc Vivo ut Volo*" gives a different interpretation to this phrase, one that appears to follow Petrarch more than Cicero.

17. See Sylvester 1968, 285; John Schaeffer 11–13; Fox 1983, 62–63; Logan 47. Logan points out this inconsistency but attributes it to an oversight of More, who "simply lost touch of one of the implications of the passage."

18. Schaeffer gives a helpful analysis of the irony of Morus's response, p. 13.

19. A. Kinney lists many of Raphael's factual errors and internal inconsistencies in 1986, 62ff and 82ff.

20. See *De off.* 3.22.86 as well as all of book 3, which examines the relationship of *utile* and *honestas*.

21. Cicero also holds that, "although it was by Nature's guidance that men were drawn together into communities, it was in the hope of safe-

guarding their possessions that they sought the protection of cities" (*De off.* 2.21.73).

22. Compare this assessment with Raphael's statement that "the whole island is like a single family," *Utopia* 149/3–4.

23. Compare *Politics* 1261b 33–39 and *Utopia* 107/9–10.

24. *Politics* 1261a 10–15; *Utopia* 107/10–11,13.

25. Morus does not use this argument directly, but since pleasure and the lack of true benevolence constitute the principal bases of Hythlodaeus's utopian society, More certainly wants his readers to reflect upon its implications.

26. Ward Allen gives a thorough and, in my view, unrefuted analysis of the literary construction and tone of this passage in his 1976 article, pp. 108–18. See Hexter's opposing view, of 1975.

27. The words in brackets replace the Yale translation: "in the estimation of the common people." For the correction, see Skinner 1987, 153n.

28. Wood 105–15. Wood claims that Cicero "is the first major thinker to give such emphasis to the notion of private property and to make it a central component of his structure of social and political ideas" (105).

29. Consider, for example, Utopia's prohibition against crying for departed loved ones (223/36). Cicero outlaws excessive mourning of the dead (*De leg.* 2.23.59–24.60), but he recognizes and values the bonds that characterize loved ones. Such bonds are never mentioned in Raphael's account of Utopia; Raphael himself seems to have no close bonds with any of the people he mentions. In speaking of his own companions who died while returning from Utopia, for example, Raphael simply says that they "succumbed to fate" (219/12).

The many cases of capital punishment should also surprise anyone who recalls Raphael's condemnation of state executions as direct violation of biblical injunctions (73/22–36). He says nothing, however, against the many instances of capital punishment in Utopia—for speaking of political matters outside the senate or the public assembly (125/1–2), for rebellion (191/34–36), or . . . whenever the senate decides (191/22ff). Yet also disturbing are the extraordinarily severe punishments for such "crimes" as premarital sex offenses (187/27–38, 193/3–8). What is the point of a policy that seems to foster correct action at any cost rather than the development of virtue that comes from free choice and hence from mistakes? Granting that these offenses should be discouraged, should not a seasoned statesman expect young lovers occasionally to fall, given the frailty of human nature and the strength of erotic ties? Moral frailty and eroticism, whether sexual or intellectual, however, have no place in Utopia. Neither does the family as More knew and cherished it.

30. As Cicero recognized, true intellectual virtue cannot be fostered where people are forced to believe propositions about God and the universe that have left philosophers in disagreement throughout the centuries (*Acad.* 2.20–48).

31. The *Utopia* also seems to invite a serious reconsideration of especially Aristotle's understanding of these matters (White 1976) as well as Plato's (see Steintrager, Gueguen 1978, Nendza, and Corrigan).

7. *Utopia 2*: Augustinian Realist

1. This chapter originally appeared in *Renaissance* 44.2 (Winter 1992): 115–35.

2. See, for example, the introduction to CW4, where Edward Surtz states that it is "difficult to gauge the Augustinian influence" on *Utopia* and that "study of the influence of *The City of God* upon the *Utopia* is much to be desired" (clxvi).

3. George Logan observes that "[s]ince More was obviously interested in Augustine's *City of God,* one might expect the Utopian construct to bear the imprint of that work." Yet Logan concludes, "In fact, the connections are neither numerous nor specific" (192n). Alistair Fox, whose book supposedly focuses upon More's Augustinian view of providence and history, also finds no direct influence of Augustine within *Utopia.* Martin Raitiere did write an article in 1973 on "More's *Utopia* and the *City of God,*" yet Raitiere concludes that "More got from Augustine no particular social or political doctrine . . . , but rather a *feeling* for the inevitable mingling of the good and bad in any social or legal order" (164, emphasis added). In this article, Raitiere identifies too readily the characters of *Utopia* with the author.

4. J. B. Trapp maintains that "throughout his career [More] cites and quotes Augustine more fully and frequently than any other author, either directly or via the gloss" (CW9 320). See also R. C. Marius in EA where he maintains that Augustine was "More's favorite saint and Father" (417).

5. All quotations are from the Modern Library edition of *The City of God,* trans. Marcus Dods (New York: Modern Library, 1950).

6. Paul O. Kristeller in "Thomas More as Renaissance Humanist" recognizes *Utopia* as dealing with "the major questions which occupied the center of traditional philosophy" (9) and as linked "with such ancient authors as Plato, Cicero, and Lucian, and also with a large body of humanist literature from the fifteenth and sixteenth century" (7).

7. In Erasmus's letter to Froben, Erasmus states that "*tot tantisque regni negociis distrahitur, ut mireris esse OCIUM vel cognitandi de libris*" (CW4 2/16–17, emphasis added). See also Budé 4/21–22,24; Desmarais 26/17–18; Busleyden 32/15–16.

8. Consider what Augustine says at 19.25: "Virtues . . . spoiled by the puff of pride . . . must be reckoned as vices."

9. It is important to note that this pleasure derived from the contemplation of truth is presented as simply one pleasure among many, not the highest.

10. For Plato, the best way of life is ordered to the activity of philosophic contemplation, an activity possible for very few. From Plato's per-

Augustinian Realist 231

spective, therefore, true virtue and true happiness can be attained only by the philosopher. This conception of the best life, which excludes the participation of most persons, poses grave problems for the city. If contemplation is not open to most people, how can it be said to guide human activity? Furthermore, what would induce the philosophically inclined to give up the peace and joy of solitary contemplation to become immersed in the endless squabbles and wars over money and property?

11. See Ward Allen 1967, 160. Compare, for example, CW4 92/29, 120/28, 218/18, 226/18, 232/3, and 232/12.

12. All the uses of *servitus* in *Utopia* have negative connotations. In each case, *servitus* is associated with undesirable slavery to a person or with the worst of punishments. See 54/26, 78/6,24, 134/18, 146/9, 156/24, 184/17, 190/8,20, 192/2, 200/8,25, 202/12, 214/14, 220/7.

13. For the significant difference between *utilitas* (the useful) and *honestas* (the morally right), see Logan 179, 51, 52n, as well as *City of God* 2.21.

14. Once a month for two consecutive days, the Utopians assemble for civil worship. This infrequency of worship would appear strange to More's fellow Christian humanists, who would be familiar with Augustine's admonition to pray always. More himself habitually practiced contemplative prayer, attended Mass, read Scripture, and said Our Lady's Psalter each day.

15. Although some may judge 223/7-8 to be ambiguous regarding the Utopians' theoretical position on free will, as a matter of practice, the Utopians simply do not acknowledge the Christian understanding of free will. And how could they? According to Augustine (see *On Free Choice of the Will*), it is known only through revelation. However, Raphael *should* recognize the centrality of this concept in evaluating the Utopians' philosophy and political institutions. By accepting private property as the root of all pride and of all social ills and by accepting the supremacy of a civil religion that modifies Christianity to its own designs, Raphael himself must deny the Christian doctrine of free will.

16. New identifies this claim as a "clearly fantastic element of Utopia" (73).

17. Logan notes this discrepancy between Utopian and Augustinian views, but sees no particular significance in it (250n).

18. One might object that the two sects in Utopia, the *haereses*, seem motivated by the love of God. Yet neither Raphael nor the Utopian priests practice or advocate this type of life. We are told that these two ascetic sects base themselves on religion, not reason—a dichotomy which Raphael often points out in his report on religion (CW4 227/17-23, for example). Considered holier, but not saner, these ascetics would never try to defend their way of life on the basis of reason. Indeed, given the introductory comments on Utopian religions (217/6-35) and the special name of these sects (*haereses*), one could imply that Raphael and his Utopian priests consider these sects as heresies, tolerated but not promoted.

After all, "Buthrescae" alludes to the superstitious cult of Bythus (227/24), and as Raphael explains: the Utopians gradually "are all beginning to depart from this medley of superstitions and are coming to unite in that one religion which seems to surpass the rest in *reasonableness*" (217/26–29, emphasis added) and is "by far the wiser" of religions.

19. Peter New draws attention to this passage (60ff). For other assessments of war in Utopia, see CW4 xlviii–lix, Steintrager 360–61, and Avineri.

20. Compare this action with Aristotle's warnings in the *Nicomachean Ethics*: "For justice exists only between men whose mutual relations are governed by law" (1133a 25); "We do not allow man to rule, but rational principle, because a man behaves then in his own interests and becomes a tyrant" (1133a 35). In light of these statements, how are we to evaluate the role of the Utopian priests?

8. The Limits of Reason and the Need for Law

1. More is not open and direct about accusing Dorp of slander, but a close reading of More's reply reveals that he believed parts of Dorp's letter were slanderous indeed. As More pointed out to Dorp, slander is the use of "cutting words" with the intention of destroying another (see CW15 112/22–24). That More minimized the potential harm to Erasmus could well be the reason that Erasmus showed little enthusiasm for More's letter (White 1987, 499–501). Nonetheless, More's rhetorical strategy achieved what More intended: he caused Dorp to change his mind and to alter his behavior (SL 112–13).

2. Although Erasmus understood these limits, he did not always live up to them. In writing *Julius Excluded,* for example, he attacks Pope Julius by name, although Erasmus never admitted to writing this personal attack.

3. Significantly, More points out that "there are limits even in self-defence" (CWE7 239/85). These limits he seems to respect.

4. For example, More wrote letters to Margaret after each of his major interrogations. They served as a public record of what occurred. He also made sure that he had a written account of what transpired when he met with the Nun of Kent. See SL 216–23, 234–39, 245–53, 196–201.

5. More recognized that he faced dangers to his own reputation by taking on Luther in the forceful way he did (CW5 11). In response to duty, however, he reluctantly took up the charge. By appealing to anger, Luther was easily stirring up hatred against institutions that were undeniably flawed, but that had been for centuries, respected and protected by law. More never denied that both church and state needed reform; he did deny that railing instead of reasoning was the way to achieve it.

9. Reform over Revolution: In Defense of Free Will and a United Christendom

1. Cromwell and Henry played upon the same greed when they decided to dissolve the monasteries in England.

10. The Limits of Government and the Domain of Conscience

1. Some recent biographers like G. R. Elton (1974b, 129ff) deny the clear evidence from Erasmus and Giustinian that More became a counselor to Henry in 1518 (CWE5 44, 410; CSPV 2.1072, dated September 18, 1518, where Giustinian writes to the Doge that More is "newly made counselor"). Oddly enough, Elton himself admits that More showed his "wider reluctance to enter the king's service" in 1516 by refusing a handsome annuity for his services on the embassy of 1515 (1974a, 131). Before his next embassy of August 1517, More had many reasons to do so again. Only *after* that embassy did Wolsey reveal his plan to pursue a foreign policy of peace (Scarisbrick 71).

In considering More's motive for joining Henry's court, the reconstructionists make much of Ammonio's remark of 1516 that "none bids my lord of York [Wolsey] good morrow earlier than" More. Even John Guy interprets this to mean that More was working to secure a political position, since "royal service was a natural avenue to advancement, the only one that offered unlimited scope" (1980, 7–8). This interpretation, however, ignores another telling remark made by Ammonio about More five years earlier (CWE2 200). Already in 1511, More's business brought him into frequent contact with the Lord Chancellor; as Ammonio commented in 1511, "[F]or never a day passes but [More] either sees the archbishop or addresses him" (CWE2 220/75–76). Are we to conclude that he was vying for a political position even then? If so, why did More not accept the King's offer in 1516?

2. More expressed this view in such early epigrams as numbers 121 and 198 and in his *History of King Richard III* (CW15 321).

3. As Gogan points out, More showed no interest in seeing the Pope's "temporal power extended and even upheld the limits imposed on his pastoral jurisdiction by the statute of *praemunire*" (262).

4. That Warham planned to oppose Henry in Thomas Becket style is clear from the speech he prepared before dying (LP 5.245, reprinted in Moyes). Warham probably knew that his only recourse was to appeal directly to the English populace at the price of his life, as Becket had done so effectively.

5. C. S. Lewis considered More's *Dialogue Concerning Heresies* to be a "great Platonic dialogue: perhaps the best specimen of that form ever produced in English" (172).

6. To put this figure in perspective, one can consider that More was among the best-paid lawyers of London at 400 pounds a year and made

850 pounds a year at the height of his professional career as Lord Chancellor of England.

Conclusion

1. Cicero speaks of the importance of humor in oratory (*De oratore* 2.216–89), but for him, it is an occasional diversion and not a characteristic or pervasive element.

2. Lucian and Plutarch are favorites of the Utopians, and of More. In his life of Lycurgus, Plutarch gives a striking illustration of how "jesting and laughter" make "the path to instruction and correction easy and natural" (*Lycurgus* 25.2, 12.4). That More reflected deeply on the lives of Lycurgus, Solon, Agis, Cleomenes, and the Gracchi brothers can be seen by the many allusions to them in *Utopia*. More would also have been aware that Aristotle praised Solon of Athens and Lycurgus of Sparta for having established not only laws but an entire way of life (*Politics* 1273b 30ff).

More refers explicitly to Aquinas's treatment of wit at CW12 82/19. There More defends the use of humor by saying that "a merry tale with a friend refreshes a man much and without harm lightens the mind and amends the courage and his stomach so that it seems but well done to take such recreation. And Solomon says I believe that men should in heaviness give the sorry man wine to make him forget his sorrow. And Saint Thomas says that the proper pleasant talking which is called *eutrapelia* is a good virtue, serving to refresh the mind and make it quick and lusty to labor and study again where continual fatigue would make it dull and deadly."

Although no major study has treated More's use of Chaucer, Alistair Fox indicates the depth of More's knowledge in his 1978b article.

A good way to get an idea of More's many allusions to the other authors cited here is to refer to the index of *The Complete Works of St. Thomas More*.

3. Part of this paragraph and a few that follow are from my article "The Political Philosophy of Sir Thomas More."

4. In CW12 74/7–9 More alludes to this passage of the *Nicomachean Ethics* (1105a). He also explains this tendency to be guided by pleasure rather than true good at EW 463. This passage of Aristotle should be kept in mind when analyzing and weighing the claims for pleasure made in *Utopia* by Raphael Hythlodaeus.

5. For example, in his letter on education, More urges that love of good advice be cultivated in his children while love of praise be rooted out (SL 106).

6. The whole of More's *Dialogue of Comfort* dramatizes the need for good counsel, as does the first book of *Utopia*. Erasmus also stresses the importance of good counsel in the first part of his *Education of a Christian Prince* (CWE27).

7. John of Salisbury made this analogy famous several centuries earlier (*Policraticus* 67, xxi).

8. Damian Grace's article on More's epigrams gives a profound analysis of the political philosophy which informs them.

9. Refer to chap. 3, n. 5.

10. It is surprising that few have even mentioned More's place in political thought as the first to give a public defense and appeal for political free speech. See chap. 3, pp. 65–66; and chap. 10, p. 188.

11. As Damian Grace points out, this view of authority expresses "the principle which Sir John Fortescue found to be distinctive of English rule, that 'in the body politic the will of the people is the source of life,' for the king of England 'rules his people not only regally but also politically'" (Grace 1985, 119–20, quoting Fortescue 31, 79).

12. Compare CW3.2, no. 198 with Aristotle's *Politics,* esp. 1286a 25ff.

13. In the Latin version of his *Richard III,* More says unambiguously that Parliament's "authority in England is supreme and absolute" (CW15 321, CW2 6/14). More also speaks positively of representation at CW8 146. The clearest and most extended exposition of his views is CW3.2, no. 198.

14. This is my title for the fourth and last great Socratic dialogue More wrote with his daughter Margaret Roper. It appears as "Letter 206: Margaret Roper to Alice Alington" (Corr 514–32), written less than one year before More's death. Some claim that this dialogue was written by his daughter Margaret, but internal evidence indicates that it is at least a joint endeavor. In this short dialogue, More speaks of conscience over forty times.

15. Nicgorski 1991, especially 238 and n.28. As Seigel points out, "Cicero gave more attention than perhaps any other classical writer to the question of the relationship between rhetoric and philosophy" (5)—and between rhetoric and statesmanship.

16. Literature, as More broadly conceived it, is the first. See the introduction and chap. 1 above.

17. Chapters 8–10 above give some indication of his considerable rhetorical skill.

18. Seigel gives a helpful summary of Plato's and Aristotle's differences with Cicero on pp. 9–16. Cicero himself recognized the dangers of rhetoric divorced from philosophy: "[E]loquence without wisdom is generally highly disadvantageous and is never helpful [for the good of the state]" (*De inventione* 1.1).

19. To appreciate the difficulties involved in working outside the law, consider Plutarch's account of Tiberius Gracchus, especially 11.

20. More would have disagreed with Fortescue's exaggerated statement: "Human laws are none other than rules by which perfect justice is manifested" (11).

21. Plutarch's *Solon,* 5.2–3. More refers to this famous tale at CW12 225. In his *History of King Richard III,* as we have seen, More made the point that Richard came to power "not by war, but by law" (CW2 6).

22. Although this famous line from Robert Bolt's play is not a direct quote from More, it does respect the depth and even the metaphors of More's position (66). Consider CW12 205/14–17, CW14 265, SL 233, CW4 99/34–35.

23. EW 381–85 is an extended exhortation to vigilance, while *The Life of John Picus* (EW 358, 361–62 esp.) and *Richard III* vividly dramatize the tragic results of small negligences. As we have seen, Pico's neglect seems to have led to his untimely death through poisoning, and in *Richard III*, the nobles' and clergymen's neglect led to tyranny and the demise of two young princes.

24. Notice the many references to diligence and negligence at CW13 21–22. More theorizes that, to help Adam and Eve and their descendants govern themselves, God arranged their lives whereby they would be aided by both fear and love to be more diligent in the future (CW13 46–47).

25. CW13 22/4–5. More explicitly faults both civil and ecclesiastical leaders on this account. For his criticism against the bishops of England see CW9 53, 145. More elaborates upon his model of diligence at CW13 83/4ff and 97/5ff especially.

26. As mentioned in n. 24 of the Introduction, More used literature or "good letters" to include history and philosophy as well as what we generally consider as literature. The Bible was also included as sacred literature.

27. CW14 217/5–6.

28. In his last work, More refers lyrically to the "brief power of darkness" as but "an instant of time always caught between a past that is gone and a future that has not arrived" (CW14 557).

29. CW7 135/21–22.

30. More used this paradox to comfort and instruct his daughter about his execution (SL 250, 237; Corr 530/589–90). More repeated the same idea at CW12 248/22–25 and Corr 190/739. In the collection of scriptural quotes that More compiled for personal reflection at the end of his life, this quotation was included: "Who is there to harm you if you are zealous for what is good? But even if you suffer anything for the sake of justice, blessed are you" (1 Peter 3:13–14, CW14 661).

Works Cited

NOTE: Abbreviations used in this list are the same as those used in in-text citations and notes, and these may be found in Abbreviations list on page viii.

Adams, Robert P. *The Better Part of Valor: More, Erasmus, Colet, and Vives, on Humanism, War, and Peace, 1496–1535*. Seattle: U of Washington P, 1962.
Allen, Ward. 1967. "Speculations on Thomas More's Use of Hesychius." *Philological Quarterly* 46.2 (April 1967): 156–66.
———. 1971. "Hythloday and the Root of All Evil." *Moreana*, nos. 31–32 (November 1971): 51–59.
———. 1976. "The Tone of More's Farewell to *Utopia*: A Reply to J. H. Hexter." *Moreana*, no. 51 (September 1976): 108–18.
Altman, Joel. *The Tudor Play of Mind: Rhetorical Inquiry and the Development of Elizabethan Drama*. Berkeley: U of California P, 1978.
Aristotle. *The Basic Works of Aristotle*. Ed. Richard McKeon. New York: Random House, 1941.
Augustine. *The City of God*. Trans. Marcus Dods. New York: Modern Library, 1950.
Avineri, Schlomo. "War and Slavery in More's *Utopia*." *International Review of Social History* 7 (1962): 260–90.
Barnes, W. J. "Irony and the English Apprehension of Renewal." *Queen's Quarterly* 73 (1966): 357–76.
Baron, Hans. *In Search of Florentine Civic Humanism*. 2 vols. Princeton, NJ: Princeton UP, 1988.
Berger, Harry, Jr. 1965. "The Renaissance Imagination: Second World and Green World." *Centennial Review* 9 (1965): 36–77.
———. 1982. "Utopian Folly: Erasmus and More on the Perils of Misanthropy." *ELR* 12.3 (Fall 1982): 271–90.
Bevington, David M. "The Dialogue in *Utopia*: Two Sides to the Question." *Studies in Philology* 58 (1961): 496–509.
Billingsley, Dale. "The Messenger and the Reader in Thomas More's *Dia-*

logue Concerning Heresies." *Studies in English Literature* 24.1 (Winter 1984): 5–22.

Blaim, Arthur. "More's *Utopia*: Persuasion or Polyphony?" *Moreana*, no. 73 (March 1982): 5–19.

Bloom, Allan, trans. *The Republic of Plato*. New York: Basic Books, 1968.

Bolt, Robert. *A Man for All Seasons*. New York: Random House, 1962.

Boyle, Marjarie O'Rourke. *Rhetoric and Reform: Erasmus' Civil Dispute with Luther*. Cambridge, MA: Harvard UP, 1983.

Bradshaw, Brendan. "The Controversial Sir Thomas More." *Journal of Ecclesiastical History* 36 (1985): 535–69.

Branham, R. Bracht. "Utopian Laughter: Lucian and Thomas More." *Moreana*, no. 86 (July 1985): 23–43.

Brooke, Z. N. "Pope Gregory VII's Demand for Fealty from William the Conqueror." *English Historical Review* 26.102 (April 1911): 225–38.

Burkitt, Francis C. *Church and Gnosis: A Study of Christian Thought and Speculation in the Second Century*. Cambridge, Eng.: Cambridge UP, 1932.

Byron, Brian. *Loyalty in the Spirituality of St. Thomas More*. Nieuwkoop, Neth.: B. de Graaf, 1972.

Carlyle, R. W. and A. J. *History of Medieval Political Theory in the West*. Vol. 6. London: William Blackwood and Sons, Ltd., 1930.

Caspari, Fritz. *Humanism and the Social Order in Tudor England*. Chicago: U of Chicago P, 1954.

Cavendish, George. *The Life and Death of Cardinal Wolsey*. In *Two Early Tudor Lives*. Ed. Richard S. Sylvester and Davis P. Harding. New Haven, CT: Yale UP, 1962.

Chambers, Richard W. *Thomas More*. London: Jonathan Cape, 1935.

Cicero. *Academica*. Trans. H. Rackham. Loeb Classical Library [LCL], 1933.

———. *Brutus*. Trans. G. L. Hendrickson. LCL, 1952.

———. *De amicitia*. Trans. W. Falconer. LCL, 1923.

———. *De fato*. In vol. 2 with *De oratore*. LCL, 1942.

———. *De finibus*. Trans. H. Rackham. LCL, 1931.

———. *De inventione*. Trans. H. M. Hubbell. LCL, 1949.

———. *De legibus*. Trans. C. W. Keyes. LCL, 1928.

———. *De natura deorum*. Trans. H. Rackham. LCL, 1933.

———. *De officiis*. Trans. Walter Miller. LCL, 1913.

———. *De oratore*. Trans. E. W. Sutton and H. Rackham. 2 vols. LCL, 1942.

———. *De re publica*. Trans. C. W. Keyes. LCL, 1928.

———. *Orator*. Trans. H. M. Hubbell. LCL, 1952.

———. "Pro Balbo." In vol. 2 of *The Speeches*. Trans. R. Gardner. LCL, 1958.

———. "Pro T. Annio Milone." In vol. 1 of *The Speeches*. Trans. N. H. Watts. LCL, 1953.

———. *Tusculan Disputations*. Trans. J. E. King. LCL, 1945.
———. *Verrine Orations*. Trans. L. H. G. Greenwood. 2 vols. LCL, 1948.
———. *Works*. Loeb Classical Library (LCL). 28 vols.
Coogan, Robert. "*Nunc Vivo ut Volo*." *Moreana*, no. 31 (November 1971): 29–45.
Corrigan, Kevin. "The Function of the Ideal in Plato's *Republic* and St. Thomas More's *Utopia*." *Moreana*, no. 104 (December 1990): 27–49.
Cousins, A. C. "St. Thomas More as English Poet." *Thomas More: Essays on the Icon*: 43–52. Ed. Damian Grace and Brian Byron. Melbourne, Australia: Dove Communications, 1980.
Crosset, John. "More and Seneca." *Philological Quarterly* 40 (1961): 577–80.
Cumming, Robert D. *Human Nature and History*. 2 vols. Chicago: U of Chicago P, 1969.
David, J. C. "More, Morton, and the Politics of Accommodation." *Journal of British Studies* 9 (1970): 27–49.
Davis, Walter R. "Thomas More's *Utopia* as Fiction." *Centennial Review* (1980): 249–68.
Dean, Leonard F. "Literary Problems in More's *Richard III*." EA: 315–25.
Derrett, J. Duncan. "Two Dicta of More's and a Correction." *Moreana*, no. 8 (November 1965): 67–72.
Donner, H. W. 1945. *Introduction to Utopia*. London: Sidgwick & Jackson, Ltd., 1945.
———. 1952. "St. Thomas More's *Treatise on the Four Last Things* and the Gothicism of the Trans-Alpine Renaissance." EA: 343–55. Originally published in *English Miscellany* 3 (1952): 25–48.
Dorsch, T. S. "Sir Thomas More and Lucian: An Interpretation of *Utopia*." *Archiv für das Studium der Neueren Sprachen und Literaturen* 203 (1966–67): 345–63. Reprinted in part in *Twentieth Century Interpretations of Utopia*: 88–99. Ed. William Nelson. Englewood Cliffs, NJ: Prentice-Hall, 1968.
Doyle-Davidson, W. A. G. "The Earlier English Works of Sir Thomas More." In EA: 356–74. Originally published in *English Studies* 17 (1935): 49–70.
Duncan, Douglas. *Ben Jonson and the Lucianic Tradition*. Cambridge, Eng.: Cambridge UP, 1979.
Elliott, Robert C. "The Shape of Utopia." *ELH* 30 (1963): 317–34.
Elton, G. R. 1974a. "Thomas More, Councillor (1517–1529)." *Studies in Tudor and Stuart Politics and Government: Papers & Reviews 1946–72*. Vol. 1: 129–54. Cambridge, Eng.: Cambridge UP, 1974. Originally published in *St. Thomas More: Action and Contemplation*: 86–122. Ed. Richard S. Sylvester. New Haven, CT: Yale UP, 1972.
———. 1974b. "Sir Thomas More and the Opposition to Henry VIII." *Moreana*, nos. 15–16 (November 1967): 285–303. Reprinted in *Studies in*

Tudor and Stuart Politics and Government: Papers & Reviews 1946–72. Vol. 1: 155–72. Cambridge, Eng.: Cambridge UP, 1974.

———. 1977. *Reform and Reformation 1509–1558*. Cambridge, MA: Harvard UP, 1977.

———. 1983. "The Real Thomas More." *Studies in Tudor and Stuart Politics and Government*. Vol. 3: 344–55. Cambridge, Eng.: Cambridge UP, 1983.

Erasmus, Desiderius. *Ciceronianus*. Trans. Izora Scott. In *Controversies over the Imitation of Cicero*. Contributions to Education, No. 35. New York: Teachers College, Columbia U, 1910.

———. *The Collected Works of Erasmus* [CWE]. Ed. Craig R. Thompson. Toronto: U of Toronto P, 1974.

———. *Epistles of Erasmus* [EE, Nichols]. 3 vols. Trans. Francis Nichols. New York: Russell and Russell, 1962.

———. *Erasmi epistolae* [EE]. Ed. P. S. Allen et al. 12 vols. Oxford, Eng.: Oxford UP, 1906–55.

———. *Erasmus and His Age: Selected Letters* [EE, Hillerbrand]. Ed. Hans Hillerbrand. Trans. Marcus A. Haworth, S.J. New York: Harper and Row, 1970.

Fenlon, Dermot. "Thomas More and Tyranny." *Journal of Ecclesiastical History* 32.4 (October 1981): 453–76.

Fleisher, Martin. *Radical Reform and Political Persuasion in the Life and Writings of Thomas More*. Geneva: Librairie Droz, 1973.

Fortescue, Sir John. *De Laudibus Legum Anglie*. Ed. and trans. Stanley B. Chrines. Cambridge, Eng.: Cambridge UP, 1949.

Fortin, Ernest L. *Political Idealism and Christianity in the Thought of St. Augustine*. Villanova, PA: Augustinian Institute, Villanova U, 1972.

Fowler, H. W. *H. W. Fowler's Dictionary of Modern English Usages*. Oxford, Eng.: Clarendon P, 1954.

Fox, Alistair. 1975. "Thomas More's Controversial Writings and His View of the Renaissance." *Parergon* 11 (1975): 41–48.

———. 1978a. "Richard III's Pauline Oath." *Moreana*, no. 57 (March 1978): 13–23.

———. 1978b. "Thomas More's *Dialogue* and the *Book of the Tales of Caunterbury*: 'Good Mother Wit' and Creative Imitation." *Familiar Colloquy: Essays Presented to Arthur Edward Barker*: 15–24. Ed. Patricia Bruckmann. Ottawa, Ont.: Oberon P, 1978.

———. 1983. *Thomas More: History and Providence*. New Haven, CT: Yale UP, 1983.

Fox, Alistair, and John Guy. *Reassessing the Henrician Age: Humanism, Politics, and Reform, 1500–1550*. Oxford, Eng.: Basil Blackwell, 1986.

Foxe, John. *Acts and Monuments of John Foxe*. New York: AMS Press, 1965.

Gabrieli, Vittorio. "Giovanni Pico and Thomas More." *Moreana*, no. 15 (November 1967): 43–57.

Gogan, Brian. *The Common Corps of Christendom: Ecclesiological Themes in the Writings of Sir Thomas More*. Leiden, Neth.: E. J. Brill, 1982.

Grace, Damian. 1977. "On Interpreting St. Thomas More's *History of King Richard III.*" *European History and Its Historians*: 11–22. Ed. Frank McGregor and Nicholas Wright. Adelaide, S. Australia: Adelaide U Union P, 1977.
———. 1985. "Thomas More's *Epigrammata*: Political Theory in a Poetic Idiom." *Parergon* N.S. 3 (1985): 115–29.
———. 1988. "Subjects or Citizens? *Populi* and *cives* in More's *Epigrammata*." *Moreana*, no. 97 (March 1988): 133–36.
———. 1989. "*Utopia*: A Dialectical Interpretation." *Moreana*, no. 100 (1989): 273–302.
Grant, Patrick. "Thomas More's *Richard III*: Moral Narration and Humanist Method." *Renaissance and Reformation* 7 (August 1983): 157–72.
Great Britain. Public Records Office. *Calendar of State Papers, Spanish* [CSPS]. London: Longmans and Co., 1866.
———. *Calendar of State Papers, Venetian* [CSPV]. London: Longmans and Co., 1871.
———. *Letters and Papers of Henry VIII* [LP]. Ed. J. S. Brewer and James Gairdner. London: Longmans and Co., 1882.
Greenblatt, Stephen. *Renaissance Self-Fashioning: More to Shakespeare*. Chicago: U of Chicago P, 1980.
Greene, Thomas. *The Light of Troy: Imitation and Discovery in Renaissance Poetry*. New Haven, CT: Yale UP, 1982.
Greg, W. W., ed. *The Book of Sir Thomas More*. Malone Society Reprints. Oxford, Eng.: Oxford UP, 1911.
Gueguen, John A. 1978. "Reading More's *Utopia* as a Criticism of Plato." *Quintcentennial Essays*: 43–54. Ed. Michael Moore. Boone, NC: Albion, 1978.
———. 1983. "Why Is There No University in *Utopia*?" *Moreana*, no. 77 (February 1983): 31–34.
Guerlac, Rita. *Juan Luis Vives against the Pseudodialecticians*. Reidel, 1979.
Guy, John. 1980. *The Public Career of Sir Thomas More*. New Haven, CT: Yale UP, 1980.
———. 1988. *Tudor England*. Oxford, Eng.: Oxford UP, 1988.
Gwyn, Peter. *The King's Cardinal: The Rise and Fall of Thomas Wolsey*. London: Barrie & Jenkins, 1990.
Hall, Edward. *Lives of the Kings: Henry VIII*. 2 vols. London: T. C. and E. C. Jack, 1904.
Hanham, Alison. *Richard III and the Early Historians, 1483–1535*. Oxford, Eng.: Clarendon P, 1975.
Hardison, O. B., Jr. "The Orator and the Poet: The Dilemma of Humanist Literature." *Journal of Medieval and Renaissance Studies* 1 (1971): 33–44.
Harpsfield, Nicholas. *Lives of Saint Thomas More*. Ed. E. E. Reynolds. New York: Everyman's Library, 1963.
Hastings, Margaret. "Sir Thomas More: Maker of English Law?" In EA 104–18.

Hexter, J. H. 1952. *More's* Utopia: *The Biography of an Idea*. Princeton, NJ: Princeton UP, 1952.
———. 1965. "*Utopia* and Its Historical Milieu." CW4 xxiii–cxxiv.
———. 1975. "Intention, Words, and Meaning: The Case of More's *Utopia*." *New Literary History* 6 (1975): 529–41.
Horace. *Satires, Epistles and Ars Poetica*. Trans. H. Rushton Fairclough. London: William Heinemann, 1926.
Hosington, Brenda. "*Quid dormitis?*: More's Use of Sleep as a Motif in *De Tristitia*." *Moreana*, no. 100 (1989): 55–69.
Hughes, Philip, ed. *Saint John Fisher: The Earliest English Life*. London: Burns, Oates & Washbourne, Ltd., 1935.
Irenaeus. *Writings of Irenaeus*. 2 vols. Trans. Rev. Alexander Roberts and Rev. W. Rambaut. London: Hamilton & Co., 1869.
John of Salisbury. *Policraticus*. Ed. and trans. Cary J. Nederman. Cambridge, Eng.: Cambridge UP, 1990.
Jones, Judith P. 1971. "The *Philebus* and the *Philosophy of Pleasure* in Thomas More's *Utopia*." *Moreana*, nos. 31–32 (November 1971): 61–69.
———. 1979. *Thomas More*. Twayne's English Authors Series, 247. Boston: Twayne Publishers, 1979.
Jonson, Ben. *Ben Jonson*. 11 vols. Ed. C. H. Herford and Percy Simpson. Oxford, Eng.: Clarendon P, 1925.
Kelly, Michael. "The Submission of the Clergy." *Transactions of the Royal Historical Society, Fifth Series* 15 (1965): 77–119.
Kennedy, William. *Rhetorical Norms in Renaissance Literature*. New Haven, CT: Yale UP, 1978.
Kincaid, Arthur N. "The Dramatic Structure of Sir Thomas More's *History of King Richard III*. EA: 375–87.
Kinney, Arthur F. 1979. *Rhetoric and Poetic in Thomas More's* Utopia. Humana Civilitas, Vol. 5. Malibu, CA: Undena Publications, 1979.
———. 1986. *Humanist Poetics: Thought, Rhetoric and Fiction in Sixteenth-Century England*. Amherst: U of Massachusetts, 1986.
Kinney, Daniel. "Christian Wisdom and Secular Learning." CW15 xlvi–lxxi.
Klein, Jacob. *Plato's Trilogy*. Chicago: U of Chicago P, 1977.
Knox, Norman. *The Word "Irony" and Its Context, 1500–1755*. Durham, NC: Duke UP, 1961.
Kristeller, Paul O. 1961. "The Moral Thought of Renaissance Humanism." In *Chapters in Western Civilization*: 289–335. New York: Columbia UP, 1961.
———. 1980. "Thomas More as a Renaissance Humanist." *Moreana*, no. 65 (June 1980): 5–22.
———. 1985. "The Active and Contemplative Life in Renaissance Humanism." *Arbeit Musse Meditation: Betrachtungen zur Vita Activa und Vita Contemplativa*: 133–52. Ed. Brian Vickers. Zurich: Verlag der Facvereine, 1985.

Lehmberg, Stanford E. 1956. "Sir Thomas More's *Life of Pico Della Mirandola.*" *Studies in the Renaissance* 3 (1956): 61–74.
———. 1970. *The Reformation Parliament, 1529–1536.* Cambridge, Eng.: Cambridge UP, 1970.
Lewis, C. S. *English Literature in the Sixteenth Century Excluding Drama.* The Oxford History of English Literature, III. Oxford, Eng.: Clarendon P, 1954.
Logan, George M. *The Meaning of Utopia.* Princeton, NJ: Princeton UP, 1983.
Lupton, J. H. *A Life of John Colet.* Hamden, CT: Shoe String Press, 1961.
Luther, Martin. *Bondage of the Will.* Vol. 33 of *Luther's Works.* Philadelphia: Fortress P, 1972.
McConica, James K. *English Humanists and Reformation Politics under Henry VIII and Edward VI.* Oxford, Eng.: Clarendon P, 1965.
McCutcheon, Elizabeth. 1971. "Denying the Contrary: More's Use of Litotes in the *Utopia.*" EA: 263–74. Originally published in *Moreana,* nos. 31–32 (November 1971): 107–21.
———. 1983. *My Dear Peter: The "Ars Poetica" and Hermeneutics of More's* Utopia. Angers, France: Moreana, 1983.
———. 1985. "More's *Utopia* and Cicero's *Paradoxa Stoicorum.*" *Moreana,* no. 86 (July 1985): 3–22.
Marc'hadour, Germain. 1962. "A Name for All Seasons." EA: 539–62.
———. 1972. *The Bible in the Works of St. Thomas More.* 5 vols. Nieuwkoop, Neth.: B. de Graaf, 1972.
Marius, Richard. *Thomas More: A Biography.* New York: Alfred A. Knopf, 1984.
Mermel, Jerry. "Preparations for a Public Life: Sir Thomas More's Entry into the King's Service." *Journal of Medieval and Renaissance Studies* 7 (1977): 53–66.
More, Thomas. [Corr]. *Correspondence of Sir Thomas More.* Ed. Elizabeth F. Rogers. Princeton, NJ: Princeton UP, 1947.
———. [EW]. *The Four Last Things.* In *The English Works of Sir Thomas More.* Ed. W. E. Campbell et al. Vol. 1. London: Eyre & Spottiswoode, 1931.
———. [EW]. *The Life of John Picus.* In *The English Works of Sir Thomas More.* Ed. W. E. Campbell et al. Vol. 1. London: Eyre & Spottiswoode, 1931.
———. [SL]. *Selected Letters.* Trans. Elizabeth F. Rogers. Princeton, NJ: Princeton UP, 1947.
———. [CW]. *The Yale Edition of the Complete Works of St. Thomas More.* New Haven, CT: Yale UP, 1963–[still in progress].
CW2 *The History of King Richard III.* Ed. Richard S. Sylvester. 1963.
CW3.1 *Translations of Lucian.* Ed. Craig R. Thompson. 1974.
CW3.2 *The Latin Poems.* Ed. Clarence H. Miller, Leicester Bradner, Charles A. Lynch, and Revilo P. Oliver. 1984.

CW4 *Utopia*. Ed. Edward Surtz and J. H. Hexter. 1965.
CW5 *Responsio ad Lutherum*. Ed. J. M. Headley. 1969.
CW6 *A Dialogue Concerning Heresies*. Ed. Thomas Lawler, Germain Marc'hadour, and Richard Marius. 1981.
CW7 *Letter to Bugenhagen, Supplication of Souls, Letter against Frith*. Ed. Frank Manley, Germain Marc'hadour, Richard Marius, and Clarence H. Miller. 1990.
CW8 *The Confutation of Tyndale's Answer*. Ed. Louis Schuster, Richard Marius, James Lusardi, and Richard Schoeck. 1973.
CW9 *The Apology*. Ed. J. B. Trapp. 1979.
CW10 *The Debellation of Salem and Bizance*. Ed. John Guy, Ralph Keen, Clarence H. Miller, and Ruth McGugan. 1987.
CW11 *The Answer to a Poisoned Book*. Ed. Stephen M. Foley and Clarence H. Miller. 1985.
CW12 *A Dialogue of Comfort against Tribulation*. Ed. Louis L. Martz and Frank Manley. 1976.
CW13 *A Treatise upon the Passion*. Ed. Garry E. Haupt. 1976.
CW14 *De Tristitia Christi*. Ed. Clarence H. Miller. 1976.
CW15 *In Defense of Humanism*. Ed. Daniel Kinney. 1986.
Moyes, James. "Warham, an English Primate on the Eve of the Reformation." *Dublin Review* 114 (April 1894): 390–419.
Munday, Anthony, et al. *Sir Thomas More: A Play Revised by Henry Chettle, Thomas Dekker, Thomas Heywood and William Shakespeare*. Ed. Vittorio Gabrieli and Giorgio Melchiori. Manchester, Eng.: Manchester UP, 1990.
Nederman, Cary. "Nature, Sin and the Origins of Society: The Ciceronian Tradition in Medieval Political Thought." *Journal of the History of Ideas* 49.1 (January–March 1988): 3–26.
Nelson, William. "Thomas More, Grammarian and Orator." EA: 150–60. Originally published in *PMLA* 58 (1943): 337–52.
Nendza, James. "Idealism in More's *Utopia*." *Review of Politics* 46 (1984): 428–51.
New, Peter. *Fiction and Purpose in* Utopia, Rasselas, The Mill on the Floss *and* Women in Love. New York: St. Martin's P, 1985.
Nicgorski, Walter. 1978. "Cicero and the Rebirth of Political Philosophy." *Political Science Reviewer* 8 (1978): 63–101.
———. 1984. "Cicero's Paradoxes and His Idea of Utility." *Political Theory* 12 (1984): 557–78.
———. 1991. "Cicero's Focus: From the Best Regime to the Model Statesman." *Political Theory* 19 (1991): 230–51.
Pace, Richard. *De Fructu Qui Ex Doctrina Percipitur (The Benefits of a Liberal Education)*. Ed. and trans. Frank Manley and R. S. Sylvester. New York: Frederick Ungar Publishing Co., 1967.
Pigman, George. "Versions of Imitation in the Renaissance." *Renaissance Quarterly* 33 (1980): 1–32.

Plato. *The Dialogues of Plato*. Trans. B. Jowett. 2 vols. New York: Random House, 1937.
Plutarch. *Plutarch's Lives*. 11 vols. Trans. Bernadotte Perrin. LCL. Cambridge, MA: Harvard UP, 1928.
Pohl, F. J. *Amerigo Vespucci: Pilot Major*. New York: Columbia UP, 1944.
Pollard, A. F. "The Making of Sir Thomas More's *Richard III*." EA: 421–31.
Quintilian. *Institutio oratoria*. Ed. and trans. H. E. Butler. 4 vols. Cambridge, MA: Harvard UP, 1921.
Raitiere, Martin N. "More's *Utopia* and *The City of God*." *Studies in the Renaissance* 20 (1973): 144–68.
Rebhorn, Wayne. "Thomas More's Enclosed Garden: *Utopia* and Renaissance Humanism." *English Literary Renaissance* 6.2 (Spring 1976): 140–53.
Reid, James, ed. *Academica of Cicero*. London: MacMillan & Co., 1885.
Reynolds, E. E. *The Field Is Won: The Life and Death of Saint Thomas More*. Milwaukee: Bruce Publishing Co., 1968.
Robinson, Ralph, trans. *The Utopia of Sir Thomas More*. Ed. J. H. Lupton. Oxford, Eng.: Clarendon P, 1895.
Rodgers, Katherine G. "A Critical Edition of Thomas More's *A Treatyse on the Last Things*." Unpublished Ph.D. dissertation, Yale U, 1992.
Roper, William. *Lives of Saint Thomas More*. Ed. E. E. Reynolds. New York: Everyman's Library, 1963.
Rudat, Wolfgang E. H. "More's Raphael Hythloday: Missing the Point in *Utopia* Once More?" *Moreana*, no. 69 (March 1981): 41–64.
Scarisbrick, J. J. *Henry VIII*. London: Eyre & Spottiswoode, 1968.
Schaeffer, John D. "Socratic Method in More's *Utopia*." *Moreana*, no. 69 (March 1981): 5–20.
Schoeck, Richard J. 1956. "More, Plutarch, and King Agis: Spartan History and the Meaning of *Utopia*." EA: 275–80. Originally published in *Philological Quarterly* 35 (1956): 366–75.
———. 1963. "Canon Law in England on the Eve of the Reformation." *Medieval Studies* 25 (1963): 125–47.
———. 1969. "'A Nursery of Correct and Useful Institutions': On Reading More's *Utopia* as Dialogue." EA: 281–89. Originally published in *Moreana*, no. 22 (May 1969): 19–32.
———. 1976. *The Achievement of Thomas More*. U of Victoria, BC, Canada: English Literary Monographs, 1976.
Seigel, Jerrold E. *Rhetoric and Philosophy in Renaissance Humanism: The Union of Eloquence and Wisdom, Petrarch to Valla*. Princeton, NJ: Princeton UP, 1968.
Seneca. *Octavia. Tragedies*. Vol. 2: 401–89. Cambridge, MA: Harvard UP, 1929.
Skinner, Quentin. 1987. "Sir Thomas More's *Utopia* and the Language of Renaissance Humanism." *The Language of Political Theory in Early-*

Modern Europe: 123–57. Ed. Anthony Pagden. Cambridge, Eng.: Cambridge UP, 1987.

———. 1988. "Political Philosophy." *Cambridge History of Renaissance Philosophy*: 412–52. Ed. Charles Schmitt and Quentin Skinner. Cambridge, Eng.: Cambridge UP, 1988.

Stanford, William B. *The Ulysses Theme: A Study in the Adaptability of a Traditional Hero*. New York: Barnes & Noble, 1964.

Stapleton, Thomas. *The Life and Illustrious Martyrdom of Sir Thomas More*. Trans. Philip E. Hallet, ed. E. E. Reynolds. New York: Fordham UP, 1966.

Starnes, Colin. *The New Republic: A Commentary on Book I of More's Utopia*. Waterloo, Ont.: Wilfrid Laurier UP, 1990.

Steintrager, James. "Plato and More's *Utopia*." *Social Research* 36 (1969): 357–72.

Surtz, Edward L. 1957a. *The Praise of Pleasure: Philosophy, Education, and Communism in More's Utopia*. Cambridge, MA: Harvard UP, 1957.

———. 1957b. *The Praise of Wisdom: A Commentary on the Religious and Moral Problems and Backgrounds of St. Thomas More's Utopia*. Chicago: Loyola UP, 1957.

———. 1958. "More's *Apologia Pro Utopia Sua*." *Modern Language Quarterly* 19 (1958): 319–24.

———. 1965a. "Sources, Parallels, and Influences." In CW 4, xliii–clxxxiii.

———. 1965b. "Utopia as a Work of Literary Art." In CW 4, cxxv–cliii.

Sylvester, Richard S. 1963. "The 'Man for All Seasons' Again: Robert Whittington's Verses to Sir Thomas More." *Huntington Library Quarterly* 26 (1963): 147–54.

———. 1967. "A Part of His Own: Thomas More's Literary Personality in His Early Works." *Moreana*, nos. 15–16 (November 1967): 29–42.

———. 1968. "'Si Hythlodaeo Credimus': Vision and Revision in Thomas More's *Utopia*." EA: 290–301. Originally published in *Soundings* 51 (1968): 272–89.

———. 1977. "Thomas More: Humanist in Action." EA: 462–69. Originally published in *Medieval and Renaissance Studies*, no. 1: 125–36. Ed. O. B. Hardison, Jr. Chapel Hill: U of North Carolina P, 1966.

Sylvester, R. S., and G. P. Marc'hadour, eds. [EA]. *Essential Articles for the Study of Thomas More*. Hamden, CT: Archon Books, 1977.

Taft, Arthur I. *The Apologye of Syr Thomas More, Knight*. Ed. with intro. and notes. London: English Text Society, 1930.

Trinkaus, Charles. *The Scope of Renaissance Humanism*. Ann Arbor: U of Michigan P, 1982.

Tyndale, William. *The Works of the English Reformers*, Vol. 1. Ed. Thomas Russell. London: Ebenezer Palmer, 1831.

Vespucci, Amerigo. *Letters to Piero Soderini*. Trans. George T. Northup. Princeton, NJ: Princeton UP, 1916.

Vickers, Brian. 1970. *Classical Rhetoric in English Poetry.* New York: Macmillan, 1970.

———. 1988. "Rhetoric and Poetic." *Cambridge History of Renaissance Philosophy*: 715–45. Ed. Charles Schmitt. Cambridge, Eng.: Cambridge UP, 1988.

Virgil. *Aeneid.* Trans. Robert Fitzgerald. New York: Vintage Books, 1983.

Vives, Juan Luis., ed. *De civitate Dei.* Basel, Switz.: J. Froben, 1522.

Wegemer, Gerard. "The Political Philosophy of Sir Thomas More." In *Saints, Sovereigns, and Scholars: Studies in Honor of Frederick D. Wilhelmsen.* Ed. R. A. Herrera, James Lehrberger, M. E. Bradford. New York: Peter Lang, 1993.

———. *Thomas More: A Portrait of Courage.* Princeton, NJ: Scepter P, 1995.

Weiner, Andrew D. "Raphael's Eutopia and More's *Utopia*: Christian Humanism and the Limits of Reason." *Huntington Library Quarterly* 39 (1975): 1–27.

White, Thomas I. 1976. "Aristotle and *Utopia*." *Renaissance Quarterly* 29 (1976): 635–75.

———. 1978. "*Festivitas, Utilitas, et Opes*: The Concluding Irony and Philosophical Purpose of Thomas More's *Utopia*." *Albion* 10 (Supplement, 1978): 135–50.

———. 1982. "Pride and the Public Good: Thomas More's Use of Pleasure in *Utopia*." *Journal of the History of Philosophy* 20.4 (October 1982): 329–54.

———. 1987. "Legend and Reality: The Friendship between More and Erasmus." Supplementum Festivum: *Studies in Honor of Paul Oskar Kristeller*: 489–504. Ed. James Hankins, John Monfasani, Frederick Purnell, Jr. Binghamton, NY: Medieval and Renaissance Texts and Studies, 1987.

Wood, Neal. *Cicero's Social and Political Thought.* Berkeley: U of California P, 1988.

Wooden, Warren W. 1972. "Thomas More and Lucian: A Study of the Satiric Influence and Technique." *University of Mississippi Studies in English* 13 (1972): 43–57.

———. 1977a. "Anti-Scholastic Satire in Sir Thomas More's *Utopia*." *Sixteenth Century Journal* 8.2 (1977): 29–45.

———. 1977b. "Satiric Strategy in More's *Utopia*: The Case of Raphael Hythloday." *Renaissance Papers* (1977): 1–9.

Zapatka, Francis. "Prose Apothegms into Rime Royal: Thomas More's Translation of Pico della Mirandola's 'Twelve Rules.'" *Actu Conventus Neo-Latini Guelpherbytania*: 395–400. Ed. S. Revard, F. Radle, A. DiCesare. Binghamton, NY: Medieval and Renaissance Texts and Studies, 1988.

Index

Abel, 139
Abraxa, 106
Academica (Cicero), 112, 113, 125, 227–29
Achilles, 38, 89, 90, 165
Adam, 29–31, 61–64, 139, 220, 236
Adams, Robert P., 71, 185, 189, 190, 204
Adeimantus, 105
advice. *See* counsel
Aeneas, 38, 225
Agamemnon, 89, 90
Agis, 121, 234
Alaopolitans, 143
Alington, Alice, 235
Allen, Ward, 124, 226, 229, 231
allusion, 109, 111, 149, 226, 227, 228, 234
Altman, Joel, 224, 225
Ammonio, 233
Annates, Restraint of, 198, 199
The Answer to a Poisoned Book (CW11), 166, 219
Anthony (character in *A Dialogue of Comfort*), 52–53, 56
The Apology of Sir Thomas More, Knight (CW9), 3, 66, 68, 72, 157, 168, 181, 188, 202, 206, 208, 210, 221, 230, 236
Aquinas, Thomas, 206, 224, 234
Aristophanes, 170, 206
Aristotle: and *Utopia*, 230, 232; his *Nicomachean Ethics*, 28, 220, 232, 234; *Politics*, 60–61, 121–23, 146, 207, 227, 229, 234, 235; *Rhetoric*, 93, 209
Art of Poetry (Horace), 1, 84

Ascham, 226
Atreus, 23
Augustine: his *City of God*, 8, 29–32, 36, 61, 128–49, 227, 230, 231; *On Free Choice of the Will*, 231. Mentioned, 12, 23, 192, 215, 216, 231
authority, ecclesiastical, 67, 187; vs. political, 13–14, 187–88, 204, 208
authority, political: absolute, 67, 207, 235; before the Fall, 61–62, 207; communism's loss of, 105–6; fear of, 192; Henry VIII's use of, 193, 197; Luther's and Tyndale's attitude towards, 13, 165, 173–74, 212; misuse of, 55–56, 66, 193, 208; Parliament as England's highest, 68, 235; proper use of, 55, 65, 102–3, 153, 155, 157, 158, 160, 165, 207; source of, 60, 187, 207–9, 221, 235; TM's understanding of, 61–62, 68, 187–89, 192, 204, 207–14, 233, 235; use of force and, 61, 73, 164–65, 221; vs. ecclesiastical, 14, 187–88, 204, 208
Autumn reader, 10, 215
Avineri, Schlomo, 232

Baal, 220
Babylons, 140
Barnes, Friar Robert, 181
Barnes, W. J., 223
Baron, Hans, 205
Basilides, 106
Bathsheba, 177–78
Battenhouse, John, 73. *See also* Letter to a Monk
Becket, Thomas, 200, 233

249

benevolence, 30, 116, 121–22, 229
Berger, Harry, 125, 142, 216, 224, 225
best form of government, 68–69, 115–16, 124
best regime, 111, 115, 116, 126
best way of life: as central issue of political philosophy, 127, 129; Augustine on, 129, 131, 134; before the Fall, 206; Cicero on, 109–10, 113–14, 116, 228; More on, 110–11, 227; Plato on, 230–31; *Utopia* on, 107–8, 131–32, 134, 227
Bevington, David M., 224
Bible, 34, 60, 70, 180, 206, 216, 236. *See also* Scripture
Billingsley, Dale, 219
Blaim, Arthur, 225
Bloom, Allan, 223
Boleyn, Anne, 189, 191, 193–94, 201
Bolt, Robert, 236
bonae litterae. See liberal arts
The Bondage of the Will (Luther), 163
The Book of Fortune (EW 338–344), 27, 39
The Book of Sir Thomas More (Munday, Shakespeare, et al.), 16–17
Boyle, Marjarie O'Rourke, 163, 164, 168, 181
Bradner, Leicester, 78
Bradshaw, Brendan, 165, 222
Branham, R. Bracht, 216
Brixius, Germanus, 158–59, 226
Brooke, Z. N., 187
Brutus, 202
Brutus (Cicero), 228
Buckingham, Duke of (Edward Stafford), 35, 190
Budé, William, 107, 132, 230
Burkitt, Francis C., 106
Busleyden, Jerome, 107, 132, 230
Buthrescae, 232
Byron, Brian, 225

Caesar, 71
caesaropapism, 14, 200, 202
Cambridge University, 186
Carlyle, R. W. and A. J., 176, 194
Carpocrates, 226
Catesby, Sir William, 36
Catherine of Aragon, 187, 191, 196, 201
Cavendish, George, 191, 196
Cerberus, 171

Chambers, Richard W., 101, 167, 216
character delineation, 93
charity, 125, 133, 149
Charles V, 3, 197
Chaucer, Geoffrey, 82, 172, 206, 225, 234
Christ: as masterful rhetorician, 57–60, 220; Luther and, 172–73, 174; TM on, 30–31, 45–48, 55, 57–60, 220; *Utopia*'s references to, 103, 136, 149. Mentioned, 32, 43, 197, 203
Christendom: Henry VIII and, 190, 193–94, 199, 212; Luther and, 159, 164, 168, 174, 175, 177; TM's concern for, 10, 13, 14, 188, 196; TM's defense of, 159, 165–67, 168, 174–76, 177, 181, 202, 208, 212
Christian humanist, TM as a, 129–30, 162, 167, 216, 224, 231. *See also* humanist
Church (Roman Catholic), independence of, 195–96
church and state, 13, 65, 145, 180, 188, 204, 208, 211, 232
Cicero: ontological foundation of his political philosophy, 228; his *Academica*, 112, 113, 125, 227–29; *Brutus*, 228; *De amicitia*, 120; *De finibus*, 121, 225; *De inventione*, 235; *De legibus*, 112, 120, 121, 124–26, 228, 229; *De natura*, 228; *De officiis*, 112, 114, 116–18, 120–21, 124, 125, 228, 229; *De oratore*, 228, 234; *De re publica*, 110, 120, 124, 131, 227; *Orator*, 167, 228; *Pro Balbo*, 227; *Pro Milone*, 227; *Tusculan Disputations*, 227, 228; *Verrine Orations*, 227
Circe, 42
citizen, 92, 93, 100, 115, 134
The City of God (Augustine), 8, 29–32, 36, 61, 128–49, 227, 230, 231
civil religion, 137, 138, 146, 231
civil society, 124, 180, 207
Cleomenes, 234
Colet, John, 9, 185, 186
Collectanea satis copiosa (Cranmer and Fox), 197
common corps, 174, 177. *See also* Christendom
common good, 4, 34, 38, 44, 55, 56, 67, 68, 73, 107, 117, 122, 170, 209–11, 213

Index 251

common law, 4, 8, 12, 201
commonwealth (republic): Aristotle on, 121; Augustine on, 134, 137; best state of, 110–11, 116, 124, 227, 228; Cicero on, 110–11, 114, 116, 120, 124–25; how to reform, 15, 57, 97–98, 102–3, 159, 160, 165, 168, 172, 181–82, 186, 212; private property and, 99, 120, 121
communism, 98, 105, 148
The Confutation of Tyndale's Answer (CW8), 30, 61, 66, 70, 74, 81, 155, 156, 168, 174–81, 194, 195, 213, 219–21, 224, 235
conscience: as surest foundation for politics, 73; as the metaphysical foundation of law, 73, 184, 210; Christ's appeal to, 57–60; collective (nation's), 12, 19, 65, 211, 213; development of, 18, 50–51, 57–60, 210; education and, 50–51, 53, 183; free will and, 60, 73, 210, 211; greatest pleasure from, 46–48, 51–52; Henry VIII and, 14, 193, 196–97, 201, 202, 204; law and, 19, 65, 73, 183–84, 210–13, 222; literature and, 18; obstacles to developing, 31, 55–56; power of, 60, 73, 156, 184, 210; statesmen and, 19, 60, 65, 211, 213; TM's appeal to, 12, 14, 168, 201, 202, 204, 206, 235; TM's develoment of, 211; *Utopia* and, 222; virtue and, 46, 50, 73, 184, 193
constitution, 217
constitutional, 61, 120
contemplation, 51, 88, 109, 130, 131, 133, 134, 144, 145, 230, 231
Convocation, 197–200
Coogan, Robert, 228
Corinthians, 220, 224
Corneus, Andrew, 43
correspondence, TM's. *See* letters
Corrigan, Kevin, 230
counsel (advice): Adam's responsibility to give, 61–62, 64; Christ's special, 30–31, 55; conflict between desire and, 29, 191; education should develop a love for, 83, 207, 234; elected officials are more open to, 66, 209; free speech needed for, 65–66; need to plant and cultivate, 28, 51; need for diplomacy in giving, 104, 191–93; need for, 28, 53, 65–67, 102, 104, 207, 234–35; TM plays Good Counsel, 16; TM's, 10, 14, 53, 185–86, 189, 191–93, 195–96, 202–3; TM's reluctance to become King's, 233; statesman's responsibility to give, 65, 211; *Utopia* and, 93, 102–4, 117–19, 128, 132, 186, 225; virtue and, 46–48, 53. *See also* deliberation, public
Coventry, Friar of, 153–54, 165
Cranmer, Thomas, 12, 194, 196–98, 201, 212
Cromwell, Thomas, 12, 14, 168, 194, 197–99, 201, 202, 204, 212, 233
Crosset, John, 119, 120
Cumming, Robert D., 132
Cupid, 38
Cynicus, (Lucian), 49

Dante, Alighiere, 34
David, King, 38, 70, 177–79, 221
David, J. C., 216
Davis, Walter R., 217
De amicitia (Cicero), 120
De copia (Erasmus), 92, 93, 99
De finibus (Cicero), 121, 225
De inventione (Cicero), 235
De laudibus legum Anglie (Fortescue), 61
De legibus (Cicero), 112, 120, 121, 124–26, 228, 229
De libero arbitrio (Erasmus), 162–63, 164
De natura (Cicero), 228
De officiis (Cicero), 112, 114, 116–18, 120–21, 124, 125, 228, 229
De oratore (Cicero), 228, 234
De re publica (Cicero), 110, 120, 124, 131, 227
De Tristitia Christi (CW14), 14, 18, 37, 55, 58, 59, 64, 70, 73, 184, 200, 201, 203, 210, 213, 214, 219–22, 236
Dean, Leonard F., 218, 221
The Debellation of Salem and Bizance (CW10), 67–69, 202, 209, 210, 219
decorum, 111, 114, 117–19, 123, 124, 127, 228
deliberation, public, 4, 65, 67, 165, 168, 181, 211, 212
democratic government, 25, 211
Derrett, J. Duncan, 68

Desmarais, John, 132, 230
dialectics: irony and, 78–79, 84–85, 222–23; literature and, 41–42, 52–53, 78–85, 89–90, 91, 149, 222–23; pride and, 56–57, 88–89
A Dialogue Concerning Heresies (CW6), 7, 18, 30, 57, 67, 69, 70, 72–74, 77, 81, 82, 161, 167, 173, 177, 195, 196, 207, 209, 210, 213, 220, 221, 233
A Dialogue of Comfort against Tribulation (CW12), 28, 30, 31, 34, 48, 51, 52, 55–57, 64, 67, 69, 70, 88, 218, 220, 226, 234–36
"A Dialogue on Conscience" or "[A Letter from] Margaret Roper to Alice Alington" (Corr 511–32), 37, 72, 183, 210–11, 235, 236
diligence/diligent: Adam's, Eve's lack of, 31, 62–64, 236; Christ's effort to foster, 57–59; Creator's effort to foster, 63–64, 236; importance of, 32, 48, 59, 62–63, 65, 213; statesman and, 62–63, 73–74, 213–14. See also vigilance
diplomacy: humanist project and, 116, 160, 162, 213; TM's style of, 3, 154–55, 191–93; TM's success in, 9–11, 192; in *Utopia*, 93–97, 103–4, 117
Discourse on Free Will (Erasmus), 162–63, 164
divine right, 67, 187, 193, 194, 204, 207
Division between the Spirituality and the Temporality (St. German), 201
divorce, 191–93, 196–98
Doctors' Common, 10
Donner, H. W., 101, 217
Dorp, Martin, 73, 156, 221, 224, 225, 232
Dorsch, T. S., 142, 148
Doyle-Davidson, W. A., 217
dualism, TM's alleged, 24, 78
Duncan, Douglas, 223

Ecclesiastes, 221, 224
education: as caring for souls, 28, 33, 50–51, 53, 56–57; conscience and, 50–51, 53, 183–84; freedom and, 4, 36; humanist program and, 4, 11, 13, 15, 114–15, 162, 212; law and, 4, 15, 114–15, 162, 183–84, 211–13, 216; literature and, 18, 25–26, 38, 52–53, 77–90; private property and, 122; rhetoric and, 4, 10–11, 115–16, 212; statesman and, 5, 28–29, 36, 77, 115–16, 212; TM's, 2, 4–6, 8–9, 205; TM's children and, 4, 12, 30, 50–51, 83, 116, 183–84, 212, 234; TM's effect on, 11; *Utopia* and, 116, 122, 126; virtue and, 4, 28, 33, 50–51, 53, 122, 216. See also deliberation, public
Education of a Christian Prince (Erasmus), 37, 217, 221, 234–35
Edward IV, King, 35, 218
Eleatic Stranger, 56, 58
Elliott, Robert C., 224
Elton, G. R., 15, 161, 162, 166, 167, 175, 190, 217, 219, 220, 233
embassies, TM's, 3, 12, 227
emotion. See passion
English Cicero, TM as the, 205
Enoch, 139, 140
Epicureanism, 112, 134
Epigrammata (CW3.2), 18, 23–25, 27, 38, 41, 54, 60, 65–67, 69–72, 78, 80, 85, 89, 146, 158, 185, 190, 207–9, 217, 222, 226, 228, 235
epistemology, 78, 80, 222
Erasmus, Desiderius: humanist reform and, 11, 13, 15, 29, 162, 196, 216; Luther and, 13, 29, 155, 162–67, 171, 174, 175, 176, 181; TM and, 9, 11, 16, 107, 132, 158, 159, 161, 215, 222, 225, 226, 230, 232, 233; *De copia*, 92, 93, 99; *Discourse on Free Will*, 162–63, 164; *Education of a Christian Prince*, 37, 217, 221, 234–35, 237; *Enchiridion*, 224; *Hyperaspistes*, 163, 164; *Julius Excluded*, 232; *Praise of Folly*, 156, 224
Eucrates, 86–88, 148
evangelical liberty, 180
Eve, 29–31, 61, 63–64, 139, 236
Evil May Day, 157
"Exhortation to True Virtue" (CW3.2), 27
Ezekiel, 62

the Fall, 29, 61, 62, 72, 206, 207, 213
fantasy: pride and, 30–31, 51, 55, 64, 73, 88, 206, 218; sound reason vs., 50–52, 56, 73, 210
Fenlon, Dermot, 208, 217
fighting words, 157, 159

figures of speech: importance of, 18, 58, 78, 222–23; allusion, 109, 111, 149, 226, 227, 228, 234; antanagoge, 93; anamnesis, 95; antimethathesis, 96; copia, 93, 97, 225; enargeia, 95; ethopopoeia, 97; ethos, 93, 94, 97; exemplum, 219; litotes, 93, 96, 224; metaphor, 32, 53, 94, 95, 97, 220, 224, 236; parable, 93–96; paradox, 110, 236; parison, 96; period, 97; periphrastic, 95–96; sententiae, 95–96; understatement, 93, 96; wordplay, 96
Fish, Simon, 13, 182, 194–95, 198, 201
Fisher, Bishop John, 196, 197, 199, 200, 204
flattery, 3, 33, 57, 59, 192, 201
Fleisher, Martin, 14
folly, 24–26, 29–30, 34, 45, 50, 70, 85, 104, 130, 140. *See also* reason, limits of
force, legitimate use of, 13, 56, 73, 159–60, 164–65, 167–68, 211, 213, 221
Fortescue, Sir John, 61, 235
Fortin, Ernest L., 129
The Four Last Things (EW 459–99), 26, 28, 30, 51, 73, 88, 210, 217, 234
The Four Voyages of Vespucci (*Mundus Novus*), 101
Fowler, H. W., 87
Fox, Alistair, 15, 17, 24, 29, 35, 78, 82, 165, 175, 181–82, 193, 197, 202, 204, 217, 222, 226, 228, 230, 234
Foxe, John, 166
free will: centrality of—to TM's political theory, 12, 29–30, 60; denying, 13, 29, 162, 176–77, 180; Erasmus and Luther on, 29, 163–64; governing the use of, 63, 73; misuse of, 31, 60, 63, 138, 210; the two cities and, 139; in *Utopia*, 112, 138, 231
Free Will, Discourse on (Erasmus), 162–63, 164
freedom: Aristotle and, 60–61; Augustine on, 61, 141, 149; Biblical understanding of, 61, 206; Cicero and, 26, 61, 115–16, 125–26; conscience and, 50–51, 60, 73, 210–11; education and, 33, 36; false, 172–73, 176–77; family and, 125, 207; force and, 13, 56, 73, 164–65, 177, 211, 213; history and, 23, 72; human nature and, 23, 26, 27, 29–31, 33, 36, 39, 53, 60–61, 162, 206–7, 211; law and, 67–68, 73, 209–10, 211; literature and, 25–26; Luther and, 13, 172, 176; pleasure and, 26, 30–31, 33; politics and, 23, 25–26, 53, 60–63, 74, 115–16, 207, 108; pride and, 30–31, 36, 49, 206; reason (intellect) and, 3–5, 25–26, 30–31, 33, 36, 50–51, 56–57, 61, 63, 65, 185–86, 188, 206–7, 212; rhetoric and, 115–16; statesman and, 4, 26, 56, 61, 65, 207, 211, 221; TM and, 4, 65–66, 164, 188, 206, 207, 210, 211, 221, 235; *Utopia* and, 78, 92, 125–27, 131, 141, 145, 149, 229; vigilance/diligence and, 26, 31, 36, 62–65, 314–15; virtue and, 3–4, 33, 36, 39, 49, 50, 65, 206, 207, 229
freedom of speech, 4, 13, 65–66, 188, 208, 211, 221, 235; not present in *Utopia*, 229
Friar of Coventry, 153–54, 165
friendship, 6, 30, 54, 59, 113, 116, 122, 209
Frith, John, 166, 182, 203
Froben, John, 230
Furnivall's Inn, 10

Gabrieli, Vittorio, 219
Genesis, 61
genocide, 143
Giles, Peter, 43, 83, 98–102, 117, 133, 149, 155
Giustinian, Sebastian, 233
gnosticism, 106, 107, 226
gnostics, the new, 181
Gogan, Brian, 208, 233
Gonell, William, 88
Good Counsel (character in "A Dialogue on Conscience"), 16
government: after the Fall, 63, 206–7; before the Fall, 61, 206; best form of, 68–69, 115–16, 124; counsel and, 65–67, 212; democratic, 25, 211; foundation for, 18; kings and, 65–67, 185–88; law and, 67–68, 204, 209–10, 235; origins of, 23; representative, 5, 65–66, 69, 188, 209, 211; rhetoric and, 115–16, 165, 235; self-governing citizens and, 60–62, 211, 236; statesmen and, 14–15, 19, 57, 65, 68, 69, 73–74, 213; TM's poems on,

government *(continued)*
    54, 60, 65, 66, 70, 71; virtue and, 14, 18, 69, 73, 116, 123, 125
Gracchi, 234, 235
grace, 63, 64, 81
Grace, Damian, 41, 60, 66, 71, 217, 218, 224, 228, 235
Grant, Patrick, 218
greed, 34, 128, 139, 233
Greeks, 18, 52, 83, 88, 90, 132, 133, 157, 192
Greenblatt, Stephen, 13, 172
Greene, Thomas, 228
Greg, W. W., 16, 17
Gregory I the Great, Pope, 175
Gregory VII, Pope, 187
Grey, Lord Richard, 35
Grievances against the Ordinaries, 195
Gueguen, John, 126, 230
Guerlac, Rita, 225
Guy, John, 10, 13, 155, 187, 194, 197–99, 201, 202, 204, 216, 227, 233
Gwyn, Peter, 185

Hall, Edward, 157
Hanham, Alison, 218
happiness, 39, 112–14, 120, 141, 144, 228, 231
Hardison, O. B., 217
Harpsfield, Nicholas, 130, 183, 196, 205, 222
Hastings, Lord, 35, 80
Hebrews, Letter to, 216
Hector, 90
Henry VII, 5, 9, 184, 190
Henry VIII, 12, 13, 55, 67, 71, 159, 185, 188, 190, 201, 203, 204. *See also* imperial ambitions, Henry VIII's
heresy: Pico and, 41; pride and, 30; TM and, 13, 162, 221; Tyndale and, 175, 178; *Utopia* and, 231
Herod, 70
Hexter, J. H., 218, 229
history: Augustine and, 129–30, 135, 138–40; democracy as prepared by, 25; as drama of free will, 72; every history the same, 72–73; Henry VIII as judged by, 204; humanities and, 216; irony's, 222; literature includes, 217, 219, 236; Luther and, 175–76, 181; prudence and, 77; TM as judged by, 204; TM's study of, 2, 8, 9, 11, 67, 129–30, 161, 184, 205, 215; TM's understanding of, 182, 218–19; TM's view of kingship and, 67, 209; in *Utopia*, 101, 117, 129–30, 135, 138–40, 147
The History of King Richard III (CW2, CW15), 6, 7, 29, 30, 35, 65, 68, 69, 71, 73, 80, 184, 185, 207, 208, 210, 215, 217–19, 221, 227, 233, 235, 236
Hitler, Adolf, 34
Hobbes, Thomas, 12
Homer, 25, 38, 85, 89, 90
Horace, 1, 18, 58, 84, 166, 169, 170, 206
Hosington, Brenda, 220
Hughes, Philip, 197, 200
humanist, TM as a, 12, 13, 18, 24, 129–30, 162, 167, 185–86, 196, 216, 224, 227, 231. *See also* Christian humanist.
humanist project: Cicero and the, 109–16, 124–25; Henry VIII and the, 185–86, 196; Luther's threat to, 13, 164, 181–82; role of diplomacy, 10–11, 116, 160, 162, 213; role of education and public deliberation, 4, 11, 13, 15, 115, 162, 167–68, 172, 181, 212, 213; role of history, 2, 11, 72–73, 182, 212; role of law, 4, 15, 57, 114, 116, 160, 167–68, 181, 211–13; role of literature, 11, 18, 25–26, 77–90, 169–72, 212, 213; role of philosophy, 2, 44, 78–79, 104–5, 113, 119; role of reason, 4–5, 11, 13, 18, 24, 172, 181, 206; role of rhetoric, 3, 4–5, 10–11, 57–60, 107–8, 114–16, 160, 167–68, 212, 216, 225; role of virtue, 2, 3, 4, 15–16, 73, 116, 206–8; Seneca and the, 119–20. Mentioned or referred to, 2, 4, 11, 12, 13, 18, 24, 107–8, 162, 165, 167–68, 185–86, 216
humility (humble): Augustine on, 31–32; Christ and, 30, 46; More's soliloquy on, 16; Pico on, 43; statesman and, 54–55, 207, 221. Mentioned, 70, 126, 133
humor: dialectics and, 85; perverse, 157; TM's diplomacy and, 3, 7, 154, 172, 205–6, 234; *Utopia* and, 95, 98, 129, 148–49
Hyperaspistes (Erasmus), 163, 164
Hythlodaeus, Raphael, 7, 24, 43, 44, 91, 92, 94, 97, 100–102, 106, 107,

127, 141, 148, 149, 154, 155, 181, 186, 220, 226, 229, 234

The Iliad (Homer), 89
imperial ambitions, Henry VIII's, 12, 13, 189, 193, 195–97, 204
inflammatory rhetoric, 163, 164, 166, 169, 173
institutions: Augustine on, 128, 131, 135–34; "good mother wit" (prudence) and, 18; law and, 114, 115, 122–23, 211, 232; Luther and, 159, 232; More and, 4, 5, 12, 14, 162, 168, 187, 211; need for, 5, 114, 115, 123; statesman and, 4–5, 211–12; in *Utopia*, 103, 108, 116, 122–26, 131, 139, 140, 231; vs. virtue as fundamental safeguard, 4, 12, 14, 18, 69, 120, 122–23, 125, 131, 212
Irenaeus, St., 226
irony: Christ's use of, 58, 60, 220; dialectics and, 78–79, 84–85, 222–23; first use of, 222; Horatian, 84, 170; Lucian, 7, 49, 84–88, 148–49; Socratic, 7, 78–79, 84, 86, 87, 222–23; TM's, 3, 7, 35, 40, 78–79, 84–85, 95, 96, 103, 110, 149, 176–78, 202, 206, 220, 222–23, 228
Isaiah, 224
Itys, 23

Jack Slouch, 177
James the Apostle, 58–59
Jerome, St., 192, 217
jest, full truth in, 3, 206
John of Salisbury, 61, 235
John of Saxony, 164
John the Apostle, 58–59
Jones, Judith, 228
Jonson, Ben, 1, 205, 215
Judas Iscariot, 58–60, 180, 184, 200
Julius Excluded (Erasmus), 232
jurisdiction, 198, 204, 208, 233
just war, 73, 160, 213, 221
Juvenal, 170, 206

Kelly, Michael, 199, 200
Kennedy, William, 98, 225
Kincaid, Arthur F., 218, 224
Kings, Book of, 179
Kinney, Arthur F., 110, 111, 117, 120, 224, 227, 228

Kinney, Daniel, 216
Klein, Jacob, 215, 222
Knox, Norman, 222
Kristeller, Paul O., 110, 129, 216, 224, 230

law: as a work of reason and tradition, 67–68, 209; as second greatest educator, 212; attitude towards unjust, 67–68, 210; conscience and, 19, 65, 73, 183–84, 210–13, 222; devil and the, 68, 210; education and, 4, 15, 36, 115, 162, 183–84, 211–13, 216; force and, 73, 164–65, 167–68, 213; foundation of, 13, 18, 73, 172, 184, 210; freedom and, 67–68, 72–73, 209, 221; government and, 67–70; Henry VIII and, 193, 197–200; humanist project and, 4, 13, 15, 57, 116, 167–68, 172, 213; importance of, 4, 18, 26, 36, 61, 65, 67–68, 114–15, 116, 153–60, 161, 196, 209–13, 218, 221, 232; inadequacy of, 36, 55, 68, 69, 213; literature and, 18, 25–26, 212; Luther and, 13, 159, 162, 164–65, 168, 173–74, 176, 178–79, 185, 232; of God, 131, 140, 178–79, 197, 218; of nature, 73, 210; public deliberation and, 4, 65, 67, 165, 168, 181, 211, 212; reformation and, 15, 162, 167–68, 181–82; rhetoric and, 114–16, 160; rule of, 4, 65, 67–68, 161–62, 211; St. German and, 201–2; statesman and the, 4–5, 26, 36, 57, 67–70, 73, 162, 165, 168, 211–14; TM's study of, 3, 6, 8, 205, 215–16; TM's practice and execution of, 5, 8, 9–10, 167–68, 174, 215–16, 227; TM's theory of, 13, 18, 67–68, 73–74, 155, 173–74, 180, 183, 201–2, 204, 209–13, 218, 221; two systems of, 13–14, 187–88, 203–4, 208; in *Utopia*, 123–24, 131, 138, 140, 143, 222; virtue and, 50, 69, 114–15, 116, 125, 216, 221
lawyer, 5, 10, 12, 39, 101, 159, 175, 179, 201, 205, 215
legitimate force, 13, 56, 73, 159–60, 164–65, 167–68, 211, 213, 221
Lehmberg, Stanford E., 219
Lenten Reader, 10, 215

Letter from Margaret Roper to Alice Alington (Corr 511–32), 37, 72, 183, 210–11, 235, 236
Letter Seven (Plato), 79, 223
Letter to Brixius (CW3.2, Corr), 158–59, 226, 228
Letter to Bugenhagen (CW7), 181, 205
Letter to Colet (SL 4–5), 57, 220
Letter to Cromwell (SL 205–15), 184, 187, 232
Letter to Dorp (CW15, SL), 9, 11, 18, 82, 83, 89, 156, 158, 212, 225, 232
Letters to Erasmus (SL) 196, 216
Letter to Gonell (Corr 102–7), 3, 18, 30, 50–51, 83, 88, 183–84, 234
Letters to Margaret (SL, Corr), 73, 183, 184, 210, 211, 220, 232, 236
Letter to a Monk, (CW15, SL), 57, 72, 88, 153–55, 158, 207, 221
Letter to Oxford (CW15, SL), 77, 157–58
Letter to Wilson (SL), 184, 236
Lewis, C. S., 233
liberal arts (*bonae litterae*/good letters), 11, 25, 81–82, 160, 217, 236
liberty, 4, 27, 30, 36, 39, 44, 65, 117, 173, 176, 180, 188, 189, 199. *See also* freedom
libido dominandi, 190. *See also* power, lust for
The Life of John Picus (EW 349–96), 39–49, 57, 70, 224, 226, 236
The Life of Sir Thomas More, Knight (Roper), 6, 9, 10, 16, 65, 67, 68, 183, 189–92, 196, 203, 204, 210, 216
Linacre, Thomas, 9, 185, 186
Lincoln's Inn, 3, 10, 215
literature, its meaning in the Renaissance, 217, 236. *See also* liberal arts
literature: as greatest educator, 18, 235; dialectics and, 41–42, 52, 78–90, 91, 96, 110, 149, 222–23; importance of, 11, 17–19, 25–26, 34, 52; interpreting, 17–18, 19, 81–82, 222; law and, 18, 25–26, 211–12; pleasure of, 83, 84, 89–90, 179, 234; politics and, 18–19, 25–26, 37–38, 77–90, 169–70, 217; prudence and, 77–78, 83; rebirth of classical, 18, 222–23; rhetoric and, 114–15, 167, 216; Socrates and, 222–24; statesman's education and, 11, 18, 19, 25–26, 42, 52, 77–90, 212; TM's study of, 9; TM's treatment of folly/irrationality in, 24–29; TM's treatment of government in, 54–55, 57, 60, 65, 66, 69, 71, 72, 221; TM's treatment of humility in, 54–55; TM's treatment of pride in, 30–36, 66, 88; TM's treatment of self-rule in, 38–53; TM's treatment of tyranny in, 23, 24, 33–36, 65, 66, 70, 71, 221; virtue and, 37–38, 217, 221. *See also* satire
Logan, George M., 14, 111, 132, 224–26, 228, 230, 231
Lover of Lies (*Philopseudes*, Lucian), 50, 84–88, 148, 225
Lucian, TM's translations of (CW3.1), 18, 34, 49, 84–86, 88, 148, 156
Lucian, 7, 25, 49, 84, 86, 142, 148, 149, 156, 206, 225, 230, 234
Lucifer, 29–31, 33
Lupton, J. H., 10
Luther, Martin: his *Bondage of the Will*, 163; Erasmus and, 13, 29, 155, 162–67, 171, 174, 175, 176, 181; free will and, 12, 29, 154; Henry VIII and, 159, 187, 194, 203; reason and, 73, 155; reform and, 13, 159; TM and, 159–60, 162–76, 179, 181, 182, 187, 201, 203, 212, 225, 232
Lycurgus (Plutarch), 234
Lynch, Charles A., 78

Machiavelli, Niccolo, 12, 14
Magellan, 101
manichean, 24
Marc'hadour, Germain, 224
Marius, Richard, 10, 15, 165, 167, 175, 217, 224, 230
Mark, Gospel of, 58
Markham, John, 221
The Marriage of Wit and Wisdom, 16–17
Martial, 147, 206
martyr, 205
Master Mock, 166
Matthew, Gospel of, 58
McConica, James K., 10, 13
McCutcheon, Elizabeth, 224, 228
melancholy, 15–17, 217
Menippus (Lucian), 49
mercenaries, 147, 173
Mercers' Guild, 10

mercy, 71, 144
Mermel, Jerry, 227
merry tales, 234
monasteries, dissolution of, 190, 233
Monk, Letter to a. *See* Battenhouse, John; Letter to a Monk
More, John, 5, 6, 216
More, Thomas: his preparation for statesmanship, 2–12, 38–39, 153–60, 205; his theory of statesmanship, 12, 23–36, 54–74, 205–14; his theory of self-rule (virtue), 37–53; his theory of literature's role in the statesman's education, 77–84, 88–90 (applications of this theory, 84–88, 91–149); questions about his motives, 14–18, 24, 161–62, 165, 167, 175, 193, 220, 233; tests of his statesmanship, 13–14, 161–204. WORKS: *The Answer to a Poisoned Book* (CW11), 166, 219; *The Apology of Sir Thomas More, Knight* (CW9), 3, 66, 68, 72, 157, 168, 181, 188, 202, 206, 208, 210, 221, 230, 236; *The Book of Fortune* (EW 338–344), 27, 39; *The Confutation of Tyndale's Answer* (CW8), 30, 61, 66, 70, 74, 81, 155, 156, 168, 174–81, 194, 195, 213, 219–21, 224, 235; *The Debellation of Salem and Bizance* (CW10), 67–69, 202, 209, 210, 219; *De Tristitia Christi* (CW14), 14, 18, 37, 55, 58, 59, 64, 70, 73, 184, 200, 201, 203, 210, 213, 214, 219–22, 236; *A Dialogue Concerning Heresies* (CW6), 7, 18, 30, 57, 67, 69, 70, 72–74, 77, 81, 82, 161, 167, 173, 177, 195, 196, 207, 209, 210, 213, 220, 221, 233; *A Dialogue of Comfort against Tribulation* (CW12), 28, 30, 31, 34, 48, 51, 52, 55–57, 64, 67, 69, 70, 88, 218, 220, 226, 234–36; "A Dialogue on Conscience" or A Letter from Margaret Roper to Alice Alington (Corr 511–32), 37, 72, 183, 210–11, 235, 236; *Epigrammata* (CW3.2), 18, 23–25, 27, 38, 41, 54, 60, 65–67, 69–72, 78, 80, 85, 89, 146, 158, 185, 190, 207–9, 217, 222, 226, 228, 235; "Exhortation to True Virtue" (CW3.2), 27; *The Four Last Things* (EW 459–99), 26, 28, 30, 51, 73, 88, 210, 217, 234; *The History of King Richard III* (CW2, CW15), 6, 7, 29, 30, 35, 65, 68, 69, 71, 73, 80, 184, 185, 207, 208, 210, 215, 217–19, 221, 227, 233, 235, 236; Letter from Margaret Roper to Alice Alington (Corr 511–32), 37, 72, 183, 210–11, 235, 236; Letter to Brixius (CW3.2, Corr), 158–59, 226, 228; Letter to Bugenhagen (CW7), 181, 205; Letter to Colet (SL 4–5), 57, 220; Letter to Cromwell (SL 205–15), 184, 187, 232; Letter to Dorp (CW15, SL), 9, 11, 18, 82, 83, 89, 156, 158, 212, 225, 232; Letters to Erasmus (SL), 196, 216; Letter to Gonell (Corr 102–7), 3, 18, 30, 50–51, 83, 88, 183–84, 234; Letters to Margaret (SL, Corr), 73, 183, 184, 210, 211, 220, 232, 236; Letter to a Monk, (CW15, SL), 57, 72, 88, 153–55, 158, 207, 221; Letter to Oxford (CW15, SL), 77, 157–58; Letter to Wilson (SL), 184, 236; *The Life of John Picus* (EW 349–96), 39–49, 57, 70, 224, 226, 236; "Nine Pageants" (CW3.2), 26; "On an Accurate Portrait" (CW3.2), 80; poems, early English (EW 327–44), 26–28, 39, 52; *Responsio ad Lutherum* (CW5), 65, 67, 68, 162, 169, 171, 172, 209, 224–26, 232; "Rueful Lamentation" (CW3.2), 27; *Supplication of Souls* (CW7), 195, 208, 236; *Treatise upon the Passion* (CW13), 29–33, 55, 59, 61–64, 67, 70, 73, 74, 88, 206–8, 210, 216, 219, 220, 236; "Twelve Properties of a Lover" (EW 389–93), 48; "Twelve Rules of Spiritual Battle" (EW 381–85), 45, 220; "Twelve Weapons of Spiritual Battle" (EW 386–88), 47; *Tyrannicida* (CW3.1), 33; *Utopia* (CW4), 3, 7, 8, 18, 30, 51, 66, 68, 69, 91–93, 98–100, 102, 107, 109, 112, 116, 118–21, 123–26, 128, 130–33, 135, 136, 137, 139–42, 144, 145, 147, 148, 186, 218, 220, 222, 224, 226, 230–32, 236
Moses, 74
motives, questions about TM's, 14–18, 24, 161–62, 165, 175, 193, 220, 233
Moyes, James, 233
Munday, Anthony: *The Book of Sir Thomas More*, 16–17

Nathan the Prophet, 179
natural state, 206
nature: bonds of, 120–21, 219, 229; evil and, 128; human, 28, 31–32, 47, 63, 65, 67, 80, 83, 113–16, 123, 130, 193, 207, 209, 212, 228, 229; law of, 73, 210, 218; of authority, 208–9, 221; of charity, 133; of civil government, 187, 228–29; of God, 131; of love, 48; of political life, 129, 130; of satire, 156; of tyranny, 23, 34, 218–19; of virtue, 40, 49, 141; reason's ability to see, 79–84, 90; second, 33; *Utopia* and, 120, 125, 136, 141, 144, 229
Nederman, Cary, 115
negligence. *See* vigilance
negotium (business), 109, 132, 133
Nelson, William, 216
Nendza, James, 230
Nephelogetes, 143
Nero, 120
New Testament, 70, 157. *See also* Scripture; individual books
New, Peter, 216, 226, 232
Nicgorski, Walter, 112, 227, 228, 235
Nicomachean Ethics (Aristotle), 28, 220, 232, 234
Nietzsche, Friedrich, 113
"Nine Pageants" (CW3.2), 26
Noah, 139
Nun of Kent, 232

Obedience of a Christian Man (Tyndale), 193–95, 197
Octavia (formerly attributed to Seneca), 119
Old Academy, 112
"On an Accurate Portrait" (CW3.2), 80
On Free Choice of the Will (Augustine), 231
Orator (Cicero), 167, 228
otium (leisure), 109, 132, 133
Our Lady's Psalter, 231
Oxford University, 6, 157–58, 165, 186

Pace, Richard, 9, 16
Pacifier, 167, 202. *See also* St. German, Christopher
Palinurus, 99, 225
papacy, 187, 198

parliament: as supreme authority in England, 68, 233, 235; TM's service in, 12, 39, 227; of 1504, 9; of 1510, 10; of 1523, 4, 65, 188–89, 216; of 1529, 196–97; in 1531, 197; in 1532, 197–99. Mentioned, 194, 202, 204, 207, 210, 216
passion (emotion): freedom and, 31, 56, 70; Henry VIII and, 201; reason and, 4, 18, 29, 31, 52, 206; TM and, 16–17; *Utopia* and, 93, 100, 147; virtue and, 3, 38, 50, 118. Mentioned, 93, 148
peace: Erasmus and, 13, 15, 29, 159, 161, 172; impossibility of lasting, 8, 134, 139–40; law and, 69; personal, 3, 46, 51, 86, 131, 132, 134, 231; political, 4, 8, 128, 131; private property and, 106; statesman and, 19, 74, 221; TM's concern for, 13, 15, 159, 167, 170–71, 185, 186, 233; *Utopia* and, 106, 131, 132, 140–41, 148. *See also* humanist project
Peasants' Revolt, 163, 173
persona, 92, 93, 95, 171, 225
Peter, St., 58–59, 180, 236
Petrarch, 228
Phaedrus, 79, 223
Philocles, 85, 86
Philopseudes (Lucian's *Lover of Lies*), 50, 84–88, 148, 225
philosophus gloriosus, 148
philosophy. *See* political philosophy
Pico della Mirandola, Giovanni, 39–45, 47–49, 57, 70, 220, 224, 226, 236
Pigman, George, 228
plain of reason, 163, 167, 204
Plato: statesmanship and, 2, 78, 215; TM's special study of, 9; tyranny and, 34, 215; *Utopia* and, 91, 103, 104, 110–11, 131, 132, 134, 220, 230. WORKS: Letter 7, 79, 223; *Phaedrus*, 79, 223; *The Republic*, 1–2, 3, 79, 105, 110–11, 129, 131, 217, 222, 225; *Sophist*, 53, 56–57, 222; *Statesman*, 1–2, 53, 222; *Theatetus*, 79. Mentioned, 4, 23, 84, 212, 228, 230, 235
Plato's Academy, 222
Plautus, 206
pleasure: Aristotle on, 28, 121–22, 207, 234; Augustine on, 131, 135; central to politics, 28–29, 204, 207, 209,

234; contemplation's, 33, 51, 133, 145, 207, 230; debate over virtue and, 111–14, 124–25, 133, 134–35, 144–47; freedom's, 26, 30, 31; governing, 33, 42, 47–48, 51, 52–53, 63–65, 170; greatest, 46, 47–48, 51, 52; literature's, 83, 84, 89–90, 170, 234; true vs. counterfeit, 26–29, 31, 33, 42, 44–47, 63–64, 206–7, 217; in *Utopia*, 78, 106, 112–13, 121–22, 125, 131, 133–35, 138, 141, 144–45, 146, 228, 229, 234
Plutarch, 206, 213, 215, 234, 235
poems, TM's early English (EW 327–44), 26–28, 39, 52
poetics, 25–26, 77–90
poet's contribution to statesmanship, 78, 80–82, 83–84, 89–90
Pohl, F. J., 101
polemic, 160, 166, 169, 175
Policraticus (John of Salisbury), 61, 235
Politeia, 1, 110, 217. See also Plato, *The Republic*
political authority. See authority
political experience, TM's practical, 3, 5–12, 152–204
political free speech. See freedom of speech
political institutions. See institutions
political martyr: TM and Cicero as, 205
political philosophy: and political science, 2; central question of, 127, 129; classical, 1–2, 3, 60–61, 109, 119–24, 227; classical vs. Christian, 133–34; modern, 4, 12, 14, 211; poetic theory and, 18, 25, 77–90; TM's study of, 2–4, 8–9, 205; TM's, 12, 18–19, 23–36, 54–74, 186–89, 206–14, 235. See also statesmanship, TM's understanding of; best way of life
political prudence. See prudence
political reactionary, TM as a, 160, 162
political realities, harsh and imperfect, 4, 5, 15, 161–62, 167
political religion. See civil religion
Politics (Aristotle), 60–61, 121–23, 146, 207, 227, 229, 234, 235
Politicus, 1. See also Plato, *The Statesman*
Pollard, A. F., 194
population of a Utopian city, 145

power, lust for (*libido dominandi*), 27, 34, 35, 71, 185, 190
praemunire, 233
Praise of Folly (Erasmus), 156, 224
pride, 17, 18, 26, 30–34, 36, 40, 44–47, 49–51, 54–56, 59, 60, 63–67, 83, 88–90, 130, 149, 191, 193, 206, 209, 212, 218–19, 230, 231
private property, 98, 99, 105, 115, 120–24, 139, 229, 231
Pro Balbo (Cicero), 227
Pro Milone (Cicero), 227
propaganda, 194
Proverbs, 72
prudence, 7, 57, 70, 77, 83, 92, 104, 123, 157, 198, 211, 222
psychological interpretations of More. See motives
public authority, 153, 155, 157, 158, 160, 165, 221
public deliberation, 4, 65, 67, 165, 168, 181, 211, 212

Quintilian, 78

rage: TM's, 15–16, 162; Luther's, 164; Henry's, 198
Raitiere, Martin N., 230
reason: before the Fall, 61–64; humanist reform project and, 4–5, 11, 13, 18, 24, 172, 181; limits of, 155, 168, 169; plain of, 163, 167, 204; power of, 23–24, 68, 172; role of, 4, 50–51, 61–65, 172; time-tested products of, 19, 67–68, 205
Rebhorn, Wayne, 217
reform, humanists' approach to, 15, 57, 97–98, 102–3, 159, 160, 165, 168, 172, 181–82, 186, 212
Reid, James, 227
religion, 41, 92, 115, 123, 124, 134, 136, 137, 144, 146, 167, 231, 232
Renaissance (renascence), 1, 4, 8, 11, 18, 24, 96, 99, 104, 109, 110, 117, 129, 165, 172, 182, 205, 216, 217, 220, 222, 226, 228, 230
representative government, 5, 65, 66, 69, 209, 211, 235
Republic. See Cicero, Plato
Responsio ad Lutherum (CW5), 65, 67, 68, 162, 169, 171, 172, 209, 224–26, 232

Restraint of Annates, 198, 199
revisionists, 17, 222
Reynolds, E. E., 233
rhetoric: Aristotle and, 93, 209, 212; Christ's use of, 58–60; Cicero and, 112, 114–16, 167, 209, 212, 235; education and, 4, 10–11, 115–16, 212; Erasmus and, 93, 163, 166; humanism and, 3–4, 10–11, 108, 114–16, 167–68, 216; importance of, 114–16, 160, 212, 216; inflammatory, 163, 164, 166, 169, 173; law and, 114–16, 160; literature and, 114, 216; Luther and, 162–65, 168–69, 171–72; Plato and, 212, 222; statesman and, 3, 4, 115–16, 212, 235; TM's mastery of, 3, 10–11, 159–60, 203–4, 205, 212, 216, 220; TM's use of, 154–55, 158–60, 166–70, 175–81, 188–89, 191–92, 195–96, 202–4, 212, 220, 221, 222, 232; in *Utopia*, 92–98, 103–4, 107, 115–16, 117–18, 149, 225
Richard III. *See The History of King Richard III*
right imagination, 51
Rivers, Lord, 35
Robinson, Ralph, 99, 100
Rodgers, Katherine G., 217
Roman civilization, influence of, 1–2, 8, 18, 109–27, 132, 133, 135, 205
Romans, Book of, 67
Roper, Margaret, 210–11, 235
Roper, William: *The Life of Sir Thomas More, Knight*, 6, 9, 10, 16, 65, 67, 68, 183, 189–92, 196, 203, 204, 210, 216
Ross, William, 171–73
Royal Academy of Physicians, 186
Rudat, Wolfgang E. H., 224
"Rueful Lamentation" (CW3.2), 27
ruler. *See* statesman; tyrant
rump Convocation, 200

sack of Rome, 173
Sadness of Christ. *See De Tristitia Christi*
St. German, Christopher, 14, 167, 180, 182, 202, 204, 208
Salem and Bizance (St. German), 202
Sallust, 215
Satan, 37, 61

satire: defense of, 156, 169–71; TM's use of, 159–60, 166, 169–82
Satires (Horace), 169–70
Saul, King, 55, 70
scaffolds, kings' games upon, 185
Scarisbrick, J. J., 185, 187, 204, 233
Schaeffer, John D., 224–26, 228
schism, 193
Schoeck, Richard J., 121, 216
scholasticism, TM's attitude towards, 224
Schuster, Louis, 194
Scripture: Church and, 208; the Fall in, 62–63, 72; interpreting, 81–82, 172, 181; irony in, 58–60, 220; misuse of, 158, 176, 179–80; Pico and, 41; the Supreme Good and, 134–35. Mentioned, 221, 225, 231. *See also* New Testament
seditious ideas, harm of 154, 164, 165, 174
Seigel, Jerrold E., 110, 216, 225, 235
self-defense, 142, 158, 160
self-rule: difficulty of, 37–53; greatest obstacle to, 49; what is needed for, 48. *See also* virtue
Seneca, 119, 120, 186
sensuality, as a help, 63
seruitus, 132, 134–36
Seth, 139
"Seventh Letter" (Plato), 79, 223
sexuality, as TM's motive, 15
Shakespeare, William, 16, 26, 34, 202, 215
sharp-sighted, 18, 35, 83, 87, 89, 212, 219, 223
shepherd, good ruler as, 2, 24, 62
Skinner, Quentin, 109, 110, 117, 224, 229
slander, 36, 155–58, 160, 168, 169, 180, 232
Socrates, 7, 52, 79, 84, 87, 105, 106, 111, 113, 206, 215, 220, 222, 223, 225, 228
Solon, 234, 235
Sophist (Plato), 53, 56, 57, 222
sophist, Raphael Hythlodaeus as, 225
soul, 26, 28, 31, 35, 46, 47, 50–52, 56, 57, 63, 66, 72, 79, 88, 125, 130, 153, 154, 161, 162, 183, 206, 210, 211, 217, 218, 220–23
sovereignty, 60, 187, 204, 208
Sparta, 234

spiders' webs (laws), 213
Stalin, Joseph, 34
Stanford, William B., 226
Stapleton, Thomas, 2, 8, 9, 11, 129, 196, 215, 222
Starnes, Colin, 14
Statesman (Plato), 1–2, 53, 222
"statesman," origin of the term, 1, 215
statesman: examples of, 69–72, 102, 201–2, 205–6; facets of the, 56–57, 61, 65, 68, 72, 73–74, 200–201, 205–6, 221; images of, 1, 65, 73–74, 207; issues to be addressed by, 221; greatest danger faced by, 34; greatest obstacles to, 41–42; law and, 4–5, 26, 36, 57, 67–70, 73, 162, 165, 168, 211–13; literature and, 77–90, 212; need for, 2, 4, 19, 35, 36, 199, 219; prudence and, 70, 77; results from absence of, 35; rhetoric and, 3, 4, 115, 212, 235; theoretical difficulties in the theory of, 2, 4; virtue and, 2, 53, 212, 216, 221; tasks of the: appealing to collective conscience, 12, 19, 65, 211, 213; consulting and giving counsel, 4, 65, 211; promoting education, 4, 28, 213; promoting law and tradition, 4, 57, 211–13; promoting prudent institutions, 5, 211; promoting peace, 13, 74, 221; use of legitimate force, 73, 159–60, 164–65, 168, 213, 221
statesmanship: Aristotle's definition of, 61; importance of, 19; TM's preparation for, 2–12, 205–6; TM's understanding of, 2, 12, 25–26, 60–74, 207–14, 216, 220, 221; elements of TM's: science of politics, 2, 56–57 (*see also* philosophy, history, law); art of ruling, 3 (*see also* diplomacy, rhetoric); virtue, 3, 4, 16, 18, 216 (*see also* virtue); 221
Steintrager, James, 230, 232
stoicism, 49, 112, 228
Submission of the Clergy, 199–200
Suetonius, 215
suicide, 52, 56
summum bonum, 113
Supplication for the Beggars (Simon Fish), 194–95
Supplication of Souls (CW7), 195, 208, 236

supremacy, royal, 194, 197, 202
supreme good, 133, 134
Surtz, Edward L., 100, 135, 223, 228, 230
Sylvester, Richard S. 102, 224, 226–28

Tacitus, 215
Teiresias, 50
Terence, 171, 172, 206
testing character, 7–8, 36
testing private inspiration, 174–76
Theatetus (Plato), 79
Thraso, 171
Thucydides, 4, 34, 215
Thyestes, 23
Timothy, Book of, 107
Tosspot, 171
Tournai, 71
tradition: Henry VIII and, 187, 193, 194, 195; institutions and, 69, 114, 188, 211, 212; law and, 67, 68, 209; Luther's and Tyndale's attitude toward, 13, 159, 165, 176; need for, 114–15, 211–12; poet's relationship to his, 25–26, 77–80, 89–90; recovery of the classical, 1, 110; TM and, 1–2, 4, 53, 60, 171, 187–88, 202, 204, 208; TM's break with, 12, 65, 220–21; in *Utopia*, 140–41
Treatise upon the Passion (CW13), 29–33, 55, 59, 61–64, 67, 70, 73, 74, 88, 206–8, 210, 216, 219, 220, 236
Trinkaus, Charles, 110
Trojans, 157, 165
Tunstall, Cuthbert, 185, 186
Turks, 73, 190
Tusculan Disputations (Cicero), 227, 228
"The Twelve Properties of a Lover" (EW 389–93), 48
"The Twelve Rules of Spiritual Battle" (EW 381–85), 45, 220
"The Twelve Weapons of Spiritual Battle" (EW 386–88), 47
two swords, 14, 188
Tychiades, 85–87, 225
Tyndale, William, 13, 73, 159, 162, 168, 170, 173–82, 193–97, 201, 203
Tyrannicida (CW3.1), 33
tyrant: Aristotle on, 232; choice to become, 23, 34; conscience in, 73, 184, 210; cruelty of, 23, 33–34, 161, 196;

tyrant *(continued)*
  Henry VII as, 5; Henry VIII as, 184–85, 189–90, 196, 198, 203–4, 221; Herod as, 70; how he arises, 33–36, 66, 185, 232, 236; law's power against, 35–36, 221, 232; lust for power in, 27, 34, 35, 71, 185, 190; Luther and the, 173, 176; Nero as, 120; passion and the, 3, 70; pride in, 33–34, 54, 66; Plato on, 2, 215; Richard III as, 5, 34–36, 218–19; Seneca's ability to restrain, 119–20, 186; in *Utopia*, 119–21, 142, 147, 232; vs. statesman, 2, 65, 207, 212, 215; what can resist, 19, 25–26, 34, 36, 211–12

Ulysses, 99, 100, 116, 225, 226
undersheriff, 101, 216, 227
Uriah, 177–79
Utopia (CW4), 3, 7, 8, 18, 30, 51, 66, 68, 69, 91–93, 98–100, 102, 107, 109, 112, 116, 118–21, 123–26, 128, 130–33, 135, 136, 137, 139–42, 144, 145, 147, 148, 186, 218, 220, 222, 224, 226, 230–32, 236

Venus, 38
Verrine Orations (Cicero), 227
Vespucci, Amerigo, 101
Vickers, Brian, 217
vigilance/vigilant: freedom and, 26, 36; justice and, 19, 188, 213; statesman and, 19, 26, 36, 58, 65, 73, 212, 213; virtue and, 44–46, 64–65, 236. *See also* diligence
Vincent (character, *Dialogue of Comfort*), 52–53, 220
violence, 13, 54, 155, 163, 168, 173, 174, 187
Virgil, 38, 225
virtue: accessibility of, 206, 230–31; attempted substitution for, 12, 14, 69, 123; Augustine on true, 141–42, 230; best way of life as, 114, 116; classical writers on, 4, 8, 14, 28–29, 107, 111–16, 120–25, 134, 207, 229, 230–31; conscience and, 46, 50, 73, 184, 193; difficulty in acquiring, 40–53, 65, 72, 193; education and, 3–4, 28–29, 33, 50–51, 53, 122, 216; family and, 207, 216; freedom and, 3–4, 33, 36, 39, 49, 50, 65, 206, 207, 229; greatest obstacle to, 49, 51; happiness and, 27, 112–14, 230–31; importance of, 2, 3, 4, 16, 18, 50–52; law and, 50, 69–70, 114–15, 116, 125, 216, 221; peace and, 131, 134; pleasure and, 111–14, 122, 125, 135, 144, 217, 234; politics and, 18, 28–29, 73, 116, 206–7; private property and, 99, 120–23; self-rule as, 39, 40, 48, 53; statesmanship and, 2, 53, 212, 216, 221; TM's preoccupation with, 3, 4, 16, 18, 39, 193; in *Utopia*, 120–25, 135, 138, 141–47, 229, 230; warfare needed to acquire, 40, 42, 45–48. Mentioned, 7, 17, 35, 78, 169. *See also* self-rule

Vivès, Juan Luis, 16

war games in *Utopia*, 142
war, just, 73, 160, 213, 221
Warham, William, 196, 198–200, 226, 233
Wars of the Roses, 5, 6, 70
Weiner, Andrew D., 142
White, Thomas, 111, 201, 218, 230, 232
William the Conqueror, 187
Wolsey, Thomas, 186, 188–90, 192, 196, 198, 233
Wood, Neal, 227, 229
Wooden, Warren W., 148, 224, 225

Xenophon, 104

Zapatka, Francis, 220
Zapoletans, 143

Thomas More on Statesmanship was composed in 10/13 Galliard by Brevis Press, Bethany, Connecticut; printed on 50-pound Booktext Natural and bound by BookCrafters, Chelsea, Michigan; and designed and produced by Kachergis Book Design, Pittsboro, North Carolina.